ENTRY AND RESIDENCE IN EUROPE

ENTRY AND RESIDENCE IN EUROPE

BUSINESS GUIDE TO IMMIGRATION RULES

Edited by

Paul Gulbenkian

and

Ted Badoux

EEIG
European Immigration
Lawyers Group

Business Editors

Lionel Harris

and

Franz Tepper

JOHN WILEY & SONS

Chichester • New York • Brisbane • Toronto • Singapore

First edition published in 1993 as *Immigration Law and Business in Europe.*
This edition published in 1997 by John Wiley & Sons Ltd,
Baffins Lane, Chichester,
West Sussex PO19 1UD, England

National   01243 779777
International   (+44) 1243 779777
e-mail (for orders and customer service enquiries):
cs-books@wiley.co.uk
Visit our Home Page on http://www.wiley.co.uk
or
http://www.wiley.com

Other Wiley Editorial Offices

John Wiley & Sons Inc., 605 Third Avenue,
New York, NY 10158-0012, USA

Jacaranda Wiley Ltd, 33 Park Road, Milton,
Queensland 4064, Australia

John Wiley & Sons (Canada) Ltd, 22 Worcester Road,
Rexdale, Ontario M9W 1L1, Canada

John Wiley & Sons (Asia) Pte Ltd, 2 Clementi Loop #02-01,
Jin Xing Distripark, Singapore 129809

British Library Cataloguing in Publication Data

A catalogue record for this book is available from the British Library

ISBN 0-471-96664-9

Typeset in 10/12pt Baskerville by Footnote Graphics, Warminster, Wilts.
Printed and bound in Great Britain by Bookcraft (Bath) Ltd, Midsomer Norton.

This book is printed on acid-free paper responsibly manufactured from sustainable forestation, for which at least two trees are planted for each one used for paper production.

CONTENTS

Skarholmens Advokatbyra AB, Advokat Hans Engström,
Box 237, S-127 25 Skarholmen. tel.: (46) 8 7401850.
telefax: (46) 8 740717

PREFACE

Entry and Residence in Europe: Business Guide to European Immigration Rules is the second publication of the European Immigration Lawyers Group (EILG). The Group is a network of European law firms represented in all EC countries who specialise in matters of national and EC immigration law. The aims of the Group are:

(i)   to work together in obtaining work permits for corporate employees within the European Community, including employees moving from one Member State to another;
(ii) to find means of transferring residence from countries of second choice to countries of first choice within the EC nationality rules; and
(iii) to provide a "one stop" comprehensive European Immigration Service to non-EC nationals.

Entry and Residence in Europe: Business Guide to European Immigration Rules is published to provide practical and basic information on immigration rules and policies within the European Community. As from 1992 it has become clear that there will be those who may enjoy the rights of an "open European society" and those who may not. The book provides a helpful guide for individuals and corporate entities interested in moving themselves or their employees to or settling in EC countries. It will help them to find out whether they may belong to a privileged European category, which privileges they might enjoy and which conditions should be met to obtain residence and/or a work permit in each of the Member States of the European Community. Others, without obvious privileges, may find in the following pages that they have certain rights in accordance with special EC Regulations or that national policies or rules may offer better opportunities in one particular Member State than in another.

Although the authors have put in considerable effort to raise the practical value of this second edition, this is not a "do it yourself" book. But for those faced with important questions as to where in Europe to do or start business, where in Europe to study, to work, to invest or enjoy a pension, the book offers help in understanding the European situation and the options available in each of the Member States.

It cannot be emphasised enough that in all European countries immigration laws and policies are very complex and that each case is considered and decided on its own merits. It is, therefore, essential, in addition to consulting this work, to obtain expert advice and guidance. The contents of this Guide should not, therefore, be regarded as constituting legal advice and should not be relied upon as such.

The European Immigration Lawyers Group accepts no responsibility for any errors this Guide may contain whether caused by negligence or otherwise or for any loss howsoever caused or sustained by any person who relies on it.

The countries participating in this work are listed in alphabetical order following the opening chapters from the United Kingdom and EC Nationals. Thanks are due to the authors of the various chapters and to everyone who gave encouragement and support for the preparation of this book. The Austrian chapter has been provided by Ms E. Scheuba of Allmayer-Beck & Stockert & Scheuba in Vienna. The author of the Luxembourg chapter is Mr P. Weinacht of Faltz and Associés in Luxembourg and the author of the Finland chapter is Mr Mikko Mali of Castren and Snellman in Helsinki. Although contributors have all followed a consistent pattern they have each been given latitude to bring in or emphasise aspects they consider especially important in their juris-diction. The law is stated as at 30 April 1996.

The law firms participating in the European Immigration Lawyers Group are specified overleaf.

EUROPEAN IMMIGRATION LAWYERS GROUP

Belgium	Mackelbert & Associés Avocats Advocaten Rechtsanwälte Avenue Clémentine, 3 1190 Bruxelles tel.: (32) 25345098 telefax: (32) 25345402
Denmark	Messrs. Norsker & Jacoby Kvaesthusgade 3 DK-1251 Kobenhavn K tel.: (45) 33110885 telefax: (45) 33937530
France	Lemann Isal Serfaty & Associés 67 Boulevard Lannes 75116 Paris tel.: (33) 145046161 telefax: (33) 145048020
Germany	Brandi Dröge Piltz & Heuer Rechtsanwälte Hochstrasse 19 D-33332 Gütersloh tel.: (49) 524158886 telefax: (49) 524158881
Greece	Messrs. Vgenopoulos & Partners 15 Kolonaki Square Athens 106 73 tel.: (30) 1 7221 832/7217 803/7220 149 telefax: (30) 1 7231 462

Ireland   Messrs. Eugene F. Collins
                           61 Fitzwilliam Square
                           Dublin 2
                           tel.:   (353) 16761924
                           telefax: (353) 16618906

Italy   Studio Legale Astoli
                           Corso di Porta Vittoria 14
                           20122 Milan
                           tel.:   (39) 255183100
                           telefax: (39) 25466743

The Netherlands   Everaert Advokaten
                           Weteringschans 28
                           1017 SG Amsterdam
                           tel.:   (31) 206271181
                           telefax: (31) 206273231

Portugal   Jose Alves Pereira & Associados
                           Av. de Berna n°4 – 1°DTO
                           1000 Lisbon
                           tel.:   (351) 17938890/4
                           telefax: (351) 17938889

Spain   Fernando Scornik Gerstein
                           Abogado
                           Alberto Alcocer 7, 3° Izda
                           28036 Madrid
                           tel.:   (34) 9 13507262
                           telefax: (34) 9 13507306

Sweden   Skarholmens Advokatbyra AB
                           Advokat Hans Engström
                           Box 237
                           S-127 25 Skarholmen
                           tel.:   (46) 87401850
                           telefax: (46) 8740717

United Kingdom   Messrs. Gulbenkian Harris Andonian
                           181 Kensington High Street
                           London W8 6SH
                           tel.:   (44) 171 937 1542
                           telefax: (44) 171 938 2059

**Member States
of the
European Union**

Contents of Chapter 1

UNITED KINGDOM

Chapter 1

UNITED KINGDOM

Paul Gulbenkian

1. Country characteristics and general principles

The United Kingdom comprises Great Britain (England, Wales and Scotland) and Northern Ireland, and is one of the Member States of the European Union. Its full name is the United Kingdom of Great Britain and Northern Ireland.

With an area of some 242,500 square kilometres (93,600 square miles), the United Kingdom is just under 1,000 kilometres (some 600 miles) from the south coast to the north of Scotland and just 500 kilometres (some 300 miles) across at the widest part.

The population of the United Kingdom is approximately 57 million. The climate is generally mild and temperate and prevailing winds are south-westerly.

With regard to the economy, in the late eighteenth and nineteenth centuries the United Kingdom became the first industrialised country, basing its wealth on coalmining, on the manufacture of iron and steel, heavy machinery and textiles, on ship building and on trade. In the twentieth century a second period of industrialisation changed the broad pattern of development and income. In the 1920s and 1930s the northern industrial centres saw their traditional manufacturing base weakened owing to fluctuations in world trade, competition from other industrial countries and, in some cases, from substitute products. In the second half of the twentieth century jobs in service industries have grown and now account for over two-thirds of employees and employment. Expansion has been particularly marked in financial and business services.

The development of the British system of government and the growth of political institutions can be traced as far back as the period of Saxon rule in the fifth century, up to the nineteenth century. The UK Constitution is to a large extent the product of historical events and has thus evolved over many centuries. Unlike the constitutions of most other countries, it is not set out in any single document. Instead it is made up of statute law, common law and conventions.

The Constitution can be altered by Act of Parliament and is therefore adaptable to changing political conditions. The organs of government overlap but can be distinguished clearly. Parliament is the legislature and the supreme body.

The three elements which make up Parliament are the Queen, the House of Lords and the elected House of Commons, which are constituted on different principles.

England and Wales, Scotland and Northern Ireland all have their own legal systems, with considerable differences in law, organisation and practice. However, a large volume of modern legislation applies throughout the UK. The main sources of law are government legislation, common law and EU law.

Immigration into the United Kingdom is controlled under the Immigration Rules made in accordance with legislation passed in the 1970s, 1980s and 1990s, resulting in a complete change in the Immigration Rules which came into force on 1 October 1994.

The Immigration Act 1978 and the British Nationality Act 1981 codified British immigration and nationality law. Since then, new laws, rules and practices have imposed increasing restrictions. The only right to family reunion in UK law was repealed in the Immigration Act 1988. Meanwhile, the primary purpose marriage rule and the support and accommodation requirements meant that, in 1990, nearly 70% of husbands from the Indian sub-continent were refused entry. Deportation was made easier and swifter by the Immigration Act 1988 and by new Home Office practices which followed that Act. The Home Office practice with regard to asylum seekers became more restrictive after the arrival of Tamils in the mid-1980s, culminating in the Asylum and Immigration Appeals Act 1993 and the Statement of Changes in Immigration Rules which were laid before Parliament on 23 May 1994 under Section 3(2) of the Immigration Act 1971 as HC 395 and which came into effect on 1 October 1994 (hereinafter referred to as the "New Rules"). The increasing visa restrictions, a loss of appeal rights and other decisions of immigration officers at ports, have made family visits more difficult for all the main ethnic minority communities in the United Kingdom. While developments in Europe have continued to remove barriers for nationals of European countries, the process of European harmonisation under the Single European Act and Maastricht Treaty on European Union, and increasing cooperation between ministers and civil servants from different countries, add to the stringency of control of non-European nationals.

2. Employment and inter-company transfers

(a) Employment

(i) Work permits

Work permits are issued by the Department for Education and Employment only where there is a clear benefit to employment and the economy of the United Kingdom, for example, to assist UK employers in their international development, to help them overcome short-term labour shortages which cannot be met by training resident workers, to ease high level skill shortages, or to enable major new investments to take place. Work permits will only be issued for board level executives, senior managers and highly skilled professionals or personnel with rare technical skills. Employers have to show that they cannot fill the vacancy with a UK or other EU national. The prospective employee should be living abroad when the employer makes the application because the Immigration Rules do not permit those admitted to the United Kingdom without work permits to switch into work permit employment.

There are special regulations for entertainers, sports people, models and people in the hotel and catering industry.

An application for a work permit is made in respect of a main worker required for a specific job with a specific employer. The employer must make the application to the Department for Education and Employment.

There is now a two-tier system in operation. Applications which clearly merit approval and satisfy the existing occupational skills criteria are dealt with under a simplified procedure in tier one. There are four categories of cases which fall into tier one, namely:

(1) inter-company transfers (see below);
(2) board level posts offering a realistic salary commensurate with the size of the company, for which there is no other suitable candidate;
(3) posts essential to an inward investment project, bringing jobs and capital to the United Kingdom; and
(4) posts requiring skills and experience which are recognised by the industry or profession as being in short supply in the European Union and where they are to be filled by a worker at present living abroad.

For all these employees there is normally no need to advertise the post in national and local newspapers or trade journals. However, advertisements in the press will still be required for applicants in the second tier who will continue to need full documentation to demonstrate the positive benefits that will arise from the overseas worker's presence in the United Kingdom. Workers included in this category are those who are using language or cultural skills not readily available in the United Kingdom or the European Union.

(ii) Exceptions on grounds of UK ancestry

A Commonwealth citizen, one of whose grandparents was born in the United Kingdom, does not need a work permit in order to come to the United Kingdom to work. If one of his or her grandparents was born in the United Kingdom a Commonwealth citizen who wishes to take or seek employment in the United Kingdom will be granted an entry clearance for that purpose. On entry, such a person will be admitted for a period of four years whether he or she has employment or intends to look for employment.

(iii) Trainees

A distinction is made between trainees and students. Trainees are those people who come to the United Kingdom specifically for training or work experience, and those who originally entered as visitors or students have been allowed to change to training. It is up to the Department for Education and Employment and not the Home Office to consider whether the offer of training is satisfactory. The Department for Education and Employment must be satisfied that the trainee intends to return abroad on completion of the training. An undertaking is usually obtained from both employer and trainee that a transfer to ordinary employment after the training period will not take place.

Special provisions are made for chartered accountants. The Department for Education and Employment will give approval for those who have newly qualified as chartered accountants to undertake employment, usually for two years, to enable them to obtain a practice certificate.

(iv) Permit-free employment

Persons coming to the United Kingdom for employment in a number of specified categories, such as ministers of religion, missionaries, private servants, diplomats, consuls or seamen joining ships in the United Kingdom, do not need work permits. Their applications are dealt with by the Home Office rather than the Department for Education and Employment. In all cases, permit-free workers need visas prior to their entry into the United Kingdom. The initial leave will vary according to the type of employment but may not exceed 12 months.

(v) Sole representatives of overseas firms

Sole representatives of overseas firms which have no branch, subsidiary or other representative in the United Kingdom will be admitted for an initial period of one year if they hold a visa granted for that purpose. However:

- they must have been recruited and taken on as an employee outside the United Kingdom as a representative of a firm which has its headquarters and principal place of business outside the United Kingdom;
- they must be a senior employee with full authority to take operational decisions and must intend to be employed full time as a representative of the overseas firm;
- they must not be a majority shareholder in the overseas firm;
- they must satisfy the immigration authorities that they do not intend to take employment other than as sole representatives and that they can maintain and accommodate themselves and any dependants adequately without recourse to public funds.

Although a visa is mandatory, one of the advantages of sole representation is that there is no obligation on the entry clearance officer to refer the case to the Home Office.

(vi) Doctors and dentists

All doctors and dentists from outside the European Union are now prohibited from entry to the United Kingdom unless they have a work permit or qualify as businessmen or women under the New Rules.

(vii) Overseas journalists and broadcasters

Representatives of overseas newspapers, news agencies and broadcasting organisations, on a long-term assignment to the United Kingdom, can be admitted without having to obtain a work permit. They must, however, obtain a visa before arriving in the United Kingdom.

(b) Inter-company transfers

Work permits are issued by the Department for Education and Employment to existing employees holding a senior post in an international company which requires the employee to transfer from abroad or for a post designed to develop the career of an employee.

3. Business

(a) Businessmen and women

Where businessmen and women are intending to take over or join an existing business, or to establish a new business, rather than entering the UK as employees by way of a work permit, they will need to obtain a visa and show the following:

- that the amount of money to be invested is not less than a minimum amount (currently £200,000);
- that until their business provides them with an income they will have sufficient additional funds to maintain and accommodate themselves and any dependents without recourse to employment (other than their work for the business) or to public funds;
- that they will be actively involved full time in trading or providing services on their own account or in partnership, or in the promotion and management of the company as a director;
- that their level of financial investment will be proportional to their interest in the business;
- that they will have either a controlling or equal interest in the business and that any partnership or directorship does not amount to disguised employment;
- that they will be able to bear their share of liabilities;
- that there is a genuine need for their investment and services in the United Kingdom;
- that their share of the profits of the business will be sufficient to maintain and accommodate themselves and any dependents without recourse to employment (other than their work for the business) or to public funds; and
- that they do not intend to supplement their business activities by taking or seeking employment in the United Kingdom other than their work for the business.

(i) Joining or taking over existing business

Where businessmen or women intend to take over or join as partners or directors an existing business in the United Kingdom they will need, in addition, to produce:

- a written statement of the terms on which they are to take over or join the business;
- audited accounts for the business for previous years; and
- evidence that their services and investment will result in a net increase in the employment provided by the business to persons settled here to the extent of creating at least two new full-time jobs.

(ii) Establishing a new business

Where the businessmen or women intend to establish a new business in the United Kingdom they will need, in addition, to produce evidence:

- that they will be bringing into the country sufficient funds of their own to establish a business; and
- that the business will create full-time paid employment for at least two persons already settled in the United Kingdom.

Businessmen or women will normally be admitted for a period not exceeding 12 months with a condition restricting their freedom to take employment. A further three-year extension may be obtained if they can prove that the business is continuing, the money (currently £200,000) has been invested and that new employment for at least two people has been created.

4. Retired persons of independent means/investors

(a) Retired persons of independent means

The New Rules make it clear that persons of independent means must be retired before they seek leave to enter the United Kingdom. Their applications must be made from abroad. Only the relatively wealthy can now retire to the United Kingdom and they must meet the following requirements.

- They must be at least 60 years old and have under their control and disposal in the United Kingdom a minimum income (currently not less than £25,000 per annum).
- They must be able and willing to accommodate and maintain themselves and any dependents indefinitely in the United Kingdom from their own resources, with no assistance from any other person and without taking employment or having recourse to public funds.

- They must demonstrate a close connection with the United Kingdom.
- They must intend to make the United Kingdom their main home.

Where these conditions are satisfied, retired persons will normally be admitted for an initial period of four years, with a prohibition on the taking of paid or unpaid employment.

It remains to be seen whether the Home Office will exercise discretion for those under the age of 60 who, for example, have income substantially in excess of £25,000 per annum.

(b) Investors

The New Rules introduce a new category of investors in order to enable those who wish to invest a substantial amount in the UK economy to engage in business and obtain residency status leading to settlement. The New Rules define, to some extent, the sort of investment which will be acceptable under the Rules.

- Investors must have money of their own under their control and disposable in the United Kingdom amounting at present to no less than £1 million.

- Investors must intend to invest not less than £750,000 of capital in the United Kingdom by way of UK government bonds, share capital or loan capital in active and trading UK registered companies (other than those principally engaged in property investment and excluding investment by way of deposits with a bank, building society or other enterprise whose normal course of business includes the acceptance of deposits).

- Investors must intend to make the United Kingdom their main home and be able to maintain and accommodate themselves and any dependants without taking employment (other than being in self-employment or carrying on their own business) or recourse to public funds.

Investors must make their applications from abroad and hold a valid visa for entry in this capacity.

5. Spouses and children

There are three types of family admission to the United Kingdom:

(1) immediate family of persons on a limited leave such as students, workers, businessmen, persons of independent means, writers, artists and composers;
(2) relatives coming on a permanent basis to settle in the United Kingdom with the rest of their family; and
(3) those who are allowed admission in order to get married or who have obtained settlement as a result of getting married.

(a) Marriage

Fiancés and fiancées must both apply for visas and satisfy the entry clearance officer that:

- it is not the primary purpose of the intended marriage to obtain admission to the United Kingdom;
- the parties to the marriage intend to live together permanently as husband and wife;
- they have met;
- adequate maintenance and accommodation will be available for the applicant until the date of the marriage, without recourse to public funds;
- after the marriage there will be adequate accommodation for the parties and their dependants in accommodation which they own or occupy exclusively, without recourse to public funds; and
- after the marriage the parties will be able to maintain themselves and their dependants adequately without recourse to public funds.

(b) Spouses

The rules for spouses are very similar. They must satisfy the entry clearance officer that:

- the marriage was not entered into primarily to obtain admission to the United Kingdom;
- each of the parties has the intention of living permanently with the other as his or her spouse;
- the parties to the marriage have met;
- there will be adequate accommodation for the parties and their dependants in accommodation which they own or occupy exclusively, without recourse to public funds; and
- the parties will be able to maintain themselves and their dependants adequately without recourse to public funds.

(c) Children

(i) Children born in the United Kingdom
A child who remains in the United Kingdom continuously for the first 10 years of his or her life can obtain registration as a British citizen. A child under 18, one of whose parents becomes settled or acquires British nationality, will also be eligible for registration as a British citizen. The British Nationality Act 1981 applies to children born in the United Kingdom after 1 January 1983 who do not become British citizens. While they remain in the United Kingdom without leave there is no need to obtain leave to remain. Leave is granted which is consistent

with that of the parents or parent. Where the parents live apart leave should be consistent with that of the parent who has the "day-to-day responsibility" of the child or children.

(ii) Other children
Admission of unmarried children under the age of 18 living in conventional families is unconditional. Admission of children of divided or single parent families is qualified and difficult. The burden of proof is on the applicant(s) who want to come to the United Kingdom that they are their parents' children or that they are the ages they claim.

(iii) Children over 18
Children over 18 (including, under the New Rules, fully dependent, unmarried daughters over 18 and under 21) must qualify in their own right unless there are the most exceptional circumstances.

(iv) Adopted children
The New Rules contain a number of additional requirements as a result of the Resolution on the Harmonisation of National Policies on Family Reunification agreed by EC Ministers in Copenhagen in June 1993. Overseas adoptions must be in accordance with a decision taken by the appropriate administrative authority or court in the child's country of origin or residence.

At the time of the adoption both adoptive parents must be resident together abroad, or one or both adoptive parents must be settled in the United Kingdom. The New Rules also specify that the adopted child should have the same rights as any other child of the marriage; and that he or she must have lost or broken his or her ties with his or her family of origin.

(v) Rights of access to a child resident in the United Kingdom
The New Rules introduce a new category for persons exercising their rights of access to a child resident in the United Kingdom. This is necessary in the light of the ECHR judgment in the case of *Yousef* (unreported) (No 14830/89) which found the United Kingdom in breach of Article 13 of the Convention (Rights of Redress). The New Rules now provide for a parent who is either divorced or legally separated to come to the United Kingdom for up to 12 months for the purpose of exercising rights granted by a court in the United Kingdom to a child resident here.

6. Temporary stays

(a) Visitors

People seeking entry as visitors must satisfy the immigration authorities that they are genuinely seeking entry as a visitor for a limited period not exceeding six months, that they intend to leave the United Kingdom at the end of the period of the visit as stated by them and that they do not intend to take employment in the United Kingdom or to produce goods or provide services within the United Kingdom. They must also satisfy the immigration authorities that they will maintain and accommodate themselves and any dependants adequately out of resources available to them without recourse to public funds or taking employment, or will, with any dependants, be maintained and accommodated adequately by relatives or friends and that they can meet the cost of their return or onward journey.

(i) Business visitors

Business visitors are persons living and working outside the United Kingdom who come to the United Kingdom to transact business (such as attending meetings and briefings, fact finding, negotiating or making contracts with UK businesses to buy or sell goods or services). These visitors must not intend to obtain employment, study at a maintained school, or produce goods and services within the United Kingdom, including the selling of goods and services direct to members of the public.

(ii) Medical visitors

In order to restrict the scope for abuse by those seeking leave to enter or remain as a visitor for the purpose of private medical treatment, the New Rules now provide that the treatment sought should be of finite duration and that an application for an extension of stay for medical treatment should be supported by a registered medical practitioner who holds a National Health Service consultant post. Overseas nationals may still be admitted for up to a maximum of six months to receive private treatment from a general practitioner or practitioner of alternative medicine.

(b) Students

Persons wishing to enter the United Kingdom as overseas students must obtain a visa from a British Embassy abroad before leaving their country, even if they are not visa nationals. They must be full-time students, able to pay for their course, and intend to return home when their studies are complete. The New Rules clarify the fact that all students are expected to be enrolled for at least 15 hours a week of full-time daytime study. The only exception relates to students enrolled on a full-time degree course at a publicly funded institution of further or higher education. Students are no longer permitted to enrol on a variety of part-time courses at a number of educational establishments in order to make up their 15 hours.

(c) Prospective students

Persons seeking leave to enter the United Kingdom as prospective students must demonstrate a genuine and realistic intention of undertaking, within six months of their date of entry, a course of study which would meet the requirements of students set out above. They must intend to leave the United Kingdom on completion of their studies and be able, without working or recourse to public funds, to meet the costs of their intended course and accommodation and the maintenance of themselves and any dependents while making arrangements to study and during the course of their studies.

Students must be admitted for a short period, within the limit of their means, with a prohibition on the taking of employment, and will be advised to apply to the Home Office for further consideration of their case.

(d) Medical students

The New Rules define what is meant by a student nurse. The Rules also require that student nurses must satisfy the immigration authorities that they intend to leave the United Kingdom at the end of their studies. Postgraduate doctors and dentists must be graduates from a UK medical school intending to undertake pre-registration house officer employment for up to 12 months as required for full registration with the General Medical Council, and must have spent no more than 12 months in aggregate in pre-registration house officer employment. Alternatively, they must be doctors or dentists eligible for full or limited registration with the General Medical Council or with the General Dental Council, who intend to undertake postgraduate training in a hospital, and who have spent no more than four years in aggregate in the United Kingdom as a postgraduate doctor or dentist, excluding any period spent in pre-registration house officer employment. They must intend to leave the United Kingdom on completion of their training period.

(e) Spouses and children of students

The spouse and children under 18 of a person admitted as a student are to be given leave to enter for the same period as the student if they can be maintained and accommodated without recourse to public funds. Employment is to be prohibited except where the period of leave being granted is 12 months or more.

(f) Au pairs

Au pair is an arrangement under which an unmarried person aged between 17 and 27 and without dependants, who is a national of a Western European country (including Andorra, Bosnia Herzegovina, Croatia, Cyprus, Czech Republic, the Faroes, Greenland, Hungary, Liechtenstein, Macedonia, Malta, Monaco, San Marino, Slovak Republic, Slovenia, Switzerland and Turkey), may come to the United Kingdom to learn the English language and to live for a time as a member of an English-speaking family. When the immigration officer is satisfied that an au pair arrangement has been made the au pair may be admitted for a period of up to 12 months with a prohibition on taking employment other than the employment so authorised. If he or she has previously spent time in the United Kingdom as an au pair he or she may be admitted for a further period provided the total aggregate period in which he or she will be in the United Kingdom does not exceed two years. There is nothing to stop a person in the United Kingdom as a visitor or in some other temporary capacity switching to "au pair".

(g) Working holiday-makers

Working holiday-makers and any accompanying children now require a visa before travelling and will not be permitted to switch to working holiday-maker status if they entered the United Kingdom in any other capacity. The employment available to working holiday-makers under the New Rules has been clarified to the extent that they are now prohibited from engaging in business, pursuing a career or providing services as a professional sportsman or entertainer. Only young British Commonwealth Citizens aged between 17 and 27 are entitled to visas as working holiday-makers. They must satisfy the immigration officer that they are coming to the United Kingdom for an extended holiday before settling down in their own country and that they intend to take only employment which will be incidental to their holiday. They will no longer be able to be accompanied by a dependent spouse unless the spouse qualifies in his or her own right as a working holiday-maker. A child of the working holiday-maker will only be able to accompany his parent(s) if he or she is under the age of five and will leave the United Kingdom before reaching the age of five.

7. Permanent residence

In order to apply for permanent residence a person, together with his or her spouse and children admitted as his or her dependants, must have legally resided for four years in any one of the immigration categories, including the category of refugee but excluding those on temporary stay and with exceptional leave to remain.

(a) Immigration categories leading to permanent residence

A person admitted to the United Kingdom in any one of the following categories may, if he or she so qualifies, apply for permanent residence:

- approved employment by way of a work permit;
- permit-free employment (*i.e.* sole representatives of overseas firms, ministers of religion, missionaries, representatives of overseas newspapers and broadcasters, employees of overseas governments or the United Nations or other international body and operational ground staff (but not other staff) of overseas owned airlines);

- businessmen and women who have set up business with others;
- self-employed businessmen and women;
- writers, composers or artists;
- retired persons of independent means;
- investors;
- workers or work-seekers who are Commonwealth citizens and whose grandparents were born in the United Kingdom.

8. Nationality

There are six categories of British nationality of which only one, British citizens, has an absolute right to enter Britain. The other five categories are people originating from British dependencies or ex colonies who had their right of entry to Britain taken away in 1962 or 1968, even though they travel on British passports. The British Nationality Act 1981 sets out the conditions for acquiring five of those nationalities (British citizenship, British dependent territories citizenship, British overseas citizenship, British subject status and British protected person status). The sixth category – British national (overseas) status – was created for people from Hong Kong in the Hong Kong Act 1985 and the Hong Kong (British Nationality) Order 1986 (SI 1986/948).

Since the British Nationality Act 1981 came into effect on 1 January 1983, those people who do not fall under any of the six categories of British citizenship can acquire it only by obtaining residence and then permanent residence in the United Kingdom, which normally involves remaining in the United Kingdom, under one of the categories of residence, for at least five years. To qualify, a person must have spent no more than 450 days outside the United Kingdom throughout the five-year period and not more than 90 days in the year prior to making the application.

However, the spouse of a British citizen may apply for naturalisation one year after permanent residence (*i.e.* three years after entry) and to qualify he or she must not have spent more than 270 days outside the United Kingdom throughout the three-year period and not more than 90 days in the year prior to making the application.

9. Refugees and political asylum

There may be many reasons for seeking political asylum, but persons are only refugees within the meaning of the Convention Relating to the Status of Refugees and the Protocol to the Convention if they seek to escape persecution for reasons of race, religion, nationality, membership of a social group or political opinion. In the United Kingdom all those who are granted political asylum are recognised as Convention refugees and are given appropriate documents. Special considerations apply when a person claims asylum in the United Kingdom where it appears that he or she might be eligible for asylum as a result of anything the person has said. All such cases are referred to the Home Office regardless of any other grounds of refusal under the New Rules. Once the cases go to the Home Office they will be considered in accordance with the Convention and the Protocol. Where the Home Office grants asylum the immigration officer will grant leave to enter. If asylum is refused, the immigration officer will consider whether the person is entitled to remain on some other basis under the New Rules.

Asylum claims made after entry are usually considered by the Home Office "Asylum Unit".

In some cases where the Home Office considers that persons do not have an entitlement to political asylum it gives leave to remain on an exceptional basis. Such "exceptional leave" is given outside the New Rules; it is not a recognition of refugee status, and holders of such exceptional leave who consider that they ought to have refugee status are given the right to appeal to an adjudicator against the refusal to grant political asylum.

10. Government discretion

It cannot be emphasised enough that the Home Office has very considerable discretion to waive or vary most of the requirements referred to in this chapter. The individual circumstances of each applicant are taken into account. The exercise of ministerial discretion outside the New Rules is an important aspect of immigration law and practice in the United Kingdom.

Three principles can be identified which must justify the exercise of discretion. These are:

(1) the interests of national security or foreign relations;
(2) compassionate circumstances;
(3) a previous pledge of public faith.

These principles are normally followed on the basis of consistency, reasonableness and fairness.

11. Sanctions

(a) Deportation

Any person who is a non-British citizen is liable to deportation on the following grounds:

- he or she does not comply with any condition of leave, for example by overstaying his or her leave or working in breach of condition;

- the Home Secretary deems his or her deportation to be conducive to the public good;
- in some cases where another member of the family, such as the father or mother, is to be deported;
- where a court recommends deportation after a conviction for an offence punishable by imprisonment.

(b) Illegal entry

To be an illegal entrant a person must unlawfully enter or seek to enter the United Kingdom in breach of a deportation order or the immigration laws. There are five kinds of possible illegal entry:

(1) entry without leave;
(2) entry in breach of a deportation order;
(3) desertion of a ship and overstay by seamen;
(4) entry through the common travel area;
(5) entry by deception.

(c) Detention

Immigration officers are authorised to detain the following categories of person, pending their removal:

- persons arriving by ship or aircraft in the United Kingdom, pending their examination by an immigration officer to see whether they need or should be granted leave to enter;
- persons refused leave to enter;
- illegal entrants if they are not given leave to enter or remain in the United Kingdom;
- members of the crew of a ship or aircraft who stay longer than permitted, or are reasonably suspected of intending to do so by an immigration officer.

(d) Detention by the Home Secretary

In addition to the powers of detention by immigration officers, the Home Secretary has wide powers to detain persons liable to deportation. This may occur in three situations:

(1) following a court recommendation;
(2) where notice has been given to a person of a decision to make a deportation order; or
(3) where a deportation order is in force against any person, he or she may be detained under the authority of the Home Secretary and pending his or her removal or departure from the United Kingdom.

12. Tax and social security

It is not possible in a work of this nature to give anything but a brief indication of the complex tax and social security provisions of UK law.

(a) Tax

(i) Individuals (employees/directors)

Generally, taxation in the United Kingdom impacts most on those who are resident and domiciled here, to a lesser extent on those who are resident but not domiciled and to the least extent on those who are not resident. Residence for the purpose of taxation is also not necessarily the same as residence for immigration purposes. If an individual is neither domiciled nor resident he or she will only be liable for tax on income arising here, *e.g.* from a UK source or trading. If he or she is resident but not domiciled then, in addition to tax on income or capital gains arising in the United Kingdom, he or she will be liable for tax on income remitted in the United Kingdom.

Whether or not domiciled or resident in the United Kingdom, inheritance tax may also be payable on the death of any individual in respect of assets situate in the United Kingdom, *e.g.* land and houses, and bank accounts (in excess of the aggregate of £200,000).

Basic rate income tax and capital gains tax is 24% at a lower rate band and 40% at a higher rate band, although there are various allowances for individuals and capital allowances for trading.

National insurance contributions are payable by employer and employee.

(ii) Companies

Corporation tax is levied on companies at a lower rate of 24% rising to 33% for higher revenue. Double tax treaties may also relieve tax. In addition, value added tax on various goods and services is levied at 17.5%. Stamp duty on certain documents, mainly in relation to land and houses, is 1%.

In certain cases, tax advantages may be obtained from the more favourable regimes of the Channel Islands and the Isle of Man which form part of the United Kingdom.

(b) Social security

Nearly one third of government expenditure is devoted to the Social Security Programme, which provides financial help for people who are elderly, sick, disabled, unemployed, widowed, bringing up children or on very low incomes.

Some benefits depend on the payment of contributions by employers, employees, and self-employed people to the National Insurance Fund, from which benefits are paid. The Government also contributes to the Fund. The other social security benefits are non-contributory and are financed from general taxation; some of these are income-related.

The following benefits are available: retirement pension, statutory maternity pay, financial assistance for widows, statutory sick pay and sickness benefits, invalidity pension and allowances, and industrial injuries benefits.

Other benefits include unemployment benefit (job seeker's allowance), income support, housing benefit, together with discretionary payments in the form of loans or grants made from the Social Fund to people on low incomes for expenses which are difficult to meet from their regular income.

As part of the EU's efforts to promote the free movement of labour, regulations provide for equality of treatment and other protection of benefit rights for employed and self-employed people who move between Member States. The regulations also cover retirement pensioners and other beneficiaries who have been employed or self-employed, as well as dependants. Benefits covered include child benefit, and benefits for sickness and maternity, unemployment, retirement, invalidity, accidents at work and occupational diseases.

The United Kingdom also has reciprocal social security agreements with a number of other countries. Their scope and the benefits they cover vary, but the majority cover most national insurance and family benefits.

13. **Domestic considerations**

An individual who has received the necessary visa to travel to the United Kingdom in order to take up the status for which he or she applied, will not only have to make the necessary arrangements in his country of origin for relocating to the United Kingdom, but also consider what arrangements must be made when he or she and his or her family have moved to the United Kingdom.

Apart from the simple and domestic matters, such as purchasing or renting a house or flat, and a new school for children, there are UK laws and local authority rules and regulations which should be identified. It would be unfortunate if an individual or a member of his or her family were to break any law or regulation due to ignorance, resulting in prosecution and imprisonment or a fine, thereby unnecessarily having such an infringement noted on his or her immigration history.

The aim of this section is to outline certain matters which should be considered when relocating to the United Kingdom and to alert the individual to potential problems. This is not an exhaustive list of matters.

(a) **Police registration certificate**

Upon an individual and his or her family being granted leave to remain in the United Kingdom, it will be necessary to register with the local police within seven days of arriving in the United Kingdom. The Central Aliens Registration Office is located in London for those residing in London, while those residing outside London, or anywhere else in the United Kingdom, would attend upon their local police.

(b) Motor cars

If a car is imported to the United Kingdom it will be necessary to check the import regulations and licencing requirements in the United Kingdom.

Before an individual can take a motor vehicle on the public roads in the United Kingdom, it must be registered, currently licensed and covered by a valid Ministry of Transport test certificate (MOT certificate) and the individual must be licensed to drive and have a valid insurance covering the use of the vehicle.

(c) Housing

When renting or purchasing a flat or house, an individual should ideally consult an estate agent to seek and identify the appropriate property. Upon identifying the appropriate property, an individual is recommended to consult a solicitor to negotiate and finalise the purchase or letting of the property.

A solicitor is able to advise on the mechanics and procedures of purchasing or letting, as well as completing the necessary legal work.

(i) Council tax

Council tax is the way in which an individual helps to pay for local services which the local authority or council provides. This includes the cleaning of roads, removal and disposal of rubbish, provision of education and similar local amenities. Each council sets the level of council tax for its own area.

The amount which has to be paid depends on the value of the property, relative to others in the local area. There is only one council tax bill for each dwelling or property and this is usually payable by the owner/occupier or tenant.

When there are two or more people who are joint owners or joint tenants, they will all be liable for the council tax regardless of whether the bill is sent to them in their joint names or just to one of them.

Non-payment of council tax may result in a court summons.

(ii) Televisions

A television licence is required for all houses or flats with at least one television, and is renewable annually. The application form may be obtained from a local post office. The relevant authorities may inspect any premises and it is an offence not to have a current licence. This may result in a court summons and the payment of a fine. A television licence is required from the time a television is being used. The amount of the penalty depends on the individual case.

This is a particular example where ignorance of the law may lead to a criminal record which can have an adverse effect on an individual's immigration history when applying for an extension of leave to remain, settlement or even citizenship.

(d) Health care

An individual may find it beneficial to register with a local doctor and dentist. If previous medical records are available, an individual may wish to have them transferred to a current doctor.

(e) Banking facilities

Unless an individual has a bank account in the United Kingdom or credit cards in current use, it will be necessary to open up a bank account and, in some cases, a business account.

A letter of introduction from an individual's current bank addressed to the bank with which he or she wishes to open an account is a good idea. This letter should also provide a reference, which the new bank can check through its overseas agents or inter bank arrangements.

(f) Schooling

If an individual relocates to the United Kingdom with his or her family, and any children of the family are of school age, the individual may make the relevant enquiries of the local authorities for a list of appropriate schools. Enquiries may also be made to the local education authority.

Messrs. Gulbenkian Harris Andonian, 181 Kensington High Street,
London W8 6SH. tel.: (44) 171 937 1542. telefax.: (44) 171 938 2059.

Contents of Chapter 2

EC NATIONALS

Chapter 2

EC NATIONALS

Ted Badoux

1. Historical overview

After the Second World War a political movement emerged in Europe which aspired to create strongly organised political and economic relations between the European nations. In the 1950s the later Benelux countries, France, Germany and Italy, founded three European Communities for the gradual integration of their economies: the European Community for Coal and Steel, the European Economic Community and the European Community for Nuclear Energy. Since the Treaty of Rome (1965) these three Communities are integrated and share the same institutions: the European Council of Ministers, the European Commission, the European Parliament and the European Court of Justice.

In 1986, the EC Member States signed the Single European Act setting out the principles and a time schedule for further political and economic integration, including the achievement of a single market by 1 January 1993.

At the Summit of Maastricht in December 1991, the EC Member States agreed on a Monetary and Political Union with the exception of the United Kingdom. A Common European Currency (ECU) will be introduced between 1996 and 1999. A Central European Bank will be founded no later than 1 July 1998. Defence, foreign policy and labour conditions will be integrated on the basis of inter-governmental cooperation. The summit finally led to the Treaty of Maastricht, signed on 7 February 1992 and effective as of 1 November 1993. By this Treaty the three European Communities were integrated into a European Union and, because of its many other activities besides merely economic, the name "European Economic Community" was changed to "European Community". In 1995 Members of the European Community were: Austria, Belgium, Denmark, France, Finland, Germany, Greece, Ireland, Italy, Luxembourg, the Netherlands, Portugal, Spain, Sweden and the United Kingdom.

The law of the European Community governs the European territories of the
Member States with the following exceptions:

- Danish nationals of the Faroe Isles are not considered as EC nationals privileged to free movement within the Community;

- French residents of the so-called French overseas departments French
  Guyana, Guadeloupe, Martinique and La Réunion, however, have the
  right of free movement within the Community;

- as to the United Kingdom and Northern Ireland, the subjects of the Channel
  Islands and the Isle of Man are excluded from the right of free movement.
  Next to British citizens, holders of a "British subject" passport stating "the
  right of abode in the United Kingdom" and those with British passports
  stating that "the holder is defined as a United Kingdom national for
  Community purposes", also have the right of free movement.

One of the aims of the European Community is to establish a Common Market.
This should be achieved, among other things, by the abolition between Member
States of obstacles to the freedom of movement for persons, services and capital.
The EC Treaty warrants the freedom of nationals of Member States to pursue
economic activities in other Member States. The EC Treaty provides for the free
movement of workers in Articles 48 to 51, the right of establishment in Articles
52 to 58, and the right to receive and be the recipient of services in Articles 59
to 66. Pursuant to Article 6, all EC nationals have the right to enjoy these freedoms without any discrimination on the basis of nationality. This principle of
non-discrimination implies that all EC nationals exercising the right of free
movement in a host Member State, whether by seeking or taking up (self-)
employment, by providing or being the recipient of services, should be able to
do what local nationals can do. In other words, they should receive national
treatment. The implementing provisions of EC law stipulate national treatment
in (self-)employment, trade union rights, vocational training, housing facilities
and education for children.

The implementation of the right of free movement is governed by Regulations
and Directives which are binding upon the Member States and have priority
over national law. In general, Regulations are to be enforced by the national
courts on the basis of the principle of direct applicability, while Directives give
binding guidelines for national legislation within a fixed time-frame. However,
EC provisions with regard to clearly defined rights of EC nationals are governed
by the principle of direct applicability, irrespective of their source in EC law.

The European Court of Justice in Luxembourg plays an important part in the
development of Community law, especially through interpretative rulings. In
the field of immigration law its jurisprudence, which is also a binding source of
supra-national law for the Member States, has had a major impact on issues
such as education, employment, family life and public policy.

In October 1991 the European Community agreed with the European Free
Trade Association (EFTA) countries (Austria, Finland, Iceland, Liechtenstein,

Norway, Sweden and Switzerland) to create a European Economic Area. The European Economic Area Agreement (EEA) is effective as of 1 January 1994. The following European countries are members: Austria, Belgium, Denmark, Finland, France, Germany, Greece, Iceland, Ireland, Italy, Liechtenstein, Luxembourg, the Netherlands, Norway, Portugal, Spain, Sweden and the United Kingdom. The Swiss have voted themselves out of the EEA by national referendum. For the purpose of this book, nationals of these countries are referred to as EEA nationals. Pursuant to the EEA Agreement EEA nationals enjoy the original EC right of free movement to pursue economic activities within the European Economic Area and can take up permanent residence for that purpose in any of those countries. On the same conditions as EC nationals they may also stay for study or retirement. Non-EEA nationals obtain a dependent status if they have family ties with an EEA national who takes up residence in a European country other than his or her own.

By the end of 1991, Hungary, Poland and Czechoslovakia entered into Agreements of Association with the European Community. Turkey, Morocco, Tunis, Malta and Cyprus have become associated with the European Community in the 1960s and 1970s. Slovenia has become associated on 11 June 1996. Jurisprudence of the European Court of Justice – the case of Mr Sevince from Turkey, the case of Mr Kziber from Morocco, the case of Mr Kus from Turkey and the case of Mr Bozkurt from Turkey – shows that the rules of these agreements may be very important for residence, the right to work and the social benefits of workers from the associated countries. (For a discussion of these cases, see **3(a)(i)** below.)

Apart from these agreements of association/cooperation, the European Community upholds extensive trade relations with countries and organisations of countries throughout the world.

2. Schengen visas

In view of the achievement of a single European market in 1993 whereby the internal European borders have been abolished, a group of European countries has agreed on a common system of controls at the external borders of their territory. In 1985 and 1990 the group signed agreements for this purpose in a Luxembourg town called Schengen. As of 26 March 1995 the provisions of the Schengen Agreements of 1985 and 1990 have been implemented within the following Schengen States: Belgium, France, Germany, Luxembourg, the Netherlands, Portugal and Spain. The Schengen provisions will be implemented in Greece and Italy at a later date. The Schengen provisions attend, amongst other things, to a common policy on visas and a uniform visa for the Schengen territory. Travellers who need visas for one or more Schengen States must travel with a "Schengen visa", which is issued by any one of the seven States and is valid for all others.

Travel between these countries will in principle be without a documentation check at immigration controls (except in France, where a full document check has been re-established since 26 July 1995).

Schengen visas should be obtained prior to arrival in the Schengen territory. Those who wish to travel to one of the Schengen States can apply for a Schengen visa at the State's embassy or consulate abroad. Visa applications may be dealt with at the diplomatic post or may be sent for investigation and instructions to the national visa authority.

As a consequence of this, visa applications can take anything from a few hours to a few months. Schengen visas are issued for a stay up to a maximum of three months. In general, for the issue of a Schengen visa a valid passport or other permitted travel document is required, as well as sufficient funds to finance the intended period of stay and the return journey. Furthermore, a person should not be registered as an alien, excluded from entry, or pose a risk to the public peace, the national security or the international relations of any of the seven Schengen States. The validity of the visa is linked to the validity of the passport and the return ticket. A Schengen visa is no guarantee that admission will be granted; the requirements for a Schengen visa, i.e. to hold a valid passport and to have sufficient financial means and so on, may be checked upon entry at the border. Possession of a valid return ticket is recommended. A Schengen visa can be annulled or not extended if a visitor fails to comply with any of the above-mentioned requirements.

A Schengen visa is valid for entry to the seven Schengen States. Holders of a Schengen visa can travel freely between the Schengen States as long as their visas are valid and up to a maximum of three months from the first day of arrival in the Schengen territory. Upon entering one of the other Schengen States, there is a duty to report to the immigration authorities either upon arrival or within three working days from the date of arrival.

Those who need to visit one or more Schengen States frequently for business purposes can obtain a Schengen business visa. This visa grants multiple entry to the Schengen territory for an uninterrupted stay of a certain amount of days, up to three months within a six-month period. In cases of specific national interest, visas can be granted up to six months within a 12-month period. In exceptional cases visas can even be granted for multiple entry within a period of one to five years.

The list of charges for visas, i.e. legal duties, is detailed and has been fixed for each of the Schengen States separately. The charge for a one-month Schengen visa for single or multiple entry is approximately $40. For a three-month Schengen visa the charge is approximately $50.

Those who are exempt from the obligation to hold a Schengen visa can travel freely between the Schengen States up to a maximum of three months within a six-month period, from the first day of arrival in the Schengen territory. Upon entering one of the other Schengen States, there is a duty to report to the immigration authorities as desired either upon arrival or within three working days from the date of arrival.

Those in possession of a residence permit or other valid title of permitted long-term stay in one of the Schengen States have the right to enter that State at all times. They also have the right to travel freely between the other Schengen

States up to a maximum of three months as long as they have a valid title of permitted long-term stay, possess a valid passport or other permitted travel document and have sufficient funds to finance the intended period of stay and the return journey. Furthermore, they should not pose a threat to the public peace, the national security or the international relations of any of the other Schengen States. Upon entering one of the other Schengen States, they have a duty to report to the immigration authorities as desired either upon arrival or within three working days from the date of arrival.

Nationals of the 18 countries of the European Economic Area (EEA) are exempt from Schengen visa requirements under EC law.

3. Visa requirement for entering the area of the European Community

On 25 September 1995 the European Council of Ministers issued Regulation 2317/95 listing the States whose nationals are required to obtain a visa to enter one of the EC Member States. The list is set out in the Appendix at the end of this book.

(a) Rights of free movement

European Community (EC) nationals who migrate from one State in the Community to another for economic purposes, take a privileged position. They may have found work either in employment or in self-employment; they may have come to seek employment or self-employment; or they may wish to provide or receive services. In addition, the right of free movement has been extended to migration within the Community for non-economic purposes, for retirement and for study.

(i) Employment
The rights of free movement of workers are set out in Articles 48–51 of the EC Treaty. Free movement of workers entails the right:

- to accept actual offers of employment;
- to move freely within EC territory for this purpose;
- to stay in the territory of an EC country for the purposes of employment;
- to remain there after having been employed.

These provisions have been implemented by Regulation 1612/68, which deals with non-discrimination and the worker's family, by Directive 68/360, which grants workers and their families the right of entry and residence, and by Regulation 1251/70, which gives workers and their families the right to remain in a Member State after retirement or permanent incapacity. EC nationals seeking employment have the right to enter and seek employment for three months as long as they do not attempt to live on welfare. They are not obliged to show sufficient means upon entry. Border officials are not authorised to question job-seeking EC nationals on sufficient means.

The three months' term is not very strict it would seem; six months may also be a reasonable term and even this term may be overstepped if it is demonstrated that efforts to find employment are still being made and that the prospects of success are realistic (ECJ 26.02.91, C-292/89, the case of Mr Antonissen).

EC nationals seeking employment must report to the local authorities in charge of immigration. These authorities, in turn, are obliged to refer job-seeking EC nationals to the domestic bodies for employment-finding. EC nationals are entitled to the same assistance from employment officials as nationals of the Member State. Having found employment EC nationals must report again to the authorities. For the issue of a residence permit they can be obliged to produce a passport or other travelling document, a certificate from their employer and may have to sign a statement with regard to their criminal record.

If the employment certificate demonstrates that the duration of the employment will be at least one year, a residence permit for five years should be issued. In case of employment for a period of three to 12 months, an EC national is entitled to a residence permit for the duration of the agreed employment. The issue of a residence card to EC nationals who will be working for more than three months is obligatory. For those working less than three months, a simple stamp will suffice.

It is important to note that the issue of an EC residence permit is a mere formality with a declaratory character; not the permit but the rules of Community law constitute the right to stay.

An EC residence card, which was originally issued for five years, can also be extended for five years. However, in cases of involuntary unemployment which has lasted for more than 12 months, the validity of the card may be limited to one year at the first extension; if the unemployment still prevails after this year, further extension can be refused.

Other possible circumstances which will put an end to a person's EC residence status are: voluntary unemployment; a break of stay of more than six months; or criminal behaviour. Military service, disability to work due to illness of accident and involuntary unemployment will not effect EC status.

Termination of temporary employment as such is not a circumstance that will end EC status. In view of the European labour market it must be assumed that a worker is not in a position freely to choose between a temporary assignment and unlimited employment. The terms "worker" and "activity as an employed person" are determined by EC law and must be given a broad interpretation. According to the European Court of Justice the essential characteristics of employment are, that during a given time one person provides services for and under the direction of another in return for remuneration (ECJ 03.07.86, C-66/85, the Lawrie-Blum case).

Part-time employment may well constitute an EC residence status. The criterion is whether the job is "genuine and effective", irrespective of motives for taking employment or the level of income (ECJ 23.03.82, C-53/81, the case of Ms Levin). Subsidiary means of subsistence supplied by public funds or private persons (family members) are also irrelevant, provided that the activities in employment are genuine and effective (ECJ 03.06.86, C-139/85, the case of Mr Kempf). In the same case the court ruled that it should be left to the national judiciary to assess whether or not a certain job would be genuine and effective. The nature of the payment is not decisive; room and board and a certain amount of pocket money can be considered as remuneration for activities in employment (ECJ 05.10.88, C-196/87, the case of Mr Steymann).

The nature of the job may determine whether the activities are genuine and effective; 15 hours per week of teaching may constitute genuine and effective employment, but a cleaning job for 10 hours a week may be disqualified as being marginal and secondary. A minimum of 40% of the usual working hours in a specific employment sector may serve as a guideline for national judiciaries.

EC nationals have the right to be employed under the same statutory provisions applicable to the employment of national employees.

Article 6 of Decision 1/80 of the Agreement of Association between the European Community and Turkey confers rights of continued employment to legally residing Turkish nationals. A Turkish employee who:

- has worked for one employer in permanent employment for one year, is entitled to renewal of his work permit if employment is available with the same employer;

- has worked for one employer in permanent employment for three years, is entitled to accept employment in the same profession from another employer if the offer concerns regular employment which has been registered with the local labour market authorities and notwithstanding priority for job-seeking EC nationals;

- has worked for one employer in permanent employment for four years, has free access to the labour market of the Member State.

Jurisprudence of the European Court of Justice has so far concentrated on the extent of the concept of legal employment. In the case of Mr Sevince (ECJ 20.09.90, C-192/89) the court ruled, *inter alia*, that Article 6, section 1 of Decision 1/80 is governed by the principle of direct applicability and that the term of legal employment does not include employment pending an appeal with suspensive effect against a decision by which a residence permit has been refused.

In the case of Mr Kus (ECJ 16.12.92, C-237/91) the court ruled, *inter alia*, that legal employment is not affected by the fact that employment was not the primary purpose of the residence permit which had been issued initially. Furthermore, the court held that Turkish workers can appeal to Article 6 direct and that – if they meet one of the conditions set out in Article 6 – they are entitled not only to renewal of their work permit, but also to renewal of their residence permit.

Case C-434/93 concerned Mr Bozkurt, a Turkish international transport driver. On 6 June 1995 the court ruled that it is up to the national judiciary to assess whether the employment is tied-in sufficiently with the territory of the Member State. If, in a case like this, a Turkish worker would be exempted from the requirement to obtain a residence permit and a work permit pursuant to a rule of national law, that employment would be legal in the sense of Article 6 of Decision 1/80. However, a Turkish worker who has been part of the legal labour market of a Member State cannot appeal under Article 6 for continued residence after permanent disablement on account of an industrial accident.

In the Kziber case (ECJ 31.01.91, C-18/90) the European Court applied the principle of non-discrimination to legal Moroccan workers and their family members in relation to national social security benefits of a Member State. This ruling and the direct applicability of Article 41, paragraph 1 of the Agreement of Association between the European Community and Morocco is also valid for identical provisions in similar agreements of the Community with Algeria and Tunisia.

(ii) Business and self-employment

The right of establishment, laid down in Articles 52–59 of the EC Treaty, confers the right of free movement on EC nationals wishing to enter a Member State in order to set up or manage a business or to become self-employed. This right extends to companies legally incorporated in one of the Member States.

The implementation of the right of establishment has been carried out in Directive 73/148, giving similar rights to enter and to reside as those given to workers and their families in Directive 68/360.

A whole set of Directives deals with the adequacy, standardisation and recognition of professional qualifications.

A five-year EC residence permit should be issued to a person who produces evidence that he or she established him or herself in business or in a self-employed occupation in the initial trial period of three to six months. Directive 75/34 gives business people and the self-employed the right to remain in the Member State after incapacity or retirement.

The right of establishment also includes the right of legally incorporated EC companies to transfer key personnel to new branch offices, affiliates and subsidiary companies in other Member States. In Article 54, paragraph 2 of the EC Treaty, key personnel is referred to as personnel of the main establishment assigned to the bodies of management and supervision of those branch offices, affiliates and subsidiary companies. Note, that on the basis of Article 54 an EC company is entitled also to transfer its legally residing non-EC key personnel. A work permit requirement imposed by the receiving Member State can only serve administrative purposes and should in no way be an obstacle to the exercised freedom of establishment. As part of an Agreement of Association with the European Community the freedom of establishment, including the right to transfer key personnel, has been confered to the nationals and the legally incorporated companies of the following East European countries: Bulgaria, Czech Republic, Hungary, Poland and the Slovak Republic.

Pursuant to single trade agreements with the European Community, the freedom of establishment, including the right to transfer key personnel, also not yet been confered to the nationals but only to the legally incorporated companies of the following East European countries: Belarus, Estonia, Latvia, Lithuania and Ukraine.

(iii) Non-economic activities and retirement

Two other Directives, 90/364 and 90/365, confer as of 30 June 1992 the right of establishment on EC nationals who wish to take up residence in another Member State for purposes other than economic activities or for the purpose of retirement. Sufficient funds and health insurance are the main conditions. As such persons do not intend to be active in (self-)employment, these Directives embody a principal extension of the right of free movement. Non-active and retired EC nationals may be joined by household and dependent family members, regardless of their nationality. This family is the same extended family as mentioned in (vi) below.

EC nationals who have exercised the right of free movement in (self-)employment are granted two years upon retirement during which they can choose where to live: pursuant to Article 5 of Regulation 1251/70 leaving the Member State during this period will not affect their right to remain. A retired EC migrant can also choose to remain in the Member State of which his or her spouse is a national, provided that the EC migrant has reached the age of entitlement to a state retirement pension in that country (Art 2 of Regulation 1251/70). Finally, a retired EC migrant worker can choose to stay in the Member State where he or she has been working. The conditions for doing so are as follows:

- reaching the age of entitlement to state retirement pension in the host Member State;
- having been employed there for at least the last 12 months before retirement;
- having been resident in the host Member State for more than three years.

Retired EC migrants opting for one of these Community rights are entitled to a five-year, automatically renewable residence permit. Family members living with the retired EC migrant have the same rights and can continue to exercise these rights after the retired EC migrant's death (Art 3 of Regulation 1251/70).

Regulation 75/34 contains identical provisions for retired EC migrants who have been self-employed.

(iv) Provision/reception of services

Articles 59–66 give a right of free movement to EC nationals wishing to provide services. The implementation can be found in Council Directive 73/148. Within the context of the EC Treaty, services are those normally provided for remuneration, including services of an industrial, commercial or craft character, as well as the activities of professionals.

Providers and recipients of services cannot claim lasting residence; they have the right to leave their own country, enter the territory of another Member State and remain there long enough to perform or receive the intended services.

For visits of less than three months a person needs only an identity card or passport. For visits exceeding three months a residence card should be issued.

The right extends to persons who wish to travel in order to receive services. In the case of *Luisi and Carbone* (ECJ 31.01.84, C-286/82 and 26/83) the European Court of Justice held that the freedom to provide services includes the freedom for the recipients of services to travel to another Member State in order to receive a service there and that tourists, persons travelling for business or educational purposes, and persons seeking medical treatment are recipients of services.

In the *Rush Portuguesa* case (ECJ 27.03.90, C-113/89), the court ruled that a company, incorporated in a Member State, which provides services in another Member State, may travel with its own staff which it brings from the main establishment for the duration of the work. In such cases the authorities of the Member State on whose territory the work is to be carried out may not impose conditions on the provider of services as to the recruitment of workers on the spot or the obtaining of a work permit for non-EC staff.

In the *Van der Elst* case (ECJ 09.08.94, C-43/93) the court repeated this standpoint in clear and principal wording: third country nationals have a right of free movement which can be deduced from the right of EC companies to provide services. Conditions imposed by the court are:

- the third country national must be part of the legal labour force of the Member State;

- his employer has been assigned to provide services in another Member State;

- his employer is established in a Member State.

A work permit requirement imposed by the receiving Member State can only serve administrative purposes and should in no way be an obstacle to the freedom to provide the acquired services.

(v) EC students
In the *Gravier* case (ECJ 13.02.85, C-293/83) the European Court of Justice ruled that access to and participation in courses of instruction and apprenticeship, in particular vocational training, are connected to Community law. Any form of education which prepares for a qualification for a particular profession, trade or employment or which provides the necessary training and skills for such a profession, trade or employment is vocational training, whatever the age and the level of training of the pupils or students, and even if the training programme includes an element of general education.

From this it follows that access to and participation in the general educational system of a Member State does not fall within the scope of the EC Treaty. However, pursuant to the provisions of Directives 1612/68 and 73/148 the children of EC workers or self-employed EC nationals are to be admitted to the general education apprenticeship and vocational training courses of the host State under the same conditions as the nationals of the Member State. Children are also entitled to state scholarships under the same conditions as for nationals of that State.

In 1990 the Council of Ministers laid down Directive 90/366 for EC students. Because of legal flaws this Directive has been replaced by Directive 93/96. As from 1 July 1992 EC students are entitled to a residence permit upon proof of matriculation at a university, college or educational institute for the purpose of a vocational training. Furthermore, they should have sufficient funds to prevent them from becoming a public charge and have health insurance for themselves, their eventual spouses and children, covering all risks in the host Member State. A residence permit is issued for one year and extended only if it can be shown that sufficient funds are still available.

(vi) Members of the family

The implementing provisions of EC law also confer the right of free movement on:

- the spouse;
- children under 21;
- children over 21 who are still dependent on their parents;
- dependent grandchildren;
- non-dependent grandchildren of workers;
- dependent relatives in the ascending line, such as parents and grandparents.

It must be assumed that the term "family members" includes the descendants and ascendants of either spouse, and also adopted children. The EC provisions stipulate that the Member States should facilitate the admission of other family members if they are dependent on the EC migrant or if they were living in the same household in their home country. Note, that these provisions for extended family reunion are reserved for EC nationals exercising the right of free movement; nationals of a Member State who have never exercised this right may be in a less favourable position (ECJ 27.10.82, C-35,36/82, the case of *Morson and Jhanjan*). Family members have the right to enter, reside and remain in the Member State where the EC migrant they are related to enjoys the right of free movement as a worker, self-employed person or as the provider or receiver of services. Family members enjoy the same rights as the person with the primary right, irrespective of nationality or sex. However, non-EC family members can be required to obtain an entry visa, but the Member State has no discretion; the issue should not be more than an administrative formality. Non-EC family members are entitled to a residence document having the same validity as the document of the EC national with the primary right.

The person with the primary right should be able to offer housing which can be considered as regular according to the local standards, and legal family ties should remain intact. It is not required that the family must live permanently under the same roof. In the *Diatta* case (ECJ 13.02.85, C-267/83) the European Court of Justice also ruled that the spouse of an EC national enjoying the right of free movement will keep the right to reside even if the household is no longer shared and divorce proceedings are pending. Admitted family members have the right to take employment anywhere on the territory of the Member State, even at a place far removed from the residence of the EC migrant.

Where an EC migrant has died before family reunion has taken place, Regulations 1251/70 and 75/34 provide that family members will obtain the right to remain if:

- the EC migrant resided continuously in the host country for at least two years before death; or
- he or she died from an accident at work or an occupational disease; or
- the surviving spouse was a national of the host country, but lost that nationality on account of the marriage with the diseased.

If an EC migrant returns to his or her home country, Article 52 of the EC Treaty and the provisions of Regulation 73/148 require the Member State to grant leave to enter and permission to stay to his or her family members who are migrating with him or her (ECJ 07.07.92 C-370/90, the case of Mr Singh).

In the *Reed* case (ECJ 17.04.86, C-59/85) the European Court of Justice ruled that if a Member State has made provisions for its own nationals to be joined by their unmarried "live in" partners, as is the case in the Netherlands, this social benefit cannot be denied to EC migrants.

Note, that the EC status of the spouse and other family members has been derived from the person with the primary right. In this sense, family members have a dependant status. They will loose their right to stay if, for example on account of public policy, further stay is denied to the EC migrant with the primary right.

(b) Social security taxes of EC migrants

Regulation 1408/71 refers to the temporary assignment of an employee from one Member State to another. For transfers not exceeding 12 months it provides that the employee may, upon request, remain subject to the social security system of his home country. The 12-month term can be extended up to five years. The Regulation also applies to EC migrant workers who are employed both in the host Member State and in their home country. As of 1 January 1994 Regulation 1408/71 also applies to EEA nationals.

(c) Limits on the right of free movement

Limits on the right of free movement may be imposed on the grounds of public policy, public security or public health (Art 48, para 3 of the EC Treaty).

In the Member States this public policy clause has been implemented in that a residence permit may be refused if an EC migrant is considered a risk to public peace, public security or public health. Refusal to renew or withdrawal is possible in case of false information or infringements of public peace or public security.

Measures taken on the grounds of public policy or public security should be based exclusively on the personal conduct of the individual concerned. A criminal conviction can be taken into account only in so far as the circumstances which gave rise to the conviction are evidence of personal conduct constituting a present threat to the requirements of public policy.

Diseases which may cause refusal of entry are listed in an annex to Directive 64/221. It may be worth mentioning that AIDS is not included.

Parts of this text are also included in an article on the Netherlands by Ted Badoux, "Immigration and Nationality Law" in *Center for International Legal Studies in Salzburg, Austria* (Kluwer).

EC visa requirement (EC Directive 2317/95)

Nationals of the countries mentioned below require a visa for entry to one of the Member States of the European Community.

Afghanistan	Georgia	Oman
Albania	Ghana	Pakistan
Algeria	Guinea-Bissau	Papua New Guinea
Angola	Guinea, Rep. of	Peru
Armenia	Guyana	Philippines
Azerbaijan	Haiti	Qatar
Bahrain	India	Romania
Bangladesh	Indonesia	Russian Federation
Belarus	Iran (Islamic Rep. of)	Rwanda
Benin (People's Republic)	Iraq	São Tomé & Principe
Bhutan	Jordan	Saudi Arabia
Bulgaria	Kazakhstan	Senegal
Burkina Faso	Korea (Democratic People's	Sierra Leone
Burundi	Rep.) (North Korea)	Somalia
Cambodia	Kuwait	Sri Lanka
Cameroon	Kyrgystan	Sudan
Cape Verde Islands	Laos	Suriname
Central African Republic	Lebanon	Syria (Syrian Arab Republic)
Chad	Liberia	Tajikistan
China (People's Republic)	Libya	Tanzania
Comores Islands	Madagascar (Dem. Rep.)	Thailand
Congo	Maldives	Togo
Cote d'Ivoire	Mali	Tunisia
Cuba	Mauritania	Turkey
Djibouti (Rep.)	Mauritius	Turkmenistan
Dominican Republic	Moldova (Rep. of)	Uganda
Egypt	Mongolia (People's Rep.)	Ukraine
Equatorial Guinea	Morocco	United Arab Emirates (U.A.E.)
Eritrea	Mozambique	Uzbekistan
Ethiopia	Myanmar	Vietnam
Fiji	Nepal	Yemen Republic
Gabon	Niger	Zaire
Gambia	Nigeria	Zambia

Territories and authorities not recognised by all Member States
Federal Republic of Yugoslavia (Serbia & Montenegro)
Former Yugoslav Republic of Macedonia
Taiwan

Contents of Chapter 3

AUSTRIA

Chapter 3

AUSTRIA

Elisabeth Scheuba

1. Country characteristics and general principles

(a) Geography

Situated in Central Europe, Austria covers an area of approximately 32,376 square miles (83,854 km), where a population of about 7.6 million is settled. Approximately 1.6 million people live in Austria's capital, Vienna.

Austria is a Federal Republic with nine federal states (Burgenland, Niederösterreich, Kärnten, Oberösterreich, Saltzburg, Steiermark, Tirol, Wien and Vorarlberg).

The country is bordered by Italy, Switzerland, Lichtenstein, Germany, Czech Republic, Slovak Republic, Hungary, Slovenia and Croatia.

The official language is German and the currency is the Austrian schilling (ATS).

Austrian natural resources are limited and Austrian industries' need for raw material is, to a significant extent, provided for by import.

(b) International status

Austria is a member of the most important international organisations, including the United Nations and most of its special organisations, the International Monetary Fund, the Organisation of Economic Cooperation and Development, the Council of Europe and the World Bank.

On 1 January 1995 Austria became a full Member State of the European Union.

(c) Economic aspects

(i) Foreign trade
Due to its small domestic market, Austrian industry depends to a great extent on foreign trade. The most important trade partner is the EEC, with about 70%

of Austria's exports going to EEC countries. Within the EEC Germany is the most important trade partner.

(ii) Structure of economy

Austria has a free, competitive system, but – as in most of the other European countries – the market is controlled by certain restrictions and incentives in order to maintain social and economic welfare.

Austria's industry is partly nationalised, *i.e.* its heavy industry, electric power stations and major banks. Privatisation of some of the enterprises is being discussed at present.

Because of its vast mountainous terrain, only about 20% of the total area of Austria can be used for agriculture.

2. Employment and inter-company transfers

(a) Employment

(i) General

Foreigners may only be employed if the employer either obtains a working permit (Arbeitsbewilligung) or the employee is the holder of a certificate of dispension (Befreiungsschein).

If this is not the case, the employer must apply for a special working permit (Beschäftigungsbewilligung) at the regional service of the labour market service.

A working permit will be issued if the foreigner has already worked in Austria for 52 weeks within the preceding 14 months. The working permit is valid for a maximum of two years and must then be renewed. For some professional branches there are special regulations for economic or social reasons.

A foreign employee will hold a certificate of dispension if he or she has been working in Austria for five years during the preceding eight years or if married to an Austrian for at least five years and living in Austria and if there are no economic interests precluding the issuing of the certificate. The certificate is valid for five years and may be revoked for certain serious reasons. Special regulations apply to foreign employees under the age of 19.

A special working permit will be issued if the current state and development of the Austrian labour market permits employment of foreigners and if there are no important public or economic reasons to preclude such employment. Such special working permits are valid for one year.

(ii) Exceptions

No working permission is needed for:

- foreigners married to Austrian citizens;

- foreigners who are citizens of an EEA/EC country as well as their spouses and children;
- refugees having a permanent residence permit.

Persons coming to Austria to work as trainees, missionaries, diplomats or consuls do not need working permits.

(iii) Sole representatives of overseas firms

Overseas firms operating no branch, subsidiary or other representative bureau in Austria do not need working permits for their sole representatives if:

- the foreigner is recruited for work for a short time only and the kind of work to be done cannot be done by an Austrian;
- if they are employed for some specialised work in connection with machines.

(b) Inter-company transfers

As there are no exceptions which exist for employees of a subsidiary bureau it is necessary to apply for a special working permit at the regional service of the labour market service if the employee is not a citizen of an EEA/EC country.

3. Business

(a) Businessmen and women

Businessmen and women need working permits if they hold less than 25% of the shares of a company with limited liability, and work for that company in a typical employee position.

(b) Permanent residence

The conditions for permanent residence apply as outlined in **7** below.

(c) Acquiring permission for running a trade business

(i) Physical persons

Foreign physical persons will be granted a permission for trade business if:

- reciprocity or equality of status with Austrian citizens in the foreigner's home country is granted;
- the general and specific requirements for running a trade business in Austria are met by the applicant.

Reciprocity can either be granted by State Treaties or other evidence to be given. Equality of status with nationals can be granted on application only.

General requirements for running a trade business in Austria are:

- personal qualification (a person must be 19 years of age);
- no reasons opposing (such as criminal procedures pending or crimes committed).

Special requirements are:

- proof of professional qualification;
- (in some special cases) market demand.

Citizens of EEA/EC countries, as a rule, do not have to prove their qualification as long as they have run the trade business in their home country according to the rules there.

The holder of a trading permit must appoint a managing director for his or her business as long as he or she decides not to reside in Austria. This managing director must meet all personal requirements for running the trade business and be a resident of Austria. He or she is then responsible for adhering to trade law regulations.

(ii) Legal entities and commercial partnerships

In order to obtain a trade permit, foreign legal entities or commercial partnerships must:

- set up an establishment (head office, branch office) in Austria; and
- appoint a managing director.

Legal entities and commercial partnerships not having either their head office or a branch office in Austria are excluded from running a business in Austria, unless otherwise provided for in State Treaties.

Foreign persons are subject to the same commercial regulations as nationals, with some exceptions.

4. Retired persons of independent means/investors

The conditions for temporary stay or permanent residence apply as outlined in **6** and **7** below.

5. Spouses and children

The conditions for obtaining a temporary or permanent permit for residence under Austrian law aim at family reunion. Therefore, special provisions for spouses and children apply as outlined in **6** and **7** below.

6. Temporary stays

According to the Law for Foreigners (Fremdengesetz) and the Law of Residence in Austria (Aufenthaltsgesetz) in order to stay in Austria a foreigner would need either a visa or a permit for taking residence.

(a) Visas

There are different kinds of visas as follows:

- usual visa;
- tourist visa;
- official visa (Dienstvisa);
- diplomat visa (Diplomatenvisa).

Unlimited usual visa

Foreigners may request an unlimited usual visa in the following circumstances:

- if they have resided in Austria for five years and earn a regular income;
- if their spouses and children (younger than 19 years of age) live in a common household and have resided in Austria for two years;
- if their children are younger than 14 years of age and live in a common household.

Citizens of EEA/EC countries need neither a visa nor a residence permit to stay in Austria. However, if they cannot prove that their living expenses and social security are insured they have the right to stay in Austria only if they can prove:

- that they have been offered work;
- that they will be self-employed;
- that they have the chance of starting employment or self-employment six months after their arrival in Austria at the latest;
- that they are relatives of an EEA/EC citizen who has the right to stay in Austria and is willing to pay for their stay.

If an EEA/EC citizen stays in Austria for more than three months he or she must apply for a special "passport".

7. Permanent residence

To establish a permanent residence in Austria a foreigner needs a permit to take residence in Austria. No permission is necessary, however, if:

- international Treaties granting freedom of settlement are applicable;

- a working permit is not also needed (see **2** above);
- the status as a refugee is established;
- the foreigner is a performing artist or journalist working for foreign information media.

The number of residence permits issued within one year is restricted by governmental decree, which is published once a year. Spouses (married for one year) and children under the age of 18 of Austrian citizens or foreigners staying in Austria for more than two years get a permit if their living expenses and housing are proved to be ensured.

The permit is valid for six months and renewable thereafter.

Foreigners holding a permit over a period of five years may request an unlimited residence permit. A permit will not be granted to a foreigner whose living expenses or housing are not ensured.

8. Nationality

There are four ways of acquiring Austrian citizenship:

- by birth;
- by grant of nationality;
- by working as a university professor;
- by declaration (for spouses and children of a university professor only).

Foreigners can be granted Austrian citizenship if they:

- have had legal permanent residence in Austria for 10 years;
- have had legal residence in Austria for at least four years and have been married to an Austrian citizen for at least one year;
- have had legal residence in Austria for at least three years and have been married to an Austrian citizen for at least two years;
- have been married to an Austrian citizen for at least five years if the spouse has been an Austrian citizen for at least 10 years;
- have had a legal permit to reside in Austria for 30 years.

Since dual citizenship should be avoided (according to the European Convention on Limitation of Plural Citizenship), an applicant for Austrian citizenship must prove abandonment of previous citizenships within two years.

Exemptions can be made for political refugees and persons who are denied release from their previous citizenship.

The applicant must also prove that his or her living expenses are ensured.

Criminality may disqualify the applicant if he or she has ever been sentenced for a severe crime, tax crime or if a procedure is pending.

9. Refugees and political asylum

The right of asylum may be granted to foreigners who have reasons to fear that they will be persecuted on the grounds of race, religion, nationality, integration in a certain social group or political opinion. These persons are granted the status of refugees and are given asylum.

Rights of asylum will be denied to foreigners if they have committed crimes against peace, war crimes or crimes against mankind (defined by the International Conventions) or if they have committed other, non-political crimes.

The application for asylum must be filed with the office for asylum (Asylbehörde) and may include the spouse and children under 18.

If a foreigner has entered Austria illegally for the purpose of obtaining political asylum and has come directly from the state where he or she fears persecution, he or she may not be punished for illegal entry if he or she makes an application for asylum one week after his or her arrival.

10. Government discretion

The Austrian immigration authorities decide at their own discretion and according to the immigration laws when considering the particulars and circumstances of each application.

11. Sanctions

(a) Deportation

Any person who is a non-Austrian citizen will be deported if:

- his or her entry or stay in Austria is illegal;
- he or she is a threat to public order;
- he or she has a conviction for certain severe crimes.

Foreigners cannot be deported to a country where they may be persecuted. The burden of proof lies with the foreigner.

(b) Detention

Foreigners may be detained (Schubhaft) until a decision is taken whether or not to deport.

12. Tax and social security

(a) Tax

The most important taxes are as follows.

- income taxes:
  - Corporation Income Tax Act (Körperschaftssteuergesetz);
  - Individual Income Tax Act (Einkommenssteuergesetz).
- taxes on transactions and property:
  - Value Added Tax Act (Umsatzsteuergesetz);
  - Net Wealth Tax Act (Vermögenssteuergesetz);
  - Trade Tax Act (Gewerbesteuergesetz);
  - Inheritence and Gift Tax Act (Erbschaftssteuergesetz);
  - Real Estate Transfer Tax Act (Grunderwerbssteuergesetz).

Corporations and individuals can either be fully or partly taxed depending on whether they are considered to be residents in Austria.

Corporations are regarded as full taxpayers if their bases and/or places of management are in Austria.

A full taxpayer is subject to tax on his worldwide income; a partial taxpayer is subject to tax on Austria-source income only.

Corporations are, at present, taxed at the flat rate of 30%.

Income tax rates for individuals are progressive. The rates reach a maximum of 50% for an income exceeding ATS700,000. per year. There is no joint taxation of married couples or households.

Austria has signed Tax Treaties with about 40 countries. Most of these Treaties aim to avoid double taxation on income and property.

(b) Social security

The Austrian social security system is highly developed. It covers health insurance, accident insurance, unemployment relief and pension insurance.

The social system is administered by social security authorities (Sozialversicherungsträger) and is based on the principle of compulsory membership.

The social security insurance coverage usually starts at the beginning of any professional activity (employment or self-employment). The employer is obliged to file a registration with the social insurance carriers once an employee has started work.

Persons who are not members of the Austrian social security system have the right to opt for voluntary participation in the social security system, provided certain conditions are met.

The benefits of the social security system are not restricted to those who pay contributions, but also extend to their families (spouses and children).

Contributions to social security are paid partly by the employer and partly by the employee by automatic deduction of his or her wages.

For citizens of EEA countries, Directives provide for exemption from social security contributions in the host country for up to a maximum of two years for employees who are working for a company with a registered office in Austria. These persons may remain insured under the social security system of their home country.

Moreover, Austria has signed social security Treaties with EU Member States, other European countries and several non-European countries.

13. Domestic considerations

(a) Civil registration

An individual taking accommodation in a guest house or apartment must register with the local police station within three days of arrival. If the status is altered or there is a change of address the local police must be advised.

(b) Housing

(i) Acquisition of real estate by foreigners
A foreigner must apply for special permission granted by the property transfer authorities (Grundverkehrsbehörde) if he or she wants to obtain the following rights on real estate:

- ownership;
- establishment of a "*usus fructus*" (Fruchtgenußrecht);
- establishment of a construction right;
- a long-term lease;
- registration of a mortgage.

"Foreigners" include foreign citizens, as well as companies, corporations and partnerships having their bases outside Austria, or which are based in Austria but are controlled by individuals with non-Austrian citizenship or by companies having their bases outside Austria.

(ii) Leasing
The Austrian law governing lease contracts is very much restricted in favour of the lessee. The provisions of the so-called Rent Control Act (Mietrechtsgesetz) are mandatory and cannot be changed by contract to the disadvantage of the lessee.

(c) Employment

(i) Employment contract
Terms and conditions of individual employment contracts are restricted by the provisions of the collective employment agreements. These collective agreements

are concluded between employees' and employers' organisations in writing and are registered with the Federal Minister of Labour and Social Affairs.

(ii) Non-discrimination
The Equal Treatment Act (Gleichbehandlungsgesetz) forbids any kind of discrimination, especially sexual discrimination.

(iii) Trade unions and chambers of Employees
The Austrian Trade Union Federation (Österreichischer Gewerkschaftsbund) is one of the most important institutions, having a great influence on politics. The Federation consists of 15 unions, and membership is voluntary. Although it is a private association, the Federation, in fact, has a semi-official function.

Apart from the Austrian Trade Union Federation, the interests of employees are protected by the chambers of employees. These chambers are organised as public corporations with compulsory membership.

(d) Health care

The social security authorities can conclude contracts with medical doctors and hospitals allowing an insured person to obtain free medical treatment and hospitalisation. These costs are directly borne by the social security authorities. Insured persons must, however, finance part of the costs of medicines themselves.

(e) Travellers

Austria has concluded social security Treaties with EU Member States and various other countries concerning mutual acceptance of health insurance for travellers requiring medical treatment.

(f) Schooling

Schools are either private or public. Attendance is compulsory for children between the ages of six and 15, who must attend schools for at least nine years. Education is free in public schools as well as at universities.

(g) Motor cars

Certain regulations concerning the import of cars must be adhered to. The car must be registered before it can be used on public roads. The owner must hold a driving licence valid in Austria (there are State Treaties for mutual acceptance with most of the countries) and the car must also be insured.

Contents of Chapter 4
BELGIUM

Chapter 4

BELGIUM

Frank Weinand

1. Country characteristics and general principles

Belgium, which has a population of almost 10 million inhabitants is the world's greatest exporter per inhabitant. The smallness of both the country (3,051,806 ha) and its home market has meant that Belgium orientated its economy naturally to exchange with foreign countries. Transformation, services and foreign trade therefore play a major part in its economy.

Belgium (with Brussels as "capital of Europe", seat of the Commission and the Council of the European Union as well as of the European Parliament) is situated a few hours' distance from all capitals and important cities of Europe. The extremely dense and developed transport infrastructure, which allows one to visit any point in the country and to come back the same day, makes professional contacts easy to establish and is certainly an asset.

The existence of two main languages has both concrete commercial and legal implications for tradesmen as it requests bilingual labelling of products or safety instructions, bilingual marketing and staff, mandatory use of certain languages in different circumstances, for example, labour relations. On the other hand, workers are well skilled and bi- or multilingual which ideally enables them to act in European-wide distribution or management.

In 1980, Belgium adopted a state structure similar to that of a federal state which has been confirmed and strengthened since. There are three main regions, being the Flemish region (in the North, Dutch-speaking, about 57% of the population), the Walloon region (in the South, French-speaking, about 35% of the population) and Brussels, with a bilingual status.

2. Employment and inter-company transfers

(a) Foreign labour and professional activity of foreigners

The Royal Decree No 34 of 20 July 1967 states that no employer may employ foreign workers and no foreign worker may work in Belgium without the prior authorization of the regional Minister of Employment (art.4 and 7). This general rule applies to all foreigners – except to nationals of EU member States – but with the exception of the following categories of workers who do not need a work permit:

- workers registered in the merchant service sailors' pool;
- ministers of public worship;
- journalists residing in Belgium and exclusively attached to newspapers published abroad;
- commercial travellers who have their main residence abroad and who visit their clients in Belgium on account of firms established abroad which do not have branches in Belgium, as long as their stay in Belgium does not exceed three months in succession;
- persons who enter Belgium in order to receive merchandise delivered by a Belgian business, on account of a business established abroad, as long as their stay in the country does not exceed three months in succession;
- persons who have their main residence abroad and who enter Belgium to participate in athletic meetings;
- students who must undertake training in pursuit of their studies.

In practice these two authorizations (to work and to employ) will both be claimed for by requests introduced at the same time and on the same application form by the employer – or a special proxyholder on his behalf such as an attorney – with the Employment and Labour Department of the Ministry of either the Flemish, Walloon or Brussels region, following the place of business of the employer. The file has to be completed by (Royal Decree of 19 December 1967) three properly filled out application forms, a medical certificate, two recent passport-type photographs and, in some cases, a copy of the employment contract (drawn up following the model fixed in Royal Decree of 5 May 1970), an information sheet containing evidence of the applicant's professional qualifications as well as a statement of the employer testifying that social security obligations will be complied with.

The competent authorities will only issue a work permit:

- if the function the applicant is supposed to fulfil cannot be exercised by a person belonging to the Belgian labour market (art.5 RD 6 November 1967);

- if he comes from a country with which Belgium has signed an international agreement on foreign labour (art.6 RD 6 November 1967);

- and if the specific requirements relating to the type of work permit are met (infra).

The procedure takes usually about three months, but this can be accelerated through the Ministry of Economic Affairs in cases where the work permit is applied for in the context of an investment project which benefits from government support.

(b) Work permits

Three different work permits can be granted:

(i) Work permit A

This is valid for an indefinite period and all types of employed labour. It will be granted if the candidate meets one of the following requirements:

- residence: five years' regular and uninterrupted residence in Belgium (three years for political refugees) on the day of application;

- work: five years of uninterrupted work covered by a regular work permit and by a worker who is authorized to stay in Belgium;

- family reunion: the spouse, the children or orphans of persons meeting the previous requirements (with restrictions).

(ii) Work permit B

This is valid for a definite period of maximum one year and limited to a given employer or a specific branch of activity. No specific requirements exceeding those laid out above are requested.

(iii) Work permit C

This is granted under similar conditions to work permit B but is only valid for specific professions where the work usually works for several employers. This applies to workers such as special skilled harbour workers, cleaners, jockeys, workers in the diamond industry, home workers etc. (see art.15 RD 6 November 1967).

The duration of the work permits B and C can be extended and they are subject to renewals. The refusal of a work permit opens procedural possibilities before the Minister of Employment and the Council of State.

3. Business

(a) Professional card

(i) General scope of application

As opposed to employed workers who work under the authority of another person, the self-employed work freelance. The picking up of such activity by a foreigner in Belgium is subject to prior authorization in the form of a professional card.

This regulation applies to all of the self-employed except:

- the foreigner's husband's or wife's support to the partner's professional activity;

- professional sportsmen or women whose activities do not exceed 60 days per year;

- musicians and artists who perform in theatre, circus or halls exclusively for shows, as long as the duration of the stay does not exceed 15 days per half-year;

- foreigners residing abroad, who make business trips to Belgium which cumulatively do not exceed 3 months per half-year.

(ii) Conditions for granting a professional card

The granting of the professional card is linked to the self-employed permission to reside in Belgium (infra). The work has to be located in a field of economic activity that has not reached saturation point. The card is used by the Minister of Middle Classes who has full power to rule on this matter.

The card is personal and non-transferable. It defines precisely the nature of the activities the holder is authorized to carry out and the conditions under which such activities may be exercised. If granted, its maximum duration is 5 years. When the original duration is shorter, it can be extended up to 5 years. After this, renewal is possible (art.3, par.2).

(iii) Procedure (Royal Decree of 2 August 1985)

The application is normally filed with the appropriate Belgian diplomatic or consular representative in the foreigner's country of residence. It has to be signed by the applicant himself. The following documents have to be attached (art.6 RD 2 August 1985): medical certificate, a certificate of good conduct and a complete questionnaire relating to personal data and the proposed independent activity, especially if the latter is subject to special legal requirements.

By exception, the application can be filed with the municipality of the Belgian residence of the candidate if he is holder of a Belgian "identity card for foreigners", a "certificate of registration in the foreigner's register" or a "certificate of registration model A" following Royal Decree of 8 October 1981.

It should be filed at the same time as the application for access and residence in Belgium.

(b) Special categories of workers

Special rules apply to specific categories of workers. The Belgian labour law generally considers them as employees but allows easier access and employment. This applies amongst others to trainees, au pairs, artists, etc.

(c) Establishing a branch or subsidiary company

Following article 196 of Belgian Company law (BCL), all companies and commercial, industrial or financial associations whose registered office is situated abroad are entitled to carry out commercial operations or act before the courts in Belgium.

However, as soon as its Belgian activity becomes permanent (e.g. as it opens an office or warehouse) it has either to open a branch office or to incorporate a subsidiary.

(i) The branch

The branch is created by a decision taken by the board of directors or any other institution of the foreign company entitled to do so. This decision should indicate as well who is empowered to represent the Belgian branch.

The main information about the foreign company, the decision to open the Belgian branch and the annual accounts of both the main company and subsidiary have to be published in the appropriate way. Therefore all those documents (their certified copies, eventually translated by a sworn translator into the language of the region of the local branch) have to be deposited at the local register of commerce (Companies Acts section) before being published in the Belgian State Gazette.

The publication concerns (art.197 Company Law):

For companies whose head office is located in a Member State of the EU:

- incorporation, articles of association, by-laws;
- name and form of company;
- the register where the company is registered following article 3 of the directive 68/151/EEC and its number of registration;
- a certificate from this register saying that the company legally exists;
- the address of the branch, its activity and its denomination if different from the company's name;
- the identity of the persons empowered to act on behalf of the company;
- the annual accounts and the consolidated accounts of the main company in the form as established, controlled and published following the laws of the country of its head office.

All other foreign companies have to publish as well:

- the indication under which law the foreign company has been incorporated;
- the register and number of registration if foreseen by this foreign law;
- annually, the amount of its capital.

(ii) The subsidiary company

The establishment of a subsidiary company with limited liability requests:

- the deposition, on a special banking account, of the part of the capital which has to be paid in at the incorporation: this amount will be held at the disposal of the board of directors as soon as the company is incorporated. If, for any reason, the incorporation should not occur, the amount will be refunded to the depositor after three months (art. 29bis and 120 BCL);
- the drawing up of a financial plan showing that the capital chosen by the founders is sufficient to allow the activity of the company for at least two years (art.29ter, 35, 6° and 120ter BCL);
- the incorporation by notarial deed (art. 4 al 2 BCL);
- the deposition of the notarial deed at the Companies Acts section of the Registry of Commerce of the registered office of the subsidiary (art.2 BCL); this deposition involves its publication in the Belgian State Gazette (art.10).

(d) Legal forms of the main companies

(i) "Société Anonyme–Naamloze Vennootschap"

This is a company with separate legal personality and limited liability of the shareholders. Its most outstanding characteristics are the following:

- at least two shareholders:
- a fully paid capital of a minimum of 2,500,000 BEF;
- a board of directors of three (sometimes two) members.

This form of company is used for larger businesses or companies who aim to raise external financing.

(ii) "Société Privée à Responsabilité Limitée–Prive Vennootschap met Beperkte Aansprakelijkheid"

This is a closely held limited liability company and best suits smaller or family businesses. Its shareholders or partners are always known. The transfer of shares requires the previous acknowledgement of the buyer by the other shareholders. The company is therefore a closed company. Its outstanding characteristics are:

- one or more partners;
- a minimum capital of 750,000 BEF paid in for at least 250,000 BEF;
- a least one director.

(iii) "Société Coopérative–Coöperatieve vennootschap" (SC/CV)
This form of company was originally shaped to allow workers' participation in the capital of the business which employs them. It therefore foresees a variable capital, a variable number of partners and large possibilities of defining the representation of the company and the internal decision-taking procedure. Following a modification in 1991, two kinds of SC/CV can be incorporated:

The SC/CV with unlimited liability of the shareholders. This is a company with a minimum capital of 3 BEF, which is incorporated by a private agreement between minimum three shareholders (art.143 BCL).

The SC/CV with limited liability. This needs a notarial deed to its incorporation (art.147bis Par.4) and a minimum capital of BEF 750,000 (art.147bis BCL).

Its main difference towards SPRL/PVBA is the variability of the capital (above the fixed minimum) and the number of partners.

4. Persons of independent means/investors

The current Belgian legislation on access, stay and establishment does not create any special category of persons of independent means/investors. It is therefore necessary to see what is said below instead.

5. Spouses and children

As a rule, one can say that the right to enter the country and to carry out professional activity both in the employed and self-employed field allows generally for the spouse and their young children to stay in Belgium and eventually to carry out professional activity.

Some situations are mentioned in this chapter, but others could lead to the same result.

6. Temporary stays and permanent residence

The principles of access to territory and residence of foreigners in Belgium are defined by the law of 15 December 1980 and its implementing decrees. In general and for all foreigners, a difference is made between:

- access to territory;
- stay up to 3 months;
- stay for more than 3 months;
- permanent residence.

The exercise of any employed or self-employed activity is linked to the right to enter the country, whilst the latter is linked to the existence of means of support and subsistence. Therefore the two procedures are discussed at the same time even though they have different purposes.

(a) Access

Foreigners intending to enter the country must be in possession of a valid passport or other comparable documents with a visa (art.2). The visa is obtained with the diplomatic or consular representative of one of the Benelux countries of the country of residence of the applicant.

Two different types of visa are granted:

- a transit visa which is valid for the period necessary to pass through the country on one's way to another country;
- a travel visa (more frequent) which enables the holder to stay for a maximum of 3 months. Successive visits to Belgium with a travel visa are limited in that the total duration of the presence in Belgium is limited to three months in the course of any 6-month period.

Specific conditions apply to nationals of numerous countries with which Belgium is bound by international treaties. They are laid out in annex to the Royal Decree of 8 January 1981 (no visa required).

Even if the foreigner is in possession of the legally requested documents, his entry and stay can be refused if he clearly has no sufficient means of subsistence (art.3), and for reasons relating to public order.

(b) Stay

(i) Short stay up to 3 months
The foreigner who legally entered the country (other than with a transit visa) and who intends to stay for longer than 8 days has to apply for a declaration of arrival at the municipality of his residence within 8 days of arrival. He will be given a certificate that proves this declaration.

Several types of persons are exempted from this formality, such as children under 16 years of age travelling with their parents, business people or tourists already registered at their hotel, or foreigners admitted to a local hospital.

(ii) Stay of more than 3 months
Foreigners who intend to stay more than 3 months in Belgium have to apply prior to entry to Belgium at the diplomatic or consular representative of

Belgium of the foreigner's residence abroad (art.9). Exceptionally, the application can be filed with the municipality of the foreigner's Belgian residence. The file has to contain a properly filled application form with five passport-type photographs, a medical certificate, a certificate of good conduct, a passport, work permit or professional card (or application for one) or any other document that proves sufficient financial resources.

The foreigner authorized or permitted to stay in Belgium for a period exceeding 3 months must, within 8 days of arrival in Belgium, request the municipal authorities to file his name in the foreigners' register. The foreigner will then be issued with a temporary residence permit which is usually valid for one year and renewable on application (art.12).

(iii) Residence

A foreigner who complies with conditions for entry into Belgium, who has obtained an authorization to reside and a temporary residence permit and who has resided legally and without interruption in Belgium for a period of five years is entitled to take up permanent residence (art.14).

He therefore has to introduce an application with the municipality of his place of residence in Belgium (art.16). Once the authorization is granted, the holder is registered in the population register (instead of the foreigners' register) of the municipality of residence. The local authorities will issue a permanent residence permit in the form of a special identity card which is valid for 5 years and which is automatically renewable (art.18).

(iv) Removal and expulsion

A foreigner can be removed from the territory if

- he has violated principles of public order or public security;
- or if he has violated the conditions imposed on his visit to Belgium (art.20).

The removal order can only be issued by the Minister of Justice against foreigners who have not (yet) obtained a permanent residence permit (art.20). The Minister of Justice has a wide margin of discretion in this respect.

Once the foreigner has obtained a permanent residence permit, he can only be subject to an expulsion order. Those are limited to foreigners who have seriously violated principles of public order or public security. The opinion of the Advisory Commission for Foreigners must be sought (art.20).

(v) Nationals of EU Member States

Special rules apply to such nationals who have the right to access the country and stay, provided they pick up employed or self-employed activity. Otherwise the general rules apply.

7. Refugees and political asylum

Asylum will be granted to foreigners who meet the criteria specified in article 1 of the International Treaty relating to Refugee Status signed in Geneva on 28 July 1951, to persons who benefit from refugee status obtained prior to the Geneva Treaty and to those who obtained refugee status in a foreign country under condition that this status is confirmed by the Belgian competent authorities.

The procedure of recognition of the refugee status has been split into two parts:

The Minister of Interior Affairs via his representative at the Foreigners' Office will examine the request for admissibility. Upon his refusal the candidate may claim re-examination by the General Commissioner for Refugees. Should the General Commissioner confirm the Foreigners' Office's decision, the foreigner will be expelled (art.48–57 law of 15 December 1980).

An admissible request will be examined by the General Commissioner (art.57–6). The candidate may appeal against the decision before the Permanent Commission for Refugees (art.57.11 ff.).

8. Nationality

The Belgian rules on nationality have been greatly reviewed by the law of 28 June 1984, in force since 1985, which increases significantly the influence of the *ius soli* as far as granting Belgian nationality is concerned.

(a) By attribution and *ipso iure* to persons

- because of their father's/mother's nationality;
- by reason of their adoption by a Belgian national;
- by reason of their birth in Belgium;
- by collective effect of an acquisition action.

(b) By acquisition

This needs a voluntary act of the candidate to Belgian nationality who will have to prove special links to the country:

- statement of nationality by foreigners born and living in Belgium between their 18th and 30th birthdays;
- adoption of nationality by foreigners aged between 18 and 22 years and who are living in Belgium for a certain time;
- acquisition by the foreign spouse of a Belgian partner;

- acquisition by possession of the status of Belgian national;
- acquisition by naturalization for foreigners aged over 18 and living in Belgium for at least 5 years.

9. Government discretion

The Belgian authorities in general, and the Ministers of Justice, Internal Affairs, the Middle Class or regional Ministers of Employment in particular, have considerable discretion to grant most of the authorizations referred to in this chapter. A jurisdictional control is generally overseen before the Council of State, the highest administrative jurisdiction of the state.

10. Sanctions

Most of the rules set out above are sanctioned on penal or criminal level. Fines, penalties, orders to leave the country, repatriations or expulsions are all applicable. Meanwhile the foreigner can be placed at the Government's disposal and so be imprisoned.

11. Tax and social security

(a) Social security

(i) Territorial scope of Belgian social security and generalities

The Belgian social securities will in general apply to workers and self-employed who carry out their activities in Belgium. The EU Council Regulation 1408/71 of 14 June 1971 rules on the conflict of jurisdiction between the different EU Member States. Furthermore, Belgium has entered into different bilateral social security conventions (Algeria, Austria, Canada, Israel, Morocco, Poland, San Marino, Switzerland, Tunisia, Turkey, the USA and Yugoslavia) which sometimes apply to both employees and self-employed or only the first category.

Within the Belgian social security, three different schemes appear:

- the general scheme for workers who are employed by a private employer;
- the scheme for self-employed persons who carry out their activities in Belgium;
- the scheme which applies to civil servants having life tenure in Belgian government institutions (this latter scheme will not be discussed here).

(ii) Contributions

The contributions are levied on employers (33.5% on top of the gross salary) and employees (13.5% on the gross salary) and paid quarterly to the National Institute for Social Security. The contributions for the self-employed have to be paid quarterly by those self-employed to special insurance funds with which they have to register.

(iii) Benefits

The schemes cover mainly child benefits, sickness payments and payments for invalids, unemployed compensation, old-age and survivors' pension and vacation allowances for workers.

Child benefits (Law of 19 December 1939). The purpose of this benefit is to supplement the income of employees who have children to support. The beneficiaries are (art.51–67) the worker, the unemployed person receiving unemployment allowances, employees who have suspended their activities, students or self-employed who work and/or live in Belgium. They are paid for any child.

- with a family relationship between the beneficiary and the child,
- if the child is being raised in Belgium,
- until the age of 18 (21 or even 25 if scholarship is not terminated yet).

Sickness payments and payments to invalids (Law of 14 July 1994 as amended and Royal Decree No 38 of 27 July 1967). These payments reimburse part of the costs of medical care and provide a replacement income for employees or self-employed struck by illness or invalidity. Self-employed should enter into private health insurance as the reimbursement is less important to them. The employee or self-employed and dependants become beneficiaries after a waiting period of six months, unless they can claim coverage by a Belgian or foreign social security system in the six months preceding their affiliation (application of both EU regulations and international conventions).

Unemployed benefits (Royal Decree of 25 November 1991). These benefits are granted to workers who have completed a minimum period of employment and who lost their employment because of circumstances beyond their control. Foreign workers are admitted to these benefits provided they are authorized to reside and to work in the country (art.43, par.1). The self-employed are excluded from this benefit.

Old-age and survivors' pension (Law of 20 July 1990 and Royal Decree of 10 November 1967). The pension is granted:

- on application;
- for workers or self-employed from the age of 60 on (with reduction of benefits for men who apply before the age of 65) who have ceased any significant professional activity;

- who do not receive other social benefits;
- and reside in Belgium (but important exceptions exist for Belgian nationals and foreigners of countries with which Belgium has entered into a bilateral agreement).

Vacation allowances. Holiday allowances for employees (white-collar workers) are paid by the employer. For blue-collar workers, those allowances are collected from the employer via the social security systems and paid annually to the worker. Again the self-employed are excluded from these benefits.

Labour accidents and occupational diseases. Special regulations (Royal Decree of 3 June 1970 and law of 10 April 1971) provide special funds or mandatory insurances to cover the consequences of such events. They protect foreigners as soon as they are legally carrying out employed activities.

(b) Tax

As a result of the federal structure of public power, the right to raise taxes are vested in the Federal Government, the regional bodies, provinces, and municipalities. This makes Belgian tax law one of the most complicated legal structures. Generally one distinguishes between direct and indirect taxes.

(i) Direct taxes

These are calculated on the income (mobile, real, salary or others) from natural persons, companies, legal entities and non-residents. Belgium has signed international double taxation treaties with most of the countries with which it has regular contacts. They are often shaped following the OBCD-model.

In 1983 a special tax status was created for foreigners with special skills or responsibilities who are transferred to Belgium on a temporary basis to work in the local branch of a foreign company or in the Belgian subsidiary being part of an international group. This status allows the employer to allocate certain costs related to the transfer (moving, housing, schooling etc.) as well as a salary splitting for duties carried out within the group but abroad. The latter will not be taxed in Belgium.

(ii) Indirect taxes

This concerns value added tax (VAT), customs and excise.

VAT and excise are levied on goods provided to the consumer. Since the introduction of the common market within the EU, VAT is ruled by the local transposition of the relevant EU directives.

Belgian customs law (law of 26 August 1822 as coordinated on 18 July 1977 and amended on 22 December 1989) is a body of rules composed of national, Benelux and predominantly EU law. There is not sufficient space to discuss the matter here.

12. Domestic considerations

(a) Civil registration

Any individual or family who enters into the country to stay at one place for more than 8 days is bound to register with the municipality of their residence within 8 days of their arrival (art.5 law of 15 December 1980). This applies as well for nationals of EU Member States.

(b) Housing

(i) Renting

The Belgian Civil Code oversees the general rules of leasing houses or apartments. As soon as the premises are rented to the tenant as his main residence, the law of 20 February 1991 applies which fixes certain mandatory rules mainly shaped to protect tenants' interests. The law fixes two different kinds of leases:

- a short-term lease of a maximum 36 months;
- all other leases are supposed to be agreed upon for a period of 9 years with tenants' right to notify termination with a 3 months' period of notice (and an indemnity if this notice is notified within the first 3 years of occupation) and landlords' rights to terminate the contract either (1) with 6 months' notice at any time if he wants to occupy himself, or (2) every three years with 6 months' notice in case he wants to transform or rebuild the premises without indemnity or for personal convenience with an indemnity.

(ii) Purchasing

When purchasing a flat or house, an individual should ideally consult an estate agent to seek the appropriate property. A barrister can advise on the mechanics and procedures (choice of a notary etc.) of purchasing as well as completing the necessary works.

(iii) Local taxes

Local taxes are raised to finance services provided by local authorities (removal of rubbish etc.). Each council sets the level of the local tax for its own area.

(iv) Television

All owners of television sets are required by law to apply for a television licence fee on an annual basis. They can in addition to this ask for signal distribution by cable, which then increases the licence fee.

(c) Employment

Labour relations in Belgium are based on individual labour agreements entered into between employer and worker. The freedom of agreement is limited by the following mandatory texts which overrule any individual agreement:

- international treaties;
- the constitution;
- the law of 3 July 1978 on labour contracts;
- recent legal rules adopted by the parliament to increase the competitiveness of Belgian companies ("Plan Global" until 31 December 1996, and other recently adopted measures);
- collective bargaining agreements agreed upon between the representatives of employers and workers in the National Labour Council and which apply to all sectors of the economy or in the Joint Committees which apply only to the sector concerned with the Joint Committee.

(d) Health care

Provided he or she has access to social security, any individual can either consult a hospital casualty department if it is an emergency or register with a local physician. Charges for the medical treatment will be claimed.

(e) Schooling

Children between 6 and 18 years of age are supposed to go to school. The relevant enquiries can be made with the local authorities for a list of appropriate schools. In larger cities, private or international schools provide appropriate education to foreigners (French, German, Scandinavian, European, Dutch schools).

(f) Motor cars

(i) Driving licence
Foreigners who are registered in the foreigners' register or in the population register of a Belgian municipality have to be in possession of a Belgian driver's licence to drive. As an exception:

- registered foreigners who are nationals of an EU Member State are entitled to drive with their local driving licence for a maximum period of twelve months since their registration; within this period they have to claim a Belgian driving licence at the municipality, where the exchange is usually made without formalities.
- foreigners driving in Belgium within the limits of the international road traffic are entitled to do so if they hold a foreign national or international driving licence.

(ii) Vehicle registration and insurance
Foreign drivers registered in Belgium for more than three months must in prin-

ciple apply for a Belgian number plate. If the stay is limited to less than three months they can apply for a temporary transit licence plate. Licence plates are issued by the Road Transport Department of the Ministry of Communications.

All vehicles driving on Belgian roads have to be insured for their civil liability for injuries or damage caused to third parties or resulting from the vehicle's use.

Mackelbert & Associés, Avocats Advocaten Rechtsanwälte,
Avenue Clémentine, 3, 1190 Bruxelles. tel.: (32) 25345098.
telefax: (32) 25345402.

Contents of Chapter 5

DENMARK

Chapter 5

DENMARK

Sys Rousing Koch

1. Country characteristics and general principles

Denmark is situated north of Germany and is surrounded by the North Sea and the Baltic Sea. Denmark has a total area of 43,000 square kilometres. There are approximately 5.2 million inhabitants; the number of inhabitants per square kilometre is 120.

Copenhagen, the capital, is the largest city in Denmark with approximately 1.3 million inhabitants.

Danish is a Germanic language.

Around 87% of the population belong to the Church of Denmark, which is Lutheran.

Life expectancy is 72.5 years for men and 77.8 years for women.

Denmark has a cool maritime climate; the weather is mild and changeable, with temperatures ranging from −2°C in the winter to +21°C in the summer.

Denmark has substantial natural resources both on land and in the North Sea. It is first and foremost an industrialised country but agriculture and tourism are also important sectors. The main trading partners are Germany, the Nordic countries and the United Kingdom, amounting to 21.4%, 18.9% and 7.8% respectively of the total exports.

The monetary unit is the kroner. The average exchange rate in 1995 was US $1 = DKK 5.60. The inflation rate in 1995 was 2%. The GNP for 1995 amounted to DKK 970.8 billion and the economic growth rate was 4.4%. The account balance for 1994 had a surplus of DKK 22.1 billion. The unemployment rate has decreased over the last few years. In April 1995, 282,000 persons were registered unemployed, *i.e.* 10% of the working population between the age of 16–66.

The average hourly wage earnings for time work of adult earners in 1994 was DKK 101 for men and DKK 91 for women.

Denmark is a constitutional monarchy; the sovereign is Queen Margrethe II.

The political system is a parliamentary democracy. The election in 1994 resulted in a government consisting of Social Democrats and two social liberal parties.

Denmark is a member of the European Union. In 1992 the Danes rejected the Maastricht Treaty and thereby forced the representatives from the EU countries to negotiate the Edinburgh agreement which was accepted in a new referendum in 1993. Apart from being a member of the European Union, Denmark is also a member of the United Nations, NATO, OSCE and the Nordic Council but is not a member of the WEU.

2. Governmental immigration policy

Danish immigration policy is influenced by the fact that Denmark borders the Nordic countries on one side and Germany, a member of the European Union, on the other. The Danish Aliens Act divides foreign nationals into three main categories; nationals from the other Nordic countries, nationals coming from the EU countries and nationals coming from the so-called "third countries".

(a) Nationals from other Nordic countries

According to section 1 of the Danish Aliens Act, citizens from Finland, Iceland, Norway and Sweden can enter and reside temporarily or permanently in Denmark without seeking permission. As a result of an agreement between these countries Nordic citizens do not have to be in possession of a passport while travelling between these countries. Furthermore, nationals from Nordic countries do not need a work permit if they want to take up paid or unpaid work in Denmark.

(b) All other nationals

In contrast to the liberal regulation of entry and residence applying to nationals from the Nordic countries, all other foreign nationals who intend to reside permanently must apply for a residence permit. Since 1969 restrictions on granting such permissions have been in force. As a result of a sudden rise in unemployment due to the oil crisis in 1972–73, a general ban on immigration was introduced and has been in force ever since.

(c) EU citizens

A major exception to this ban is nationals coming from Members States of the European Union. Denmark joined the European Union almost at the same time as the ban on immigration was introduced. Nationals from other EU countries have a legal right to obtain employment in Denmark unless, out of consideration for public policy, public security or public health, this legal right should be denied. EU citizens may also be denied employment that implies exercise of official authority in the host country.

EU citizens who do not want to obtain employment are allowed to stay in Denmark provided they possess sufficient means which will prevent them becoming a burden on the social system of the host country.

While EU nationals have a legal right to seek employment in Denmark, the overall intention of the immigration ban was to prevent nationals from third countries taking up work in Denmark. In the following sections the very limited exceptions to the general ban on immigration are described. Furthermore, regulation of obtaining work permits, temporary visits, expulsion, etc, is described at **3**, **4**, **5** and **8** below, while regulation concerning EU citizens is described at **9** below.

3. Foreign nationals from outside the EU and Nordic countries

The Danish Aliens Act distinguishes between foreign nationals who intend to enter Denmark temporarily and those who intend to reside permanently. Furthermore, the rules divide foreigners into two groups depending on their nationalities: those included in the annual visa list and those not included.

Thus, before arrival all foreign nationals must decide whether they intend to stay permanently or temporarily in Denmark.

(a) Permanent residence

If a foreigner wants permanent residence he or she must apply in advance according to the few limited possibilities in the Danish Aliens Act.

(b) Temporary visits

Nationals who do not need a visa and who intend to stay only temporarily can enter the country if they hold a valid passport. The frontier control, however, can deny entry if there are reasons to believe that the foreigner intends to reside permanently or to take up work, *e.g.* if the foreigner is not in possession of a minimum amount of money to pay the cost of a temporary visit.

Nationals who need a visa before entry can apply for reasons such as business meetings, participation in cultural or scientific arrangements or tourism. The granting of a visa can be denied if the Danish authorities have reasons to believe that the stay will be permanent. Even though a visa is granted, the border control is authorised to reject the foreigner if there are reasons to believe that the visit is not temporary. The general trend in the Danish visa policy has been to lay down visa requirements for countries from which a number of visitors have "changed their minds" and after arrival have applied for political asylum, or have married etc.

In **4**, **5** and **6** below, regulation concerning residence and work permits is described simultaneously because of the very narrow connection between these two kinds of permits. This is followed by a discussion of the regulation concerning naturalisation at **7** and expulsion at **8** below.

4. Permanent immigrants

(a) Employment

(i) "The rule of specialists"

The main reasoning for this provision is to maintain the possibility of allowing the assistance of foreign workers in the interest of Danish society.

In relation to the ordinary labour market this provision is only used to solve major problems of a commercial character. It is a precondition that the foreigner is qualified to do a particular kind of job which no one in Denmark is qualified to do, and that getting the job done is urgent according to the interests of production. In such cases a work permit and, consequently, a residence permit will be granted. This residence permit, however, is usually granted for the purpose of a temporary stay. Furthermore, the residence permit is given on the condition that the person works only at a specified task or for a particular employer. If these conditions change, for instance if the person is offered another job, a new application form must be filled in and approved by the authorities before the person can take up the new job.

Outside the ordinary labour market, special rules apply to a number of working categories, as follows.

(ii) Businessmen and women

In connection with the establishment of a private firm, residence permits are only granted if the establishment of the firm serves special Danish interests. Such interests are not constituted by the mere fact that investment is made or more jobs are created in Denmark. Only rarely are permits granted to retailers or owners of restaurants, etc.

(iii) Trainees

Trainees between the ages of 18 and 30 can be granted a residence permit for 18 months. The permit may be extended to cover a period of two years. Denmark has made special stage agreements with certain countries concerning exchange of trainees. Permission to work is not granted unless the work is an integrated part of the program.

(iv) Superior employees from foreign firms

Permits are granted to directors and to heads of technical or administrative departments of local branches in Denmark.

(v) Housemaids

In private households, residence permits are granted for a maximum period of two years and cannot be extended. Permission is only granted if the household usually employs housemaids and if it provides food and accommodation and pays a minimum salary in accordance with Danish standards.

(vi) Instructors etc

A Danish firm buying technical equipment which needs to be installed or about which the firm needs instruction can invite foreign instructors etc for a period of three months. At the end of this period it is necessary to apply for work and residence permits. If a visa is required on arrival, the Danish authorities consider this visa application in relation to the information received from the Danish firm.

(vii) Education

Professors, teachers and scientific employees can be employed for a three-month period without work permits. Persons coming from countries from which a visa is required must apply for a visa in advance. Residence permits are not required in cases of temporary stays of a maximum of three months. This applies whether or not the person comes from a country from which visas are required.

In cases of residence for more than three months, residence and work permits are required for all third country nationals.

(b) Persons who used to have Danish citizenship

Pursuant to section 9.1.1 of the Danish Aliens Act foreign nationals who have previously had Danish citizenship have a legal claim for a residence permit. The major category consists of Danish citizens who, by marriage, changed citizenship and left the country.

All persons coming from third countries, except refugees, must have a work permit if they wish to take up work. This also includes former Danish citizens. However, after five years of permanent residence in Denmark a work permit is no longer required.

(c) Family reunification

(i) Foreign nationals

Danes and foreign nationals who have been living legally in Denmark have a legal right to apply for family reunification with spouses. It is up to the married couple to provide a marriage certificate or similar documentation from the country of origin to prove that the marriage is lawful. The marriage must not be in conflict with basic Danish standards (a husband lawfully married to two wives according to the traditions of the country of origin is not allowed to be reunited with both wives).

(ii) Common law marriage

Persons who have been living together in a stable marriage-like relationship (common law marriage) for at least one-and-a-half to two years have the right of reunification under the same conditions as mentioned above. Such common law marriages are usually heterosexual but homosexual partnerships are also accepted by Danish law.

In both situations it can be required that the person residing in Denmark substantiates that he or she is able to provide for the family in accordance with Danish standards. It is required that both persons have reached the age of 18.

(iii) Formal engagements

Formal engagements do not qualify for family reunification unless there has been such a prior common law marriage as mentioned above. Furthermore, it is almost impossible to be granted a visitor's visa if the Danish authorities receive information that the applicant intends to marry a person who has a permanent residence permit in Denmark. In one case the Danish Ombudsman criticised this practice because the person residing in Denmark was a refugee and was consequently prevented from returning to his country of origin to be married to his fiancée there.

(iv) Children under 18

There is a right to reunification with under age children, *i.e.* children under 18. The applicants must provide the Danish authorities with documentation, *e.g.* a birth certificate to prove that the child is under age. Reasonable consideration is given in relation to the legislation and administration in the country of origin which, in some cases, make it impossible to produce such documentation.

(v) Parents

Unification with the parents of a person who has resided in Denmark for more than five years is permitted when the parents reach the age of 60. It is required that the residing person is able to support the parents when they arrive in Denmark. If the parents have other children in their country of origin, permission for reunification is not granted unless the person residing in Denmark is recognised as a refugee.

Persons who are granted a permanent residence permit conforming with the rules of family reunification can apply for a work permit. Spouses and children are usually granted permission; but, generally, parents are denied a work permit.

(vi) Family relations other than nuclear family

Pursuant to section 9.2 of the Danish Aliens Act foreigners who apply in the following situations can be granted a residence permit, but it is not a legal right. When a person fulfils the requirements in the following situations Danish authorities are said to have an optional possibility of granting a residence permit.

Foreign nationals having other family relations than the relationships mentioned in section 9.1 of the Danish Aliens Act or with similar close relations to a person living permanently in Denmark can obtain a residence permit. The intention of this provision is to create the possibility of reunification between a permanent resident and a person who the resident is under an obligation to support because of, for example, a prior foster-parents relationship.

In connection with adoption of foreign children by Danish citizens the children are automatically granted Danish citizenship when the child – as in the majority of cases – is under 12 years of age. Children above that age will become Danish citizens provided they express their interest in becoming so.

(vii) Other relatives

It must be underlined that the provision does not open up possibilities of reunification with nuclear members who fall outside the scope of section 9.1, *e.g.* children over the age of 18 or parents under the age of 60.

These family members have no possibilities of reunification at all. Furthermore, close family members from visa-restricted countries often have difficulties in obtaining a visitors visa because the authorities fear that they intend to reside permanently with their relatives.

5. Students and temporary workers

While the provisions above concern exceptions from the ban on immigration to meet Danish demands, the last provision in section 9.1 opens up the possibility of taking the special circumstances of the applicant into account.

(a) Students

Students coming from third world countries on special educational programs sponsored by the Danish Ministry of Foreign Affairs are granted residence permits. Residence permits are also granted to persons in order that they can receive an education provided only by the Danish educational system. Finally, the provision opens up an exchange of students process arranged by Danish and foreign organisations.

If a foreign student wants to receive further education after completing the education on the basis of which he or she was granted a residence permit, a renewal is not given automatically. If there is a natural link between the two education courses a new permit may be granted.

The main rule concerning work is that students are denied work permits. However, as an exception students are allowed to take up work in June, July and August. After 18 months they can be granted permission to work for a maximum of 15 hours a week.

(b) Temporary workers

(i) Au pairs

Au pairs can be granted residence permits for a maximum period of two years. In general, permissions are only granted to nationals from the Nordic countries, the EU countries or countries of a similar standard of development. Only under special circumstances are permits granted to persons coming from third world countries.

(ii) Ministers

Ministers connected with non-State religious communities operating in Denmark can be granted temporary residence permits for a maximum of two years.

Finally, residence permits may be granted on the basis of the provision in section 9.1 if special circumstances are present, *e.g.* a previous long term of residence in Denmark or a long employment period with a Danish firm abroad. The application of this provision is extremely restricted.

It must be noted that even though the immigration ban was introduced due to rising unemployment, Danish policy does not allow foreign persons to enter Denmark with the purpose of staying during their retirement. It makes no difference that they do not perform any professional activities and are able to pay all costs related to their residence in Denmark. The only exception to this is family reunification.

6. Refugees and political asylum

Asylum seekers have a right to stay in Denmark if they fall within the scope of the UN Convention Relating to the Status of Refugees 1951. The same applies where other weighty reasons or reasons similar to those listed in the Convention why the person should not be required to return to the country of origin are in question.

Asylum seekers waiting for the authorities' final decision are not permitted to take up paid or unpaid work. If asylum is granted the refugee does not need a work permit and can seek employment on equal terms with Danes.

In order to cope with the massive refugee influx from the former Yugoslavia in 1992, the Danish Parliament adopted a law according to which it became possible to postpone the examination of asylum applications for two years. During this period this group of asylum seekers had very limited rights. After expiration of the two-year period applications for asylum are resumed.

There are two asylum procedures in Denmark; a normal procedure and a procedure for applications which are deemed manifestly unfounded.

(a) The normal procedure

In case of refusal in the normal procedure the applicant has a right to appeal the decision of the Directorate for Aliens to the Refugee Appeals Board. The Board can uphold or quash the decision of the Directorate for Aliens.

If, typically, a man is granted asylum by the Directorate for Aliens or by the Refugee Appeals Board, his accompanying wife and children are also granted a permanent residence permit automatically. If the family is still in the country of origin they have the right to family reunification.

(b) The manifestly unfounded procedure

Applications which are clearly abusive or unrelated to the criteria for the granting of asylum are considered manifestly unfounded. In addition, applications which are considered without any prospect of success according to the case law of the Refugee Appeals Board falls within this category. Consequently, this special procedure covers a broader category of applications than those normally defined in international instruments as "manifestly unfounded". Only a limited number of refusals given by the Directorate for Aliens in the manifestly unfounded procedure are given with a right to appeal.

(c) Humanitarian residence permit

In a very limited number of cases the Ministry of Interior can permit residence due to special humanitarian reasons. So far, permits have primarily been given to families with under age children coming from war-ridden areas.

If the applicant is refused by the Refugee Appeals Board and the Ministry of Interior he or she is obliged to leave the country, if not voluntarily then with the assistance of the police. There is no possibility, like the German "duldung", that the applicant can stay after the final refusal to grant asylum.

7. Nationality

To obtain Danish citizenship it is necessary that the applicant has lived in Denmark for at least seven years and presently also resides in the country. Furthermore, a good knowledge of Danish is required and the person involved must be ready to give up his or her former citizenship. Criminal offences and the unlawful receipt of social benefits which must be repaid to the Danish State will normally postpone the granting of citizenship.

More liberal rules granting Danish citizenship apply to foreigners who have been married to Danish citizens for at least three years, as only four years' permanent residence is required before an application can be filed. With regard to refugees, six years' permanent residence from the date they were granted refugee status is required, before an application can be filed.

In general, foreign persons cannot acquire Danish citizenship unless they are married to a Danish citizen. Furthermore, persons who have lived permanently in Denmark for five years prior to reaching the age of 16 can acquire Danish citizenship by handing in a special application form. This must be done before reaching the age of 23.

8. Sanctions

(a) Denial of entry at the border or expulsion

Foreigners who do not fulfil the legal requirements on arrival, for example possessing a valid passport or visa when required, are denied entry at the border. If such persons claim to be asylum seekers, the police are not authorised to deny entry in the first place. In such situations the decision to deny entry is taken by the Directorate for Aliens which assesses whether there is a risk of persecution in the former country or residence. If there is no such risk, such persons are denied entry by the Directorate. However, this decision can be appealed to the Minister of Interior. Such an appeal has no suspensive effect.

Foreigners holding a valid passport, visa etc are usually allowed entry without further requirements. However, the Danish border control is authorised to ask whether the holder of *e.g.* a tourist visa is in possession of an adequate amount of money to cover all expenses in the period for which the visa is valid. If not, the authorities may deny him or her entry at the border.

(b) Withdrawal of residence permit

If a foreigner has been admitted into the country with the intention of permanent residence, Danish law provides a far-reaching protection against having the residence permit withdrawn. If the reason for giving the permit has ceased to exist, the general rule in the Danish Aliens Act is that the permission can be withdrawn. However, if a person has stayed legally in the country for three years, the residence permit cannot be withdrawn, even if the reasons for giving it have ceased to exist. The most common example is when a couple gets divorced more than three years after the time when family reunification was granted. A permission can always be withdrawn if the information given by the applicant was false.

(c) Expulsion

In criminal cases, a decision to expel a foreign national from the country can be part of the court verdict. The Aliens Act enumerates the reasons why foreign citizens can be expelled. The main principle followed is that the longer a foreign national has stayed in Denmark, the more serious a crime must be committed in order to be expelled.

9. Special rules applying to nationals from EU countries

(a) Professional activities

The basic intention of the Treaty of Rome was to establish a Common Market, which included the right of free movement of EU citizens and the right to seek and to take up employment in any other Member State without any restrictions on the grounds of nationality.

Thus, nationals from other Member States have a right to take up employment in Denmark without applying for a work permit. A residence permit for at least five years is given, and this permission is renewed if applied for, even if the person concerned reaches the age of retirement and has a pension.

Furthermore, unemployed nationals from other Member States have the right to enter Denmark with the intention of seeking employment.

(b) Non-professional activities

Council Directive 90/364/EC has extended the right of residence to a number of persons who perform non-professional activities. The Danish Aliens Act was amended in June 1992, and consequently it is now possible for the following categories of EU nationals to obtain residence permits.

(i) Pensioners

In order to obtain a residence permit it is a precondition under this head that the applicant receives old age benefit, invalidity or early retirement pension or a pension in respect of an industrial accident or disease of an amount sufficient to avoid becoming a burden on the social security system. A sufficient amount is an amount which is higher than the level of the minimum social security pension paid by the host country to its own citizens.

(ii) Students, their spouses and dependent children

When a student assures the national authority that he or she has sufficient means not to burden the social system of the host country he or she may qualify for a residence permit. The student must be enrolled in a recognised educational establishment for the principal purpose of following a vocational training course and must be covered by sickness insurance in respect of all risks in the host country.

(iii) Other EU citizens

Member State nationals who do not enjoy the right of residence under other provisions of Community law may obtain residence permits provided they and the members of their families are covered by sickness insurance in respect of all risks in the host Member State and they have sufficient means to avoid becoming a burden to the social assistance system of the host country during their stay.

10. Tax

The Danish tax system is founded on the principle that a high income results in a high taxation. The personal allowance lowers the tax relatively more for low income earners than for high income earners. Thus, Denmark has a progressive tax system.

Foreigners coming to Denmark must have either a personal or an economic relationship with Denmark before they are required to pay tax. Depending on the relationship the foreigner will be considered either as fully or partially liable to duty. The principal taxes in Denmark are ordinary and special income taxes, capital levy, property tax and labour market contributions. It is impossible to give a detailed description of the tax legislation due to the limitation of space. Only one relevant type of regulation will be outlined.

(a) Researchers and specialists

Special regulation exists regarding taxation of foreign researchers and other specialists. According to the regulation, 30% of what is earned must be withheld by the employer. The taxation is, thus, lower for these groups than for others; however, these groups do not have a personal allowance.

Researchers can choose between normal taxation and the regulation already outlined, while specialists must prove that their monthly salary amounts to DKR 44,100 (1993). The size of the salary governs whether or not this kind of taxation is applied. For researchers as well as specialists it is a condition that the working period is for a term of between six to 36 months' duration.

The employer must contact the regional custom and tax administration within eight days after the conception of the contract.

11. Domestic considerations

(a) Civil registration

After obtaining a permanent residence and work permit a foreigner can approach the local civil registration office in order to receive a civil registration number which entitles him or her to free medical services on an equal footing with Danes.

(b) Schooling

Children normally go to school at the age of six or seven and receive free education in public schools for nine or 10 years. High school is also free of charge. Education from private schools and high schools is available. After high school many people continue their studies at universities or technical colleges and generally receive subsidies.

Messrs. Norsker & Jacoby, Kvaesthusgade 3, DK-1251 Kobenhavn K.
tel.: (45) 33110885. telefax:(45) 33937530

Contents of Chapter 6

FINLAND

Chapter 6

FINLAND

Mikko Mali

1. Country characteristics and general principles

Finland, along with Sweden and Austria, became a member of the European Union at the beginning of 1995. Therefore, EU principles on movement of people are also applicable in Finland.

Finland is not yet party to the Schengen Agreement. However, the Nordic countries (Denmark, Finland, Iceland, Norway and Sweden) entered into a Treaty which guarantees passport-free movement for the citizens of Member States. No passport is, therefore, required when a citizen of a Nordic country travels to another Nordic country.

Finland, a prosperous country with good social security, has a high standard of living and advanced technology. It is one of the most northerly countries in the world, situated between 60 and the 70 degrees of latitude. Finland shares borders with Sweden, Norway and Russia.

With its 338,000 square kilometres, Finland is the seventh largest country in Europe. Approximately 190,000 lakes cover 10% of the country's surface, forests 70% and cultivated land about 8%.

The population of Finland is approximately five million, of which 71,000 are foreign citizens. Population density is 15 inhabitants per square kilometre, and life expectancy is 70 for men and 78 for women.

Finland is officially bilingual. Of the total population, 93% name Finnish, a language belonging to the Finn-o-Ugrian group, together with Estonian and Hungarian, and 6% Swedish, as their mother tongue. The Swedish-speaking Finns live mainly along the coast.

Finland is a Western democracy with a president elected for a six-year term and a 200-member, single-chamber parliament elected every four years. After the parliamentary elections in 1995 a majority government was formed under the leadership of the Social Democratic Party, together with the conservative Coalition Party, the former having 63 and the latter 39 members of parliament.

The great majority of Finns belong to the Evangelical Lutheran Church (85.9%), and 60,000 to the Orthodox Church.

The total labour force in Finland is 2.5 million, of which 8% earns its living from agriculture, 27% from industry and 65% from services. The average monthly salary is FIM 11,520 for men and FIM 9,326 for women. Due to the recession at the beginning of the 1990s, some 500,000 workers were unemployed. In 1996 the unemployment rate is still 16%.

Finland's most important branches of industry are metal and engineering which account for 38%, and forest industry, which accounts for 23% of the total industrial production (1994). Furthermore, the food and the chemical industries have a 10% share of the total output; 37% of metal and 46% of forest industry production is exported mainly to other EU countries. The most important trading partners outside the European Union are the United States and Japan.

2. Employment and inter-company transfers

(a) Employment

(i) Required permits
A person wishing to work in Finland is generally required to have a work permit. However, a work permit is not required where the number of days worked is less than five. In order to get a work permit a person must have either a visa or a residence permit. Therefore, a combination of either a work permit and a visa or a work permit and a residence permit must be applied for.

(ii) Work permits
A foreigner who intends to stay and work in Finland for longer than five days must have a work permit. This also applies to work on a vessel registered in Finland.

An application for a work permit must be made prior to entry into Finland. However, a work permit can also be granted after entry, if the reasons for working in Finland came about after the entry, or if it would be unreasonable to refuse the permit in the circumstances. When applying for a work permit for the first time, the employer in Finland must first fill in an application, receive a favourable labour office statement concerning it and then send the application and the statement to the employee, who must apply for a work permit and a visa or a residence permit at the Finnish embassy or consulate in his or her home country. An employment certificate must always be attached to the application. No permit will be issued if the applicant does not already have work available for him or her in Finland when applying for the permit.

Finland joined the European Union at the beginning of 1995 and had earlier become party to the European Economic Space (EES) Convention which entered into force at the beginning of 1994, citizens of other EU Member States are free to move and work within the Union. Hence, citizens of a country which is a Member State of the EES are not required to have a visa or work permit.

There are other exceptions to the requirement of a work permit. A work permit will not be required if the foreigner:

- holds a residence permit for an indefinite period;
- holds a residence permit for a specified period and has been a Finnish citizen, or one of the foreigner's parents is or has been a Finnish citizen, or the foreigner is married to a Finnish citizen or to a person residing in Finland, or the foreigner is a refugee; or
- is a student (students do not need a work permit for part-time work during the semester, and full-time work during the vacation period).

Normally, a work permit will be granted for at least one year. It is not necessarily restricted to a certain employer but usually to a certain branch. It may also include specifications as to the territorial validity of the permit and the nature of the work.

(iii) Visas

A visa is required if a person comes to Finland for purposes other than short business trips or a vacation. A visa is always required if the relevant country and Finland have not made a Treaty on visa-free entries. Such Treaties have been made with over 80 countries.

Although a person may ordinarily stay in Finland without a visa for a period of three months during any six-month period (provided he or she has not stayed in any other Nordic countries during the period), if a work permit is required for working more than five days, a visa is required accordingly. A visa with which a work permit may be issued is a multiple entry visa. A visa may be issued for up to three months for each entry.

(iv) Residence permits

A residence permit is required if the stay exceeds three months. A temporary residence permit may be issued for a period no longer than two years, after which it can be renewed. Normally, a residence permit is issued for one year at a time.

A permanent residence permit may be issued to a person who has stayed in Finland for more than two years. However, a stay of more than two years in Finland does not automatically entitle a person to a permanent residence permit. In case of temporary employment, a residence permit will normally be renewed for a specific period of time. As mentioned above, a person who has a permanent residence permit is not required to have a work permit.

Although a work permit is not necessary for citizens of other EES Member States, such people are required to obtain a residence permit if their stay in Finland is extended beyond three months. A residence permit will be issued to citizens of EES Member States for a period of five years on application.

Approximately 30,000 applications for a residence permit were filed in 1995, most of which were decided favourably. It should be noted that there may have been several persons on a single application, and, conversely, several applications per person.

(b) Inter-company transfers

A work permit may be issued to managers, executives and experts who come to work temporarily in Finland in a subsidiary or branch office of a foreign company, or at least a partially foreign-owned Finnish company. There are no strict requirements on the percentage of ownership in the Finnish company by the foreign company.

A work permit may be issued to a person who is to act as a manager or executive. A foreign company may generally nominate its personnel to management of its branch office or subsidiary, provided the personell's contribution is essential to the company. Consequently, a work permit may be issued to a person coming to work for a Finnish company when he or she is transferred from a subsidiary of a Finnish company abroad and possesses such essential skills. Transfers within the same group of companies on a managerial or executive level are generally treated favourably by the Finnish immigration authorities.

A work permit may also be issued to an expert who possesses such essential expertise in his or her field of work that the work generally cannot be performed by Finnish nationals available for work. Hence, the foreign person may not be a worker who could be replaced by a Finnish employee who would be otherwise available. The necessity of expertise of the person is evaluated on a case-by-case basis.

It should be noted that an intra-group transfer is not necessarily required. On the above-mentioned grounds a work permit may also be issued to a person who comes to work in Finland, although he or she has not previously been employed by a company of the group.

(c) Specially skilled workers

A work permit may be issued to a professional in a field of work which cannot be undertaken adequately by native Finnish workers, for example foreign language teachers, lecturers, scientists etc.

(d) Exceptions on grounds of Finnish ancestry

There are no exceptions based on Finnish ancestry with regard to the requirement of a work and residence permit. However, persons who are at least 50% Finnish by nationality (rather than by citizenship) will be granted a residence permit for a specified period of time, because they are considered as returning to Finland. Nationality, in this case, means that such persons have been registered as Finns by nationality in the former Soviet Union, although they have been Soviet citizens. The 50% rule means that either parent or at least two of the grandparents of the person have been Finns by nationality.

(e) Other workers

The list of workers who may be granted a work permit is not exhaustive. Naturally, a work permit may also be issued to persons doing other kinds of work. Decisions on applications are made on a case-by-case basis.

3. Business

(a) Businessmen and women

Persons belonging to the business community will not usually encounter problems in acquiring a business visa to Finland for a period up to three months. If the stay will be for more than three months, a residence permit will be needed, and probably even a work permit. Businessmen and women do not necessarily need a work permit when their stays do not exceed three months. The five-day rule applies mainly to persons who come to Finland to work for companies located in Finland and who receive a remuneration from Finland (*i.e.* become part of the Finnish labour force).

There is no special treatment for investors and business persons. If they plan to stay in Finland for more than three months, they must follow the same procedure as described above.

A foreigner living in the area of the European Economic Space regardless of his nationality, or a corporation which has a registered branch office in Finland and which has been established and has a registered office in one of the countries of the European Economic Space, may generally conduct business activities of good practice in Finland. The Ministry of Trade and Industry may give a permission to corporations from other countries.

(b) Foreign investment regulations

Due mainly to European integration, new laws have come into force and changes to old laws have been made abolishing most of the restrictions concerning ownership of real property and shares of companies in Finland. The new laws and changes came into effect on 1 January 1993.

(c) Shares of corporations

The limited liability company (osakeyhtiö, abbreviated "Oy") is the dominant form of business in Finland and usually the most suitable for a foreign enterprise wishing to establish operations in Finland. All shares in a limited liability company must be of equal nominal value, the total amount of which has to be at least FIM 15,000, although a recent Government proposal on amending the Companies Act would increase the minimum amount to FIM 50,000. Certain categories of shares may be given voting rights up to 20 times more than those of other categories of shares.

A limited liability company may be established by persons at least half of whom have their domicile within the European Economic Space. The same applies to the members of the board of directors. The managing director must also be domiciled in an EES country. The decisive factor is therefore the domicile, not the nationality, of the founders, the board members or the managing director of the company. Exemptions may be granted by the Ministry of Trade and Industry, but in practice at least one board member must reside in an EU country.

Investments which do not aim at obtaining a controlling power in a corporation are free from any kind of restriction. The rules on restricted shares which cannot be owned by foreigners have been repealed, and existing restricted share clauses have become null and void.

Direct investments, the purpose of which are to acquire controlling power in a corporation, are controlled only under special preconditions. These rules set forth in the Act on the Control of Acquisitions of Finnish Companies by Foreigners (the Control Act) apply to companies where:

- the number of employees exceeds 1,000; or
- the turnover exceeds FIM 1 million; or
- the balance sheet total exceeds FIM 1 million.

Such corporations are subject to special control by the Ministry of Trade and Industry. The same applies to all companies which manufacture defence supplies, regardless of the size of the company. However, with the exception of acquisitions of companies manufacturing defence supplies the Control Act is not applicable to persons or companies from EES or OECD countries.

According to the Control Act a foreign owner who, acquires shares thereby obtaining at least one-third of all votes or, alternatively the controlling power in such corporation, or a company manufacturing defence supplies, is under an obligation to apply for confirmation of the acquisition from the Ministry of Trade and Industry. A "foreign owner" is a foreigner not having domicile in Finland, a foreign corporation or foundation, or a Finnish corporation in which foreigners have at least 50% of the voting power of the shares.

The obligation to apply for confirmation does not apply to issuing additional shares or capital stock requiring that shares shall be subscribed in proportion to the old shares. Neither does it apply to situations where shares are received under the law of inheritance or family laws.

The application must be made within one month from the day of the acquisition, or it can be given in advance. The report must include information about the corporation or commercial unit where controlling power has been acquired, and the details of the agreement entitling the purchase of controlling power. The report is dealt with and preliminarily decided by the Ministry of Trade and Industry. In case of a company manufacturing defence supplies, the application is dealt with by the Ministry of Defence. On rare occasions matters will be submitted to the Council of State when a more detailed study of prohibition is considered necessary. A decision concerning prohibition can be made only by the Council of State.

A transaction can be prohibited only if it endangers important national interests. These important national interests are defined to be securing national defence, preventing severe economical, social or environmental problems concerning a certain industrial sector or geographical area, and securing public order or citizens' health and safety.

Where the Council of State prohibits an acquisition, the acquiring party has the obligation to assign the ownership of so many shares that the law does not apply after the assignment. In case of prohibition, the right to vote will be removed. The parties to the contract also have the right to revoke the contract. If the prohibition concerns the transfer of business activities rather than of shares, the contract will be dissolved in any case.

The legislation does not apply to deposit banks or insurance companies, which are covered by special laws that include restrictions concerning ownership of shares in other companies and engagement in trade, or in other areas than banking and insurance activities.

(d) Real estate and housing companies

Foreign persons, foreign companies and companies with foreigners having the majority of all votes only need authorisation from the Government for acquiring real property under special circumstances. Citizens of a foreign country who reside in Finland need authorisation only if the real estate is located in the border zone or in a so-called protected area, meaning an area important for military purposes. The border zone is defined as the border between Finland and the Russian Federation. The same rule applies to foreign corporations and corporations controlled by foreigners.

Non-residents, foreign corporations and corporations controlled by foreigners always need to obtain an authorisation from the county government for acquiring real property for recreational purposes or as a secondary residence. This liability does not apply to real estate acquired for permanent residence or for agricultural or forestry purposes. Authorisation will not be needed if real estate is received under the law of inheritance or family law, or when the assignor is a close relative of the assignee or when spouses acquire real estate together and only one of them would otherwise be required to obtain authorisation. The purchaser must apply for authorisation within three months from the day of the acquisition. If this duty has not been fulfilled or the application has been rejected, the real estate must be transferred to a party who does not require authorisation. If this does not happen within one year, the county government can order the property to be sold in a compulsory auction.

Unlike a limited liability company where, if ownership of a limited liability company which owns real estate in Finland changes so that the majority of shares is owned by foreigners, authorisation would be required as of the date of the change in the ownership; ownership of shares in a housing company is in no way restricted.

4. Persons of independent means/investors

A residence permit may be granted, for example, if the applicant can secure his living in Finland. Therefore, there is no formal hindrance for persons not actively working or for investors to get a residence permit for a specified period of time if they have sufficient personal wealth.

There are no legal rules governing the amount of investment to be made or the duration of the investment. As in other cases, a residence permit may at first be granted for a limited period of time only.

Citizens of other EU countries can retire in Finland without restrictions.

5. Spouses and children

A spouse of an EES citizen residing in Finland will be granted a residence permit for a period of five years. Such a person does not need a work permit.

A spouse of a non-EES citizen residing in Finland will normally also be granted a residence permit for a shorter period of time. If a non-EES citizen has been granted a permanent residence permit, his or her spouse who has been granted a residence permit for a specified period of time is not required to apply for a work permit.

A foreigner who has cohabited for at least one year with a person residing in Finland may, in practice, also be granted a residence permit. The same applies to a foreigner who has a child with a person residing in Finland.

A child under the age of 21, either of whose parents is a EES citizen residing in Finland, will be granted a residence permit for a period of five years. No work permit is necessary.

Children of non-EES citizens residing in Finland and supported by their parents will normally also be granted a residence permit for a shorter period of time.

6. Temporary stays

(a) Visitors

Tourists and others foreigners who stay in Finland for private reasons for a short period of time must have a visa. However, no visa is required of a foreigner who is a citizen of a State with which Finland has made a Treaty on visa-free entries. Such Treaties have been made with over 80 States. Neither is a visa required of a foreigner who is a citizen of a country being a Member State of the European Economic Space (EES).

If a visa is not required, a passport will be sufficient to enter the country. No forms need to be filled and usually no questions are asked at the border control. Although a visitor must be able to pay for his stay in Finland, it is seldom checked at the entry.

No passport is required for citizens of the Nordic countries. There are, additionally, approximately 10 countries with which Finland has made bilateral agreements according to which an identity card issued in the relevant country will be accepted in place of a passport.

The maximum stay without a visa depends on the relevant agreement. Usually the stay may not exceed three months.

If a visa is required, an application must be made prior to entry at the Finnish consulate or the Finnish embassy in the home country of the visitor.

There are different types of visas. A single entry visa is valid for one entry and a maximum stay of three months. Repeated entries from the Nordic countries (Denmark, Sweden, Norway and Iceland) are not considered to be new entries. Therefore, travel back and forth between the Nordic countries can be accomplished on a single entry visa. Repeated entry from any other country is not possible with a single entry visa.

A multiple entry visa is issued for a number of entries. Each visit is limited to no more than three months. Multiple entry visas are not usually available to tourists.

A transit visa is granted for a specific number of transit passages within a specific period. The stay under a transit visa is limited to five days per passage.

A return visa for the purpose of returning from a single or multiple voyage may be issued to an alien residing in Finland.

(b) Business visitors

The same rules apply generally to business visitors as for tourists. Business visitors will normally have no problems obtaining the relevant visas and permits if they are coming to Finland on legitimate business.

(c) Students

Foreigners who wish to study in Finland for more than three months need a residence permit. The residence permit may be granted if the foreigner is accepted by a Finnish university or vocational school.

The foreigner has to prove to the Finnish authorities that he or she is able to pay for his or her own living during the stay in Finland. The authorities may require that the necessary amount be deposited in a Finnish bank account. The foreigner will then be allowed to use that money during the stay in Finland.

As a foreign student, the foreigner is allowed to work part time during the semester and full time during the vacation period without a work permit. The expected earnings may be taken into account when estimating the amount needed.

(d) Spouses and children of students

The spouse and children of a foreign student in Finland also need a residence permit which may be granted, provided that the family is able to pay for their stay in Finland.

7. Permanent residence and nationality

(a) Permanent residence

A permanent residence permit entitles a person to stay in the country without any limitation of time and can be applied for by a foreigner who has resided in Finland legally, (for an uninterrupted period of two years) unless the purpose of the foreigner's stay or other special reasons dictate otherwise. The purpose of the foreigner's stay implies otherwise, for example, if the foreigner comes to Finland to study. A student is expected to leave the country after finishing the course of studies.

(b) Nationality

There are some 71,000 foreigners living in Finland with a residence permit. Approximately 36% are from the former Soviet Union, 20% are refugees, and 10% are Swedes. Most of the nationalities of the world are represented.

According to the Finnish nationality law, dual citizenship must be avoided. However, there are some exceptions based on bilateral agreements with certain countries. A person may have dual citizenship until he or she is 18 years old, after which he or she normally has to choose between the nationalities.

Finnish citizenship can be acquired either at birth, upon declaration or upon application. Upon application, a foreigner may be granted Finnish citizenship, provided that:

- the applicant is 18 years old;
- for the past five years the applicant's permanent residence and domicile has been and still is in Finland;
- the applicant leads a respectable life and is able to support his or her family; and
- the applicant has adequate knowledge of the Finnish or Swedish language.

A former Finnish citizen may be naturalised after being resident in the country for two years, simultaneously may his or her children under 18 acquire Finnish citizenship. Finnish ancestry, however, is not a sufficient reason to speed up the naturalisation process.

The Ministry of the Interior will refer applications to the President of Finland for a decision.

If a foreigner is married to a Finnish citizen or if there are otherwise special reasons, exemptions may be made to the five-year rule and the conditions listed above.

It takes approximately two years from the application until a decision is made. The conditions for granting Finnish citizenship are investigated by the police and the social security authorities, among others. In 1995, 2,182 applications were received and an additional 379 persons were granted Finnish citizenship on applications filed earlier.

8. Refugees and political asylum

A foreigner can be granted asylum in Finland if he or she leaves his or her country of origin or habitual residence and does not want to return for reasons of a justified fear of persecution on account of race, religion, nationality, social class or political opinion in that country.

Thus, Finland complies with the United Nations Convention on the Status of Refugees and its protocol, both of which are in force in Finland. According to these provisions, the applicant has no personal right to asylum and the state has a right to exercise discretion freely.

Asylum can be refused if there are reasons concerning the security of Finland which justify the refusal. This also applies if the foreigner has committed crimes which are, according to international agreements, crimes against peace and humanity, war crimes or other serious crimes, which would not be defined as political crimes.

Asylum can also be refused if the foreigner came from a state which granted asylum or where asylum could have been requested. This is not the case, however, if the foreigner's stay in that state was very short and for the purpose of changing transport.

A request for asylum must be filed upon entry or soon thereafter. The application can be filed with the police, the passport control officer at the point of entry, the Directorate of Immigration or the Alien's Counsellor. Asylum can also be granted after a longer stay in Finland, if conditions in the foreigner's country of origin or habitual residence radically change during his or her stay in Finland, creating grounds for asylum.

The request for asylum is decided by the Ministry of the Interior. If the Ministry proposes to refuse the asylum, it must ask the Asylum Committee for a statement.

If a request for asylum is refused, the foreigner can, nevertheless, upon an application, be granted a residence permit if he or she cannot return to his or her country of origin or habitual residence for reasons originating within that country.

9. Government discretion

The rules for immigration have been set out in the Foreigners Act and other relevant legislation. The Government does not participate in case-by-case decision-making. However, the Council of State has the power to decide in what cases, others than those specifically stipulated in the Foreigners Act, a residence permit may be granted abroad.

10. Sanctions

(a) Criminal sanctions

A foreigner who resides in Finland without a required passport, visa or residence permit or who works without a required work permit is subject to a fine.

An employer who employs a foreigner who does not have a required work permit is subject to a fine or a maximum of one year's imprisonment. An employer who gives authorities false information about the salary or other terms of employment or work assignment of a foreigner working for him or her is subject to a fine.

A person smuggling or organising smuggling of a foreigner to Finland or giving a counterfeit passport, visa or residence permit to a foreigner to be used for entry into Finland with the purpose of obtaining economic benefits to himself or herself or someone else, is subject to a fine or a maximum of two years' imprisonment.

(b) Deportation

Deportation is possible where a foreigner:

- resides in Finland without a required passport, visa or residence permit or works without a required work permit;
- is unable to take care of himself or herself through his or her own fault;
- has committed a crime, the punishment for which, according to the law, may be at least one year's imprisonment, or who has repeatedly committed crimes;
- has proven to be a danger to other people's safety; or
- has taken or, according to his or her previous behaviour, can be assumed likely to take actions resulting in sabotage, espionage or other activities jeopardising the safety of Finland.

A refugee or an EES citizen may only be deported for a special reason according to the last of the above reasons. A refugee may also be deported if he or she
has been adjudged guilty of an exceptionally serious crime.

11. Tax and social security

(a) Tax

A foreigner who plans to work in Finland for several years or for an indefinite
period of time will normally be considered a resident for tax purposes. Finland
has entered into bilateral agreements with most countries to avoid double taxation.

Foreign employees do not normally have to report to the tax authorities
unless they intend to stay in Finland for more than one year, in which case they
must register shortly after their arrival.

A personal registration number is important in Finland and is also used in
taxation. A personal registration number may be received from the local
population registration authorities after arrival to Finland, if a residence permit
has been granted for at least one year.

The Finnish level of income tax is one of the highest in the world. Employment
and otherwise earned income is taxed progressively. Earned income is divided
into a fixed municipal tax of approximately 15–20% depending on the municipality and a progressive State tax. The maximum total tax rate is approximately
70%.

As of the beginning of 1996 some foreigners working in Finland receive
special tax treatment. A 35% flat tax rate is applied to specialists meeting certain
conditions concerning, for example, their earnings and their stay in Finland.

The relatively new system of taxation of capital income was introduced in
1993. The taxation of capital income has been separated from the taxation of
other income, and a 28% flat tax rate is applied. The same tax rate is applied to
all capital gains.

The corporate income tax rate is 28% and the tax base is considered broad.
The tax rate applies to all legal entities.

In Finland, the avoir fiscal system is applied with regard to corporate taxation, which means that companies pay a 28% tax on their income from which
the receivers of dividends may benefit on certain conditions. This applies
mainly to shareholders living and taxed in Finland. There are a few countries
with which Finland has a bilateral agreement on cross-border application of the
Finnish avoir fiscal system.

(b) Social security

Finland is one of the most advanced industrial countries in the scope and
extent of a social security system. It is, however, questionable how long the

social welfare system may be maintained, due to growing national debt causing compulsory cuts in the public sector.

The social insurance system includes several categories of insurance such as health, pension and unemployment insurance, by which all Finns are covered. Cover is extended to foreigners who have resided in Finland with a valid residence permit for at least one year or who have received a residence permit for longer than one year.

Notwithstanding, citizens of other EES countries are covered by insurance on the basis of working in Finland.

Work injury insurance is financed by employers and covers all workers.

If a person is ill or must stay at home to take care of sick children, he or she receives a taxable daily allowance to cover the lost income. The amount of the daily allowance depends on the salary of the person. In most cases the daily allowance is approximately 60% of the salary.

Most hospitalisation and laboratory fees are paid by society. Drugs and medicine are also heavily subsidised, but the part paid by an individual is no longer tax deductible.

When a child is born, the mother is legally entitled to a total of 263 days' leave, for which she receives a daily allowance calculated as mentioned above. The father is entitled to three weeks' leave with the same benefits. It is possible for the father to use some of the leave of the mother in her place. After the 263-day period, a parent is entitled to leave until the child is three years old. During that time the parent staying at home with the child is entitled to a subsidy of FIM 1,500 per month.

A national occupational injury system pays all health care costs for work-related accidents.

A basic old-age pension financed by both employees and employers is payable to everyone over the age of 65.

12. Domestic considerations

(a) Introduction

In Finland, as in other Nordic countries, equality between men and women is an important factor in society. At least half of the students in universities are women. Most women work outside their homes, and chores at home are shared. Before starting school, all children are entitled to care in a communal kindergarten starting, in many cases, before their first birthday.

The labour legislation grants everyone at least four weeks' vacation per year, which is extended to five weeks after one year of employment with the same employer. Overtime work is restricted to a maximum of 200 hours per year, with some exceptions.

(b) Housing

Due to the relatively cold climate, houses must be well-built. Good quality housing is available all over the country. Most Finns in major cities live in apartment buildings, but duplex and terrace houses are also common. Single family houses are also popular in the suburbs. In the countryside, people almost exclusively live in single family houses.

Expatriates usually rent an apartment or a house during their stay in Finland. Professional agencies can provide assistance in finding accommodation.

As mentioned earlier, no permission is required for a foreigner to purchase real estate to be used as a residence (or an apartment – *i.e.* a share in a housing company), regardless of his or her nationality.

(c) Health care

All Finns have access to a good and extensive health care system provided by the public sector. Foreigners living legally in Finland have, to some extent, access to the same services. The scope of the social security system covering foreigners depends on the status of the foreigner. Although some foreigners may not be covered by insurance, they can be treated when the need arises.

(d) Schooling

Almost all schools in Finland are operated and funded by the State. However, some private schools exist in some major cities. Children start school at seven years of age (some, exceptionally, at the age of six) and receive free education in public schools for nine years, with free instruction, books and lunches. Children have nine years of compulsory school attendance.

A free, three-year high school education is offered in public schools. University studies are in expensive, with tuition fees amounting to approximately FIM 400 per year.

Adult education is available in various forms with considerable State subsidies.

Castrén & Snellman, P.O. Box 233, (Erottajankatu 5A), 00131 Helsinki.
tel.: (358) 228 581. telefax: (358) 680 1250

Contents of Chapter 7

FRANCE

Chapter 7

FRANCE

Brigitte Serfaty

1. Country characteristics and general principles

France has always been a dominant European country, being 500,000 square kilometres in size.

France's long and historical past has made it the fifth economical power of the world. France has always been a country of immigration rather than emigration. The French population is composed of people from various countries originating from former colonies in Africa and Asia, as well as Eastern Europe.

After the Second World War, General De Gaulle considered it necessary, in order to rebuild the country and to compensate war losses among the working population, to increase the immigration of foreign labour. Therefore, the French Government encouraged immigration and, in particular, labour immigration from North Africa by facilitating their integration into France. As a result, a true immigration policy was implemented to bring stable foreign labour into France. Decisions were made to facilitate foreign labour access to work. At that time, French demographs estimated a need for three to four million foreign workers to participate in the European economic boom.

Approximately three million foreigners now reside in France.

Laws regarding the acquisition of French nationality were passed, indicating a clear intention to assimilate foreign population. Prior to 1973 (the first oil crisis), the economy enjoyed an ongoing economic development which favoured labour immigration. After 1973, when the economy began to feel the effects of the first economic crisis, the Government began to impose certain controls over labour immigration. Immigration laws were amended, introducing limitations making it more difficult to emigrate to France. However, this was not sufficient to stop the continuous flow of immigration into France. Unemployment increased and the French population began to resent the presence of a foreign labour force, pressuring the Government to limitate foreign immigration. In

1993, the employment situation became critical (the unemployment rate reached 13% of the working population). Therefore, the Government decided to take all necessary measures to implement the new policy of "zero immigration" and to stop illegal immigration completely. Nevertheless, as Third World countries became more poor, citizens of those countries risked their lives to illegally penetrate European countries, and France in particular.

As a result of increasing unemployment, the cost of labour also increased. (The amount of unemployment indemnities distributed to ever-growing numbers of unemployed people is paid by the working population in the form of social security charges.) In spite of severe legal penalties and sanctions, some French employers engaged illegal employees, paying salaries which were inferior to the legal minimum wage.

One of the most important aims of the French Government now is to encourage the integration of legal immigrants (composed of several ethnic minorities primarily from North Africa) into French society. These immigrants make up the majority of the unemployed population. However, unemployment and poverty is leading to increased delinquency, making successful integration more difficult.

2. Employment and inter-company transfers

(a) General employment conditions

In order to enter French territory all foreigners must have certain documents, which are listed in the Ordonnance of 2 November 1945, Article 5. These documents are as follows:

- documents and visas as required by various international Treaties;
- documents regarding the purpose, conditions of stay and financial resources of the applicant (*e.g.* for a business trip a foreigner must produce information regarding his or her activity, his or her position in the company, if any, as well as information regarding companies located on French territory);
- documents regarding the practice of a professional activity (residence and work permits).

Article L 341–2 of the Labour Code provides that any foreigner who wishes to settle in France, in order to work as an employee, must produce a working contract or an authorisation to work. Temporary working contracts cannot be assimilated to regular working contracts, and therefore cannot give access to a work permit. The foreigner must also provide a medical certificate, established in his or her country of origin.

With the exception of a passport, foreigners coming to join their spouses are not required to produce any of the documents listed above.

The granting of a residence and work permit is supervised by "L'Office des Migrations Internationales" (OMI). The OMI is a government institution which has exclusive control over the procedure regarding entry of foreign employees into France. Failure to respect the procedure imposed by the OMI can lead to penalties. Before any "introduction procedure" (procedure of legal entry) is initiated, every French employment agency is entitled to verify that no un-employed French residents are available to fulfill the task of the foreign candidate.

The introduction procedure requires that the following additional documents must be produced:

- specific information regarding the job;
- a commitment to pay the OMI fee (F 1,000, plus an additional fee for social contribution, which varies from F 4,000 to F 8,000);
- an application regarding lodging accommodation.

The whole introduction procedure takes approximately two months.

(b) Inter-company transfers

Foreign companies which wish to send employees to France either to work in their French subsidiaries or in a related French company, can organise this transfer and obtain the necessary working and residence permits in one of two ways.

(1) Transferred employees may apply through the regular procedure of introduction of employees (as discussed above, and in more detail at **7** below). This procedure consists of obtaining a working contract from the company located in France and submitting a whole file to the OMI, which will then decide whether or not the transfer is authorised. Usually, authorisations are granted if it is established that the future employee has specific skills, and benefits from a very high salary.

(2) Application may be through a bilateral Treaty on expatriation and trans-fer of employees. A number of countries, such as the United States, Canada, Israel and Switzerland, have signed bilateral Treaties on employ-ment transfer with France, which allow easier transfer of employees.

The second procedure is subject to conditions as follows:

- the transfer must be for a short period of time;
- the employee must remain an employee of the foreign company and under its subordination authority;
- the employee must show specific skills and must benefit from a high salary.

When such conditions are met, the employee can be granted a temporary work authorisation for 18 months and, exceptionally, for a longer period. The procedure is similar to the regular procedure (introduction procedure) although it does not refer to the same laws and regulations. It takes approximately two months to obtain a temporary authorisation. One of the most important legal consequences of this status is the fact that since the employee remains an employee of the company of his or her country of origin, he or she remains subject to the law of that country. In some countries, such as the United States (whose laws are particularly in favour of the employee) it is important for a US company to keep its employees under US law. European law in general, and French law in particular, is also favourable to the employee. In case of a dispute, for example regarding termination of a contract, the employee is often entitled to important indemnities if the procedure for terminating the contract, as required by French law, is not respected.

Foreign employees in France maintain rights to social security in their countries of origin, as a result of bilateral social security Treaties signed with Algeria, Austria, Benin, Canada, Congo, the Ivory Coast, the United States, Gabon, Israel, Jersey, Madagascar, Mali, Morocco, Niger, Norway, Quebec, Romania, Switzerland, the Czech Republic, Slovakia, Togo, Tunisia and Turkey.

3. Business

(a) Independent business visitors

Visitors who intend to do business in France without settling in the country can receive assistance from French consulate offices all over the world. Instructions are given readily to grant business visas, giving a right to enter France for short visits over a long period of time. In order to obtain the visa, business people are required to provide documents proving their professional activity, and documents relating to their contracts in France, such as professional correspondence and invitations.

Business visitors who intend to become legal officers of French entities, such as directors of companies incorporated in France or directors of French agencies, or of a branch of a foreign company, are likely to be granted a commercial card.

(b) Commercial cards

The holding of a commercial card is a prerequisite for any foreigner who intends to participate in a commercial or industrial activity in France. If the company is incorporated in France, the commercial card is mandatory for business people who:

- intends to become a partner in a French company which is a "société en nom collectif", or a "société en commandite simple ou commandite par action";

- intends to become a manager (gérant) of a "société à responsabilité limitée", a president of the board of administrators of a "société anonyme" a director of a "société anonyme à directoire";

- intends to act as an administrator empowered to act in the name of an economic interest group with regards to third parties.

Commercial cards are also required for salesmen (commercial agents) travelling around France to sell their products.

French administration enjoys complete discretionary authority to grant or refuse a commercial card to any foreign applicant. Decisions are made according to the amount and quality of information obtained from the applicant regarding his or her personal situation, as well as the activity of the company.

In any event, it must be understood that a commercial card is *not* an immigration entitlement and that it has no effect on the right to enter or remain in French territory. It is merely an authorisation for foreigners to undertake certain commercial activities in France.

(c) Foreign investment

Foreign direct investments in France are subject to a procedure of control (déclaration spéciale) which is less restricted in relation to EU residents than non-EU residents (Decree Nos 95–98 January 1990 and 91–1079 of 18 October 1991). The following operations qualify as direct investments in France:

- the buying, creating or extension of a store, goodwill, agency or personal business;
- any operation which alone or as a group gives or extends the control of foreign residents of French commercial, agricultural or industrial entities.

Therefore, all direct investments performed by non-resident individuals or resident companies under foreign control must be subject to the procedure of a prior declaration (déclaration préalable) to the Ministry of Treasure. These investments are deemed authorised if no opposition has been officially made within the month following the declaration. However, certain operations, whether performed by EU or non-EU residents, are not subject to prior declaration, but only to the filing of a report within 20 days of their completion. These are as follows (the list is not definitive):

- creation of a branch office or new businesses;
- extension of existing business;
- increase of share holding in a French company;
- direct investments of an amount inferior to F 10 million.

The following activities are not subject to the procedure of reporting the operation 20 days after completion:

- creation of branch offices or new companies when the whole operation does not exceed F 5 million;
- an operation, the purpose of which involves the building of a construction to be rented or sold.

4. Pensioners/persons of independent means

In certain situations it is possible to reside in France without obtaining a work permit. This kind of residence entitlement only concerns foreigners who intend to reside in France for a uninterrupted period of time and who intend to live off their own financial resources. These foreigners are considered by French law as "visitors", and their residence permit bears the reference of "visitor". Usually, such foreigners have important financial resources coming from abroad. Their income may, according to the relevant tax Treaty, be declared to French tax authorities and eventually taxed in France.

Some foreigners, as a result of their age of physical condition, need to be financially supported by members of their families who live in France. This category of foreigners can also apply for a visitor residence permit. The procedure is different from that described at **5** below, because although it also concerns relatives of the individual foreigner legally residing in France, it does not entitle the foreigner to work in France; it is merely a residence authorisation.

The French administration has rights to control the level of financial resources at the foreigner's disposal and eventually to refuse to grant authorisation renewal. For instance, the French administration is entitled each year to check the amount of available financial resources in a bank account.

After three years of legal residence, foreign pensioners or foreign residents of independent means, can apply for a permanent residence card for a period of 10 years, which is usually granted without difficulties. In case of refusal, the foreigner can apply for a temporary residence card.

The visitor residence permit is also valid for foreigners working freelance in professions not requiring a work permit, such as translators, interpreters, artists and writers. However, these applicants must also prove that they have adequate financial resources to support themselves and their dependants without working. The minimum acceptable income is the net equivalent of the legal minimum wage (currently F 5,000 per month) for each dependant. Applicants must also show evidence of insurance protection and adequate housing for themselves and their dependants.

5. Spouses and children

French law (Ordonnance of 2 November 1945) provides that foreigners legally residing in France are entitled to apply for admission in France of their families (spouses and children). As a result, all beneficiaries are allowed to work and reside legally in France. However, this law imposes certain conditions which will be discussed below.

Spouses, minors, children of political refugees and stateless persons also enjoy a preferential system. They are lawfully entitled to a 10-year residence card.

The conditions for the admission of spouses and children are as follows:

(1) *regarding the applicant*:
- the applicant must hold a valid residence permit operating for at least one year;
- the applicant must not be a student;
- the applicant must have resided in France for a period of more than two years;
- the applicant must enjoy "normal" living accommodation (43 square metres for four people);
- the applicant must prove that he or she has stable and sufficient financial resources;

(2) *regarding the marital status*:
- concubinage and polygamy are not regarded by French law as fulfilling the required marital status.

The legitimate or illegitimate status of children does not restrict their rights to benefit from the provisions on family reunion.

Foreigners from Morocco and Algeria may benefit from a bilateral Treaty which suppresses some of the legal conditions. Foreigners coming from Burkina Faso, Gabon, Mauritania, Togo, Republic of Central Africa are, under other bilateral Treaties, totally exempted from fulfilling the admission conditions.

Families (spouses and children) of professors or scientific researchers are not subject to any of the conditions provided by the law and can join the applicant as long as he or she is legally residing in France, and can obtain the same residence authorisation as the applicant.

6. Temporary stays

(a) Visitors (tourists)

As a general rule, foreigners who wish to enter French territory merely for a visit must hold a valid passport bearing a tourist visa, delivered by the French consulate of his or her country of origin. The visa is usually granted for a period of at least two months or with a definite date, provided that date is established in accordance with the length of stay.

Before granting a visa, the French administration will check that the applicant has sufficient financial means to sustain himself or herself or provides some guaranty as to his or her possible repatriation.

No visa is necessary for EU visitors or visitors coming from Poland, Hungary, the Czech Republic, Slovakia, the United States, Canada or Israel). These visitors are able to enter the country for a period of up to three months with a valid passport or, in some cases, with only a national identity card.

(b) Students and trainees

Non-EC students must apply for a long-stay visa from a French consulate issued from their country of origin, and must also produce an immatriculation or pre-immatriculation certificate from an accredited French university or other institution of higher education. Applicants are required to show sufficient financial resources to support themselves without working, as well as health insurance and the positive result of a medical examination performed by a consulate-approved doctor. Once in France, the student must apply for a student residence permit which is valid for one year and renewable, but which does not allow him or her to work.

Students covered by intergovernmental Treaties in medicine, dentistry and pharmacy who work in hospitals or clinics as an integral part of their academic education are not required to furnish a work permit.

(c) Au pairs/family helpers

With the exception of EU nationals, it is necessary for all au pair applicants to obtain a long-stay visa and residence card in order to work for a host family. As they are usually also of student status, au pairs must apply for a student residence permit.

The function of an au pair is to help a family with their children. Au pairs must be enrolled in a French language course and sign a contract for three to 12 months with a resident host family.

Au pairs may not work more than five hours per day and must be given at least one full day off per week (which must include at least one Sunday per month). They live and eat with the host families and are entitled to receive a salary which corresponds to 75–90% of the monthly minimum wage.

(d) Temporary workers/seasonal workers

Temporary workers are foreigners who intend to visit or work for less than nine months (sometimes 18 months). These workers must obtain an immigration entitlement, called an "ATP" (autorisation provisoire de travail). Such authorisations are granted to foreigners who cannot apply for a CST (temporary residence card) and although they are renewable, they are restrictive and the name of the employee is specified on the document. Therefore, these people are not free to have another professional activity other than that for which the ATP was granted.

In certain cases, foreigners can work in France under a temporary permit granted to seasonal workers (agriculture and tourism). The hiring of a seasonal worker is subject to the condition that the employment contract cannot exceed six months but can be extended from eight to 12 consecutive months for certain activities, such as agricultural production. Seasonal workers are not entitled to be bound by more than one contract.

7. Permanent residence

Foreigners who intend to reside in France on a permanent basis can be divided between those who wish or need to work, and those who can afford to live in France without working, or have no intention to work.

The legal status of foreign pensioners or foreign individuals with independent means who do not wish to work in France was discussed at **4** above. The purpose of this section is to analyse the different categories of foreigners who wish to settle and also work in France.

A distinction must be made between those who are employees of a company located in France and, therefore, subject to French labour law, and those who have a professional activity while they remain independent (*e.g.* liberal professions such as physicians, architects, lawyers, etc).

(a) Employees

(i) Temporary residence permit

In order to live and work as an employee in France for more than one year, foreigners must obtain a residence permit (carte de séjour) and a work permit (carte de travail). These two permits are issued jointly in the form of a combined work and residence permit according to the introduction procedure.

This procedure can only be implemented by foreigners located outside of France. An employee in France must normally apply for a long-stay visa while he or she is still abroad. An undetermined term work contract is required and the employment must be bona fide, although the work may be full or part time. The minimum contractual salary of regular employees should not be less than four times the legal minimum wage (currently, this must be at least F 25,000 per month). The employee must demonstrate that he or she is in a position to have adequate housing in France. When all the conditions are fulfilled, the file is sent to an administrative authority (Direction Départementale du Travail des Etrangers) which gives an opinion and makes a decision regarding the employment of specific foreign candidates. If the administration renders a positive decision, the candidate, after completion of a medical examination, will be attributed a temporary residence card bearing the employer's reference. This combined work and residence permit is valid for one year and is renewable yearly for a maximum of two years. This permit may be subject to geographical limitations, particularly to lower echelon jobs.

Authorisation to work can be obtained relatively easily by senior executives with a salary of 13 to 14 times the legal minimum wage (including contractual benefits, houses and other related employer benefits) or highly qualified employees with valuable technical expertise. In the case of refusal to grant a work permit, the administrative authority is required to give the applicant a written statement setting out the reasons for refusal (which are commonly an unfavourable employment outlook in the field of activity and the geographic area concerned). Such a decision may be appealed against if the reasons given are unjustified.

Holders of one-year residence permits should begin the reapplication procedure two to three months before the current permit expires. At the time of reapplication, the applicant must be able to prove adequate, stable, financial resources from a job, or other resources.

Foreigners already staying in France and holding a legal visa may wish to regularise their situation by lodging a complete application file at the police administration (Préfecture de Police) located near their place of residence. At present, as a result of increasing unemployment, it has been extremely difficult to obtain a work and residence permit through the regularisation procedure in France.

(ii) Ten-year work and residence permit (permit de travail et carte de resident)
After three years of holding any type of temporary residence permit, foreign individuals are eligible for a 10-year work and residence permit, which may be renewed automatically every 10 years and which authorises the holder to work anywhere in France and in any field of activity not specifically regulated by law.

A combined work and residence permit may be renewed as a 10-year work and residence permit, since both allow the holder to work. French authorities are reluctant to grant 10-year permits to non-working residents, although substantial financial resources can tip the balance in the applicant's favour.

After 10 years of continuous legal residence in France, the authorities must grant the 10-year permit automatically, unless the applicant has committed a crime serious enough to warrant his or her deportation. A 10-year permit expires if the holder leaves France and does not re-enter for three consecutive years, although extensions may be granted under certain conditions.

The 10-year permit is automatically granted to certain categories of residents, such as officially recognised refugees, parents of residents, dependent French children, non-French children of French nationals, spouses of French nationals, and spouses and dependent family members of 10-year permit holders.

Favourable regulations apply to the nationals of the following countries with special relations to France: Andorra, Monaco, Central Africa, Togo, Gabon, Algeria, Tunisia, Cambodia, Laos and Vietnam.

(b) Independent professionals

Certain professions, independent or liberal, are subject to internal organisation rules which can be extremely complex and restrictive. Some professions exclude all non-French nationals (*e.g.* civil servants). Other professions, such as architects, lawyers, auditors, physicians, dentists and veterinarians, are organised under the rules of the profession which may, in cases of bilateral Conventions, assimilate a foreigner as a French national. In such a case, if the independent professional can justify sufficient financial means, he or she may apply for a visitor's permit and work in his or her professional field.

(c) Permit-free employment

Nationals of the European Union and the following countries are not required to obtain work permits: Andorra, Monaco, Central Africa, Gabon and Togo.

Work permits are also unnecessary for non-French nationals in the following professional categories: diplomats, consuls and personnel of embassies and consulates; private servants of diplomats and consuls; personnel of international organisations who are not international administrative employees; ministers of religion; husbands and wives helping to run companies owned by a spouse; representatives of overseas newspapers, news agencies, or broadcasting organisations; personnel of transport companies in transit in France; crew members and navigators or pilots of ships or aircraft whose home port is overseas; private servants accompanying tourists (maximum stay of three months); resident representatives of overseas firms having no branch or subsidiaries in France; and au pairs.

8. Nationality

Citizenship and nationality are governed by the Nationality Code as amended by Law No 93–933 of 22 July 1993 which restricted the conditions upon which French citizenship is granted to foreigners.

This law clearly reflects the recent immigration policy established by the French Government which considered that acquisition of French nationality does not necessarily constitute a passport for integration into French society.

(a) French nationality from birth

(i) Child of a French national
Any child, whether legitimate or illegitimate, of a French native is a French national. If only one parent of the child is French, and the child was not born in France, the child can decline French nationality within six months before turning 18 years of age, unless the foreign parent becomes French while the child is still under 18.

(ii) Child born in France
A child born in France of unknown parents is French. A child born in France of stateless parents is French, as well as a child born in France of foreign parents who does not acquire his or her parent's nationality under the parent's national law. A child born in France is French if at least one of his or her parents was born in France.

An individual born in France of foreign parents becomes French when he or she turns 18, and if on that date the individual's usual residence is in France and has been in France for the previous five years. However, the French administration can always veto this acquisition of French nationality if it considers that the candidate is unworthy and/or has totally failed to integrate into French society.

Whatever the conditions to obtain French nationality, a child is presumed to have been French since his or her birth even if his or her nationality is established long after birth.

Parenthood has an effect on the nationality only if it is established while the child is under 18.

(b) French nationality obtained after birth

A foreigner married to a French citizen can apply for French citizenship if at the time of the application (a declaration) the couple is living together and the French administration is convinced that it is not a phony marriage.

(c) Naturalisation

Naturalisation can be granted to foreigners by decree upon request from the applicant. It is then considered as a privilege and certain conditions are required, as follows:

- there must be long and continuous residence in France; and
- the foreigner's talent and capacity must be of great value to France.

(d) Loss and recovery of nationality

A foreigner can renounce his French nationality or nationality can be lost by a court or governmental decision. Recovery of French nationality is also the decision of the court or government.

9. Refugees and political asylum

(a) Refugees

In accordance with the Geneva Convention, persons seeking official refugee status in France who arrive from a third country where they could have applied for refugee status are generally compelled to return to their country and apply for asylum from there.

When asylum seekers have escaped their countries and have arrived in France they must apply for refugee status without delay upon arrival. The requests of foreigners who have entered France illegally are usually refused. Applicants are then given a temporary residence permit until a final decision has been made by the French Office for the Protection of Refugee and Stateless Persons (OFPRA). The decision must be rendered within at least six months from the application date. If the applicant is denied refugee status by OFPRA, he or she can file an appeal to the Commission de Révision within one month from the refusal notification. Since 1991, such applicants are not permitted to work.

(b) Stateless persons

Stateless persons officially recognised as such by OFPRA are eligible for a temporary work and residence permit. Individuals who hold this type of permit for a period of more than three years will be granted a 10-year work and residence permit automatically. In accordance with the Geneva Convention, France decided upon a restrictive definition of political asylum and does not open its territory to economic refugees. In 1995, very few individuals were granted political refugee status in France and the number of successful applicants decreases every year.

10. Government discretion

The French Government and the administration enjoy full discretionary powers in matters of immigration law in general. This is the result of French policy implemented since 1990 on "zero immigration". However, judicial power has been given some tools to act as a safeguard against overwhelming administration excess of power.

When the administration refuses to grant visa or immigration entitlements, administrative courts, or local commissions can interfere on the foreigner's behalf and amend the negative decision. However, many decisions made by the French administration are not subject to any judicial control.

11. Sanctions

(a) Sanctions against employers

Article L 341–6 of the Labour Code provides that the employment in France of a foreigner who does not hold legal entitlement constitutes a crime.

The Law of 1994 introduced the idea of criminal responsibilities of companies. According to Article L 364–10 of the Labour Code, corporate entities may be declared legally responsible and may be subject to severe sanctions such as:

- penalties, which are five times the amount applicable to individuals;
- prohibition from carrying out the activity which employed employees illegally. In case of infringement of the codes, criminal sanctions are also applicable to the employer as an individual;
- three years' imprisonment and F 30,000 penalty for employing a foreigner who does not hold a valid permit;

- five years' imprisonment and F 200,000 penalty for interfering as an intermediary in the procedure of immigration introduction.

(b) Deportation

Illegal entry of a foreigner to work in France is subject to a number of sanctions against the employer which vary according to the employer's motivations or the consequences of the entry. The most efficient sanction is deportation of the foreigner.

There are several stages of deportation depending on the circumstances.

(i) Procedure of "reconduite à la frontière" (reconduction to the border)

The Law of 10 January 1990, completed by the Decree of 25 January 1990, allows the "préfet" (chief administrator of a department) to send back to the border any foreigner who:

- is unable to establish legal entry into French Territory or is in a situation that has not been legally regularised;
- remained in France for a period of over three months without being entitled to;
- remained in France although he or she had been denied a residence permit renewal;
- has been convicted of forgery or falsification of documents.

However, as provided in Article 25 of the Ordonnance of 2 November 1995, certain foreigners who fulfill certain conditions can escape the above-mentioned sanctions. Such foreigners are:

- those under 18;
- those who can prove that they have been residing on French Territory since they were 10 years old;
- those who can prove that they have been legally residing in France for a period of at least 10 years;
- those who have been married to a French national for over six months;
- those who are the father or mother of a child legally residing in France.

(c) Expulsion

Foreigners whose presence in France is considered a threat to French public order may be expelled. Expulsion is a measure which concerns foreigners who, although they legally reside in France, have been sentenced to jail for more than one year, or have been convicted of specific crimes. Whatever the sentence, the foreigner is then notified to appear before the "Commission d'expulsion" (Ejection Commission) which is composed of magistrates. This Commission decides whether or not the foreigner can be considered a threat to

French public order and, therefore, whether or not he or she should be expelled.

Notwithstanding the above, certain categories of residents (see above) are not subject to expulsion.

Article 27 of the Ordonnance of 1945, and Law No 91–1383 of December 1991, provides that in case of infringement of the expulsion decision, the judge is entitled, at his or her sole discretion, to sentence the foreigner to imprisonment.

A foreigner cannot appeal against the expulsion decision.

In cases of "national security", a foreigner can be expelled without appearing before the Commission.

(d) Extradition

Extradition is governed by a bilateral Convention signed by France and other countries, which was implemented by the Law of 10 March 1927.

Any request by a foreign government for the extradition of a foreigner is submitted to the "Chambre d'Accusation" (the jurisdictional authority responsible for setting the accusation against a criminal), which renders an opinion on the extradition after hearing the foreigner plead his case. The nationality of the foreigner is determined at the time of the crime.

Under the provisions of the Law of 10 March 1927, the Chambre d'Accusation examines the facts to determine whether they constitute \a crime under French law and under the law of the requesting government. It also verifies that the crime is not political and that extradition is not requested for a political reason.

The Chambre d'Accusation operates under different or complementary verifications, based on the applicable bilateral Convention, which take precedence over the Law of 10 March 1927. If the Chambre d'Accusation does not recommend extradition, the extradition will not take place; if it does recommend extradition, the French Government has discretionary power to decide upon the extradition.

12. Tax and social security

(a) Tax considerations

(i) Tax residence in France
Persons who are tax residents are subject to French tax on their world-wide income. Therefore, careful tax planning is advised for well-compensated employees and persons with significant assets. Persons falling into the following categories are considered residents for tax purposes: persons whose permanent home is in France; persons who spend more than 183 days in any calendar year in France; persons who exercise professional activities in France. Similarly, income derived from real estate is generally taxable in France. France has Treaties with many countries which eliminate or reduce double taxation.

When a foreigner is considered to be a tax resident of another country according to the application of the relevant Treaty, he or she is no longer regarded by French authorities as a French tax resident.

Bilateral Treaties usually list a number of exceptions to the principle of taxation in France on a foreigner's world-wide income. For example, most Treaties consider that real estate property should be taxed according to the laws of the country in which it is located.

(ii) Tax residence outside France

Foreigners who are not considered (as described above) as French tax residents can only be taxed on their income from French origin. If they dispose of real estate property in France they will be subject to a taxation package which ensures that their income from French origin is practically an investment. However, if the amount of income is superior to the package taxation base, the foreigner is taxed exclusively on his or her income from French origin.

Income from French origin can include:

- income from real estate property;
- income from bonds or share capital;
- income from professional activities, etc.

(b) Social security

France has developed a very complex and protective social security system which gives employees extensive protection in cases of sickness, unemployment, retirement, pregnancy etc. This protection corresponds to payments which are borne, to a large extent, by the employer. Payments represent a significant part of the total tax burden on earned income. Such payments are compulsory and entitle every employee or French worker to a broad, inexpensive social protection.

All employees, whether foreign or French, must be affiliated and registered at the Social Security Organisation which controls the status of all employees.

Transferred employees may, according to the existence of the Bilateral Social Security Treaty, continue to benefit from the advantages of social security of their country of origin. This is the case for foreign employees sent to France, as well as French employees sent abroad.

13. Domestic considerations

(a) Civil registration

Apart from all the regulations described above at **4**, **6** and **7** above there are no registration requirements for foreign citizens entering France.

(b) Housing

(i) Purchase
It is relatively easy to buy real estate property in France. The procedure is conducted by the notary who has exclusive competence in real estate matters. Both parties must sign a promising sale agreement which allows the buyer to obtain a purchase loan and check on the conditions of the property (*e.g.* mortgage etc). This preliminary contract is usually concluded for a period of one month, at the expiration of which the purchase deed can be signed and results in transfer of ownership.

The deed must be registered at the Land Registry Office and various taxes (7% of the purchase price) must be paid at the same time in order that the transfer of ownership is legal.

(ii) Signature of lease
Lease agreements are not required by law, but in cases of dispute it is always advisable to have a lease agreement in order to prove the terms of the lease. Regular leases are signed for a period of a minimum of three years, renewable for additional periods of three years. However, the tenant is always entitled to terminate the lease by giving six months' notice. The landlord usually requires advance payment of two months' rent as a guarantee.

(iii) Residence tax (tax d'habitation)
All residents, whether real estate owners or tenants, must pay residence tax once a year. Residence tax is calculated according to the value of the neighbourhood and the size of its population.

(iv) Water, electricity, gas and telephone services
The supply of water, electricity, gas and telephone services is the responsibility of governmental companies which have complete monopoly.

(c) Employment

French labour law is strictly regulated and is protective of the employee. Unions have succeeded in imposing working conditions upon the employer which are often more favourable than the law itself. These conditions concern, inter alia, termination contracts, indemnities and the number of vacation days.

In order to preserve employees' rights, all disputes between employees and employers remain under the exclusive jurisdiction of the Labour Court (Tribunal des Prud'hommes), which is composed of employees and employers.

(d) Health

France has developed a very efficient health system accessible to every French resident. The principle is to provide the same quality of health services to every resident notwithstanding his or her financial resources.

(e) Schooling

Schooling is compulsory from the age of 6 to 16. The French education system is free and secular, from grammar school to university level.

Lemann Isal Serfaty & Associés, 67 Boulevard Lannes, 75116 Paris.
tel.: (33) 145046161. telefax: (33) 145048020

Contents of Chapter 8

GERMANY

Chapter 8

GERMANY

Franz Tepper

1. Country characteristics and general principles*

(a) Country characteristics

The Federal Republic of Germany occupies an area of 356,900 square kilometres in Central Europe. The territory comprises in the north the North and Baltic Seas and in the south the Alps. The climate is moderate with a frequent change of weather. The average temperatures range from 1°C in winter to 17°C in summer. The population in 1994 was 81 million, with a rising trend. The capital city is Berlin with a population of 3.5 million. The official language is German which is also spoken in Austria and Switzerland. English is widely spoken, particularly within the business community.

Germany is a member of the European Union and of NATO.

In 1994 the inflation rate was 2.8% and the unemployment rate for the first half year in 1994 was 17.8% in the former East Germany (new Laender) and 9.7% in the former West Germany.

The system of government is a parliamentarian democracy with a President as the head and representative of the Republic. The Government is led by a Chancellor. Germany is a federation of 18 federal states (Bundesländer).

(b) General principles

Except in certain specified circumstances, individuals seeking entry into Germany must obtain a residence permit, and if they seek to work while in Germany, they must obtain a work permit.

* The author wishes to acknowledge the assistance of Peter D. Guattery of Whiteford, Taylor & Preston, Baltimore, Maryland, United States, and Olaf Posten, Bielefeld, Germany, in the preparation of this chapter.

German immigration law is covered by several statutes, Directives and regulations.

The most important statute is the Foreigners Act or Ausländergesetz of 9 July 1990 with its Directive (Verordnung zur Durchführung des Ausländergesetzes) of 18 December 1990.

EC nationals, however, are treated separately by the EC Residency Act (Aufenthaltsgesetz/EWG) of 31 January 1980, as amended in 1981 and 1990. In general, EC nationals have the right to travel, work and reside freely in Germany. More in-depth information on this topic is provided in Chapter 2 on European law.

Work permits are regulated by section 19 of the Law to Promote Employment (Arbeitsförderungsgesetz) of 25 June 1969 as amended in 1991 and the Work Permit Directive (Arbeitserlaubnisverordnung) of 12 September 1980, as amended in 1990.

Asylum is covered separately by the Act on the Rules of Procedure for Asylum (Asylverfahrensgesetz) of 9 April 1991.

All persons visiting or wishing to do business in Germany must check whether he or she is required to apply for a residence permit (Aufenthaltsgenehmigung) and a work permit (Arbeitserlaubnis). Additional issues of asylum and taxes and social security also arise.

2. Employment and inter-company transfers

(a) Employment

According to section 19 of the Law to Promote Employment (above) every foreign national who wishes to work in Germany needs a work permit. The permit will be granted depending upon the situation of the labour market and the particular circumstances of each individual case. In general and due to its relatively high unemployment rate it is quite difficult for a foreign national to obtain a work permit in Germany.

The Work Permit Directive (above) was enacted in order to advise the competent authorities on how to apply the vague language of section 19.

It should be noted that a residence permit must be applied for before the application for a work permit can be made. According to section 5 of the Work Permit Directive, a work permit will only be granted to foreign nationals who legally reside in Germany. Thus, a work permit will be issued only if a residence permit has previously been granted. Furthermore, the work permit will automatically become null and void if the residence permit should become invalid (s 81, No. 1 of the Work Permit Directive).

(i) Exceptions

A work permit is not required if a person is self-employed.

A work permit is only necessary if the employment is for consideration in the form of wages or at least typically is expected to be for payment. Therefore, a foreigner is permitted to perform voluntary work without a work permit.

A work permit is necessary notwithstanding the nature of employment, its duration or otherwise, provided prior permission or qualification is obtained to perform certain services (*e.g.* for physicians).

The following list of examples details the most relevant cases where a work permit is either necessary or unnecessary.

(ii) Work permit required

A work permit is required in the following cases:

- for household work and childcare if performed for payment and if the salary is not paid in compliance with an obligation to provide maintenance;
- for vocational industrial or other similar training;
- for nursing staff, including trainees;
- for au pair employment;
- for models if not self-employed;
- for certain visiting physicians if a permit according to a German statute regulating medical practice is required;
- for fraternal workers.

(iii) Work permit not required

According to section 9 of the Work Permit Directive a work permit is not required in the following cases:

- individuals referred to in section 5 II of the Works Constitution Act (Betriebsverfassungsgesetz), *i.e.* individuals not regarded as employees, and executives who have been granted general power of attorney (General-vollmacht) or full power of attorney (Prokura);
- certain employees engaged in the international carriage of goods and passengers and, with certain exceptions, the staff of vessels and aircrafts;
- foreign nationals who remain domiciled in a foreign country and who are sent by their employer to Germany in order to:
  - carry out erection or maintenance work or repairs for plants or machines,
  - inspect plants, machines or other goods for acceptance or to provide instruction on the use of said machines or goods,
  - complete company training in the course of export, delivery, and licensing agreements;
- foreign nationals who come for a speech or other presentation of particular scientific or artistic value or for sports events, for a period not exceeding three months;
- foreign speakers who offer only daily presentations on an irregular and non-permanent basis;

- professors and certain other members of the scientific staff and university assistants if certain further requirements are met;

- school children and students at universities for a temporary employment of not more than two months per year and school children and students for vacation jobs;

- individuals working in consular or diplomatic missions or with international organisations;

- journalists, correspondents and reporters if accredited by the Press and Information Office of the Federal Government;

- professional sportspersons;

- individuals falling under the NATO Status of Forces Agreement (NATO-Truppenstatut);

- individuals employed by a German employer as commercial employees in a foreign country, who in the course of their employment work in Germany for a period not exceeding three months;

- individuals who have been granted a residence authority (s 27 of the Foreigners Act).

(iv) Other cases
Although section 9 of the Work Permit Directive sets out the exemptions in detail, there are some relevant borderline cases:

- a work permit is not required for the practical education of pharmacy and medicine students if necessary for their studies in Germany;

- a work permit is not required for foreign nationals receiving practical training in judicial or other legal work in Germany after having passed the first German state examination (Rechtsreferendare);

- a work permit is not required for foreign physicians if not practising in Germany, particularly physicians whose stay is brief (days or weeks) for a congress or for further education;

- concert soloists are not required to apply for a work permit. Other musicians are exempt from applying for a work permit only if they play at purely private events or solely for their private entertainment;

- a work permit is not required for radio presentations if the foreign national is economically and socially independent from the radio station. A freelance worker under certain circumstances, however, may be an "employee" for work permit purposes.

(v) Types of work permit
There are two types of work permits: general and special. The special work permit is usually applied for only after a general work permit has been issued.

General work permit

The general work permit will be granted where the current and future needs of the employment market permit. Due consideration must be given to the circumstances of the individual case (s 19 I 2 of the Law on the Promotion of Employment; s 1 I of the Work Permit Directive).

Although the "circumstances of the individual case" must be considered, a work permit will generally be denied in industrial centres and in unfavourable economic situations.

Where the application is made to renew a work permit, the requirements of *section* 19 I 2 of the Law on the Promotion of Employment must also be fulfilled. In general, a foreign national who has already received a work permit will be granted a renewal if his or her employer can establish that he or she wants to further employ this employee in Germany for business reasons in accordance with section 19 I 2 of the Law on the Promotion of Employment.

Typically, a general work permit is valid only for employment within the district of the local employment office (s 3 I of the Work Permit Directive).

The general work permit will be granted for the time of the employment only and its maximum duration will be limited to three years (s 4 I of the Work Permit Directive).

Special work permit

A special work permit will be granted in accordance with section 19 VI of the Law on the Promotion of Employment and section 2 of the Work Permit Directive. A special work permit is normally sought after a longer period of integration of a foreign national.

In general, a special work permit is valid for employment within Germany without any geographical restriction (s 3 II of the Work Permit Directive). In certain exceptional cases, however, a geographical restriction may be imposed.

A special work permit is typically granted without any time-limit (s 19 VI of the Law on the Promotion of Employment; however, *cf* for time-limits s 4 of the Work Permit Directive).

The prerequisites for a special work permit are independent of the present state and future development of the employment market and, in particular, a special work permit will be granted in the following cases.

Section 19 VI of the Law on the Promotion of Employment

A special work permit will be granted to a foreign employee if within the eight years preceding the validity of the special work permit he or she lawfully worked for a total period of five years in Germany. "Lawfully" in this context denotes that the said employee had a valid general work permit during this time period.

In calculating the five-year time period, the following periods of work will not be considered:

- work performed by the employee in Germany in order to fulfill an agreement for work and services concluded between his or her foreign employer and a German enterprise;

- work performed during the time period the employee was, due to the Work Permit Directive or due to an international Treaty, exempt from applying for a work permit;

- work performed by the employee prior to leaving Germany and giving up his ordinary residence (gewöhnlicher Aufenthalt) in Germany;

- work which prepares the employee for an occupation abroad;

- work for which no contribution to the Federal Employment Office is required according to section 169a of the Law on the Promotion of Employment (*i.e.* short-term employment with a weekly working time of less than 18 hours – s 102 of the Law on the Promotion of Employment).

Section 2 of the Work Permit Directive
A special work permit will be granted:

- if a foreign national lives together with a German member of his or her family and has been granted a residence leave according to section 23 I of the Foreigners Act;

- if a foreign national has been recognised as having a right to asylum;

- if a foreign national has a valid passport for refugees issued by a German authority;

- to certain refugees according to a special Act on humanitarian support of 22 July 1980 as amended in 1990;

- to a foreign national who has been "taken over" according to section 33 of the Foreigners Act and who has been granted a residence authority;

- to a foreign national who has been in Germany for six years and who has been granted a residence leave or residence authority (ss 15, 17 or 30 of the Foreigners Act);

- to a foreign national who has been granted a residence leave or residence authority (ss 15, 17 or 30 of the Foreigners Act) if he or she came to Germany under the age of 18 and graduated here from an accredited secondary school or received an education in an officially accredited or comparably regulated vocational training program, participated in a special practical training program or concluded a contract of apprenticeship in an officially accredited apprenticeship trade;

- to a foreign national who has been granted a residence leave according to section 16 I or II of the Foreigners Act;

- if, under the individual circumstances, a denial of the work permit would be an undue hardship to the foreign national.

In so far as the foreign national is required to stay in Germany for a certain period of time, a temporary absence of up to six months will not interrupt the time periods required for a work permit.

(vi) Time

Application for a work permit must be made prior to the commencement of employment or before expiration of an existing work permit.

Under section 5 of the Work Permit Directive, an application for a work permit is without success and, therefore, an application should not be filed, before the applicant has been granted a residence permit.

(vii) Competent authorities

Under section 11 of the Work Permit Directive, the foreign national must file a written application with the local employment office (Arbeitsamt). The employment office having jurisdiction over the application is the office at the place of employment of the applicant. The place of employment is the place of business of the factory or establishment. If the place where the employee works changes constantly, the place of employment is at the place of business where payroll accounting is performed.

A sample application form for a work permit is set out in Annex IV at the end of this chapter.

(b) Inter-company transfers

All employees need to obtain a work permit as described above. No special rules apply to inter-company transfers. However, as a general rule work permits for senior management positions or positions requiring very particular skills not available on the German employment market are usually obtained without any major problem.

3. Business

Persons who do not intend to work in Germany, or self-employed people, do not need a work permit. However, they still need a residence permit.

German immigration law does not give businesses with a particularly high investment the right to obtain a residence and work permit. However, it may be easier to convince the public authorities in Germany to grant a residence permit (and a work permit if necessary) to such persons if the applicant is in a position to prove that he or she will not be dependent upon welfare etc. An additional and usually strong argument is the fact that the potential investor will employ German nationals, since Germany presently has a particularly high unemployment rate.

4. Retired persons of independent means/investors

German immigration law does not deal with retired persons of independent means or investors separately. Such persons must comply with the general standards required for any individual who wishes to stay and/or work in Germany. Although the "independent means" or the sum to be invested may be used as an additional and perhaps convincing argument to obtain a residence and work permit, this is not a problem frequently dealt with in practice since Germany, due to its high taxes and social security payments, is typically not a country which people with independent means tend to choose as their domicile.

5. Spouses, children and relatives

Spouses, children and other relatives of foreign nationals are entitled to receive a residence permit (ss 17–22 of the Foreigners Act) as well as foreign spouses, children and parents of a German national domiciled in Germany (s 23 of the Foreigners Act). The competent authorities have no discretion in deciding whether or not to grant the permit (s 6 I of the Foreigners Act).

In all these cases the foreign national needs to prove, however, that:

- a residence permit (Aufenthaltserlaubnis or Aufenthaltsberechtigung, *cf* below at pp. 134–135) has been obtained;
- sufficient living space is available; and
- he or she can secure the support of his or her spouse, children or relative from his or her own employment, from his or her own assets or from other means owned by the foreign national.

After the marriage is dissolved (*e.g.* on divorce or death) the foreign spouse has a right to stay independent of her former husband' right (s 19 of the Foreigners Act), provided that:

- marital cohabitation in Germany legally existed for a minimum of four years; or
- marital cohabitation in Germany legally existed for a minimum of three years and in order to prevent particular hardship it is necessary to enable the further stay of the spouse; or
- the foreign national died during the marital cohabitation in Germany.

A common requirement for the spouse's right to stay is that the foreign national's residence permit (*cf* below) had not expired, unless it was not the foreign national's fault that it had expired.

6. Permanent and temporary stays

In general, German immigration law requires that each foreign national seeking entry into Germany must apply for a residence permit. There are, however, certain practical and important exceptions to this general requirement.

(a) Exceptions

Three general categories of foreign nationals are exempt from the requirement of possessing a residence permit.

(i) Tourists

Tourists, as defined in section 1 of the Foreigners Act Directive, are nationals of the countries listed in Annex I (at the end of this chapter) to that Act, and are exempt from the requirement of a residency permit provided that:

- their stay in Germany does not exceed three months; and
- they have a passport or other identification document that according to bilateral or multilateral agreements allow visa-free entry; and
- they are not working.

(ii) EC nationals

EC nationals looking for work or short-term employment and their family members if the stay is limited to three months (s 8 of the EC Residency Act) are exempt from the requirement of possessing a residence permit. Notification of the appropriate German authorities is required if the national's prospective stay exceeds one month (s 9 of the EC Residency Act), *i.e.* one month after entry, not one month beyond the three months of section 8 of the EC Residency Act.

(iii) Others (ss 2–8 of the Foreigners Act Directive)

Sections 2–8 of the Foreigners Act Directive also provide for the following miscellaneous exceptions:

- children under 16 of EC or EFTA countries, or from (the former territory of) Yugoslavia, Morocco, Turkey or Tunisia if they meet certain other requirements;
- members of foreign consulates or embassies;
- nationals with special passports, such as EC Parliamentarians;
- nationals of countries listed in Annex II (at the end of this chapter) of the Foreigners Act Directive provided that they hold passports of the kind mentioned in Annex II;
- as may be provided for in bilateral or multilateral agreements;
- nationals of certain neighbour territories and in cases of emergency;
- flight personnel and passengers if they meet certain requirements; special provisions apply for passengers from countries listed in Annex III (at the end of this chapter) of the Foreigners Act Directive;
- crew and passengers on ships and pilots if they meet certain requirements.

(b) Residence permit

If an individual does not meet any of the above exceptions, he or she must apply for a residence permit.

(i) Right of residence

Certain classes of individuals are entitled to receive a residence permit and the competent authorities have no discretion in deciding whether or not to grant the permit (s 6 I of the Foreigners Act):

- EC and EFTA nationals according to the EC Residency Act;
- individuals recognised as having a right of asylum;
- foreign nationals over the age of 15 but under the age of 21, provided they grew up in Germany and meet certain minimum residency and financial support requirements;
- the spouse, children and other relatives of foreign nationals if the foreign national living in Germany meets certain requirements (ss 17–22 of the Foreigners Act, *cf* above);
- foreign spouses, children and parents of a German national domiciled in Germany (s 23 of the Foreigners Act, *cf* above);
- foreign nationals who have lived and worked in Germany for an extended period of time (*e.g.* eight years) including their spouses and children if certain other requirements are met (ss 24–27 of the Foreigners Act).

(ii) Discretionary permits

In all other cases the foreign national has no entitlement to a residence permit and hence largely depends upon the discretion of the German authorities (see **9** below).

(iii) Types of residence permits

There are six different types of residence permits (s 5 of the Foreigners Act; s 1 IV of the EC Residency Act; s 20 of the Act on the Rules of Procedure for Asylum). The names of the different residence permits are basically descriptive terms, as is the translation.

Residence leave (Aufenthaltserlaubnis)

When the foreign national's stay is permitted without any restriction as to its purpose, the residence permit will be granted as a residence leave (s 15 of the Foreigners Act). In general, however, a residence leave will only be granted for a limited period of time.

A residence leave should be applied for if foreign nationals intend to work in Germany for an extended period of time or if they want to apply for a residence permit for their family members.

The Work Residency Directive (Arbeitsaufenthalteverordnung) of 18 December 1990 permits a residence leave to be granted in the following circumstances:

Residence leave with time-limit

- For the duration of the employment of domestic servants of a diplomatic or consular representative.

- For not more than five years – school and university language teachers meeting specified requirements.
- For not more than three years – highly qualified cooks.

Residence leave for duration of specified employment for:
- Highly qualified scientists for employment in research and teaching where such employment is in the public interest.
- Highly qualified specialists with a university or other comparable degree where such employment is in the public interest.
- Executives and specialists employed with a business located in Germany, having its principal place of business in the home country of the executives or specialists (note: an important factor in determining whether an applicant is "specialist" is whether he or she has special knowledge or information which is peculiar to the business he or she is employed by).
- Executives in a German-foreign joint venture established in conformity with the terms of a bilateral Treaty.
- Skilled individuals engaged in social work for foreign nationals and their families provided the individuals are sufficiently proficient in the German language.
- Pastors meeting certain specified requirements.
- Members of religious orders meeting certain specified requirements.
- Nurses meeting certain minimum qualifications. Nurses from European countries enjoy preferential status.
- Artists, including their support personnel.
- Professional sportspersons and trainers employed by German clubs and who meet certain eligibility requirements.

Section 24 of the Foreigners Act permits residence leave to be extended without time-limit
- If the applicant has had a residence leave for the past five years (No 1).
- If the applicant is an employee and has a special work permit (*cf* above).
- If the applicant has all other required permits for permanently conducting his or her occupation (No 3).
- If the applicant has a basic ability to communicate in German (No 4).
- If the applicant has sufficient housing available for himself or herself and any dependants if living together (No 5).
- If the applicant gave no reason for expulsion.

Residence entitlement (Aufenthaltsberechtigung)
A residence permit is granted as a residence entitlement (s 27 of the Foreigners Act) only if the foreign national, after a period of time (usually eight years) has

adapted to German society and has adequate maintenance and housing available. Residence entitlement is not limited in time or by geographic area.

Residence approval (Aufenthaltsbewilligung)

A residence permit will be granted as a residence approval if the stay is for a definite and temporary purpose (s 28 I of the Foreigners Act). A residence approval may be granted for only two years, and may only be extended in certain defined circumstances.

The Work Residency Directive permits residence approval in the following circumstances.

Residence approval for educational purposes

- Graduates of German or foreign universities or other trainees to be mainly employed for further training in German universities or other institutions licensed for such training.

Residence approval for educational purposes with a two-year time-limit

- University graduates seeking practical work experience in areas of training.

- Skilled individuals and executives working in German businesses or commercial associations in accordance with the provisions of bilateral or multilateral Treaties or certain other agreements.

Residence approval for educational purposes with an 18 months' time-limit

- Guest workers for professional and language training in accordance with bilateral or multilateral Treaties.

- Foreign nationals temporarily employed by a German business partner with the purpose of being introduced to business practices or work methods.

Residence approval for educational purposes with a one-year time-limit

- Foreign nationals in a temporary training programme in Germany or who are in Germany in order to carry out an export or licensing contract.

- Foreign nationals under the age of 25 engaged in au pair employment.

Residence approval for employees for contracts for work and services

- Employees who are working to fulfill contracts for work and services may be granted a residence approval under certain circumstances.

Residence authority (Aufenthaltsbefugnis)

A residence authority may be granted if the requirements for a residence leave (Aufenthaltserlaubnis) are not met, but the applicant shall have a right to stay due to humanitarian, public international law or political reasons.

Residence allowance (Aufenthaltsgestattung)
Residence allowance is a very restricted residence permit and will by law be effected by an application for asylum (s 20 of the Act on the Rules of Procedure for Asylum (Asylverfahrensgesetz) (see below).

EU Member State residence permit (Aufenthaltserlaubnis-EU)
This particular residence permit will be granted to foreign nationals from EU Member States only. In general, citizens from EU Member States have a right to stay and work in Germany. For further information see Chapter 2 on European law.

(c) Time

In general, an application for a residence permit must be filed with the competent authorities *before* entry into Germany. It is not permissible, for example, to enter Germany as a tourist and then apply for a residence permit (ss 8 I, 71 I 2 of the Foreigners Act).

However, EC and EFTA nationals and US citizens are allowed to apply for a residence permit after entering Germany.

(d) Competent authorities

In general, an application for a residence permit must be filed with an authorised German consulate or embassy in the applicant's home country (s 63 III of the Foreigners Act). If the applicant intends to work or stay more than three months in Germany the consent of the local foreigners office (Ausländerbehörde) of the applicant's intended place of residence is required.

If the application is filed after entry into Germany, it must be filed with the foreigners office having jurisdiction over the applicant's actual place of residence.

7. Nationality

The general statute regulating naturalisation of foreign nationals is the Reich-Citizen and Nationality Act (Reichs- und Staatsangehörigkeitsgesetz) of 22 July 1913, as amended in 1986. Some foreign nationals, however, are privileged if they meet the requirements of sections 85 *et seq* of the Foreigners Act.

(a) Sections 85 *et seq* of the Foreigners Act

(i) Privileged naturalisation of young aliens
A foreign national over the age of 16 but under the age of 23 at the time of application may be naturalised, if he or she:

- renounces or loses his or her nationality (some exceptions may be made with respect to this requirement under s 87 of the Foreigners Act);

- has had a lawful primary residence in Germany for eight years;
- attended school in Germany for six years, four years of which were at a secondary school (allgemeinbildende Schule); and
- has not been convicted of a crime.

(ii) Privileged naturalisation of aliens with long residence

A foreign national who has lawfully resided in Germany for 15 years and has applied for naturalisation by 31 December 1995 will be naturalised in accordance with section 86 of the Foreigners Act, if he or she:

- renounces or loses his or her nationality (some exceptions are made with respect to this requirement under s 87 of the Foreigners Act);
- has not been convicted of a crime; and
- can pay his or her own and his or her dependants' living expenses without utilising state welfare benefits or unemployment relief; if the applicant is not able to meet such living expenses through no fault of his or her own, the authorities might dispense with this requirement.

(b) General requirements for naturalisation

According to section 8 of the Reich-Citizen and Nationality Act a foreign national residing in Germany may, upon application, be naturalised by the State in which he or she is residing if he or she:

- has acquired legal capacity according to the laws of his or her former home country, if he or she would have acquired legal capacity according to German law, or if his or her application is filed according to section 7 II 2 of the Act by his or her legal representative or with the consent of his or her legal representative;
- has conducted a "respectable way of life" (unbescholtenen Lebenswandel);
- maintains his or her own residence; and
- is in a position to maintain himself or herself and his or her dependants at this place of residence.

8. Refugees and political asylum

The German Constitution (Basic Law or Grundgesetz) in article 16 II 2 unequivocally provides that: "Persons persecuted for political reasons enjoy the right of asylum".

Asylum is regulated by the Act on the Rules of Procedure for Asylum (Asylverfahrensgesetz). According to section 20 of this Act, by operation of law the application for asylum permits the applicant a residence allowance (see **6(b)** above). Thus the applicant is allowed to stay in Germany during the time period in which his or her application is pending.

Although the term "political asylum" is not defined by the Act, the German courts have provided guidance for its interpretation. In general, the inquiry will focus on the question of whether the reason for the persecution of the applicant is "political". "Political" has been defined very narrowly and does not include a mere criminal persecution. In addition, economic reasons for residence in Germany will not be taken into account by the competent authorities.

A foreign national has no right of asylum if he or she previously obtained safe leave from political persecution in a different country, or the reason for political persecution has been created after entry into Germany.

Applicants with a right of asylum enjoy the status of refugees according to the Convention of the Status of Refugees of 28 July 1951.

The application for asylum may be filed after entry into Germany. The application may be refused and entry into Germany denied only if it is obviously without merit.

Thus, the law of asylum is under much reconsideration and discussion and a change of the constitution might be expected in the near future. The heavy influx of asylum seekers and the political and social problems related thereto in recent years have provoked a strong consensus for reconsideration of Germany's asylum law.

9. Government discretion

In all cases where the applicant has no entitlement to a residence permit (see above), the competent foreigners office is permitted the exercise of considerable discretion (s 7 I of the Foreigners Act) in the grant or denial of a residence permit. Predicting when a residence permit may be granted in such circumstances is thus extremely difficult. The availability of a residence permit instead depends upon the specific circumstances of each individual case. The Foreigners Act only stipulates when the residence permit is to be refused.

The residence permit, other than in exceptional circumstances, will be refused (s 7 II of the Foreigners Act) if:

- there is no reason for expulsion (Ausweisung) (s 45 of the Foreigners Act);
- the foreign national cannot pay or his or her maintenance;
- German public policy may be impaired or jeopardised if residence is permitted.

The residence permit will always be refused (s 8 of the Foreigners Act), if:

- the foreign national:
  - entered Germany without the required visa,
  - entered Germany with a visa which due to the information provided by the applicant was granted without the necessary consent of the foreigners office,
  - has no required passport, or
  - the identity or nationality is unknown and he or she has no right to return to another country.

10. Remedies and sanctions

(a) Remedies

(i) Residence permit

If the applicant is not satisfied with the decision of the foreigners office or any other competent authority he or she may file a formal objection (Widerspruch) to the particular decision (ss 68 *et seq* of the Rules of Procedure of the Administrative Courts (Verwaltungsgerichtsordnung). The objection will then be considered and ruled on.

If the applicant remains unsatisfied with the agency's decision the applicant may institute legal proceedings before the competent administrative court (Verwaltungsgericht) to overturn the decision.

(ii) Work permit

If not satisfied with the decision of the local employment office, the applicant can make a formal objection against the particular decision (ss 78 *et seq* of the Social Courts Act (Sozialgerichtsgesetz).

If he or she is not satisfied with any subsequent decision, the applicant may then institute legal proceedings before the competent social court (Sozialgericht).

(b) Sanctions

According to section 42 I of the Foreigners Act a foreign national is not or no longer permitted to stay in Germany if he or she has no valid residence permit. The obligation to leave Germany always requires that the stay is or becomes illegal. Therefore, the following individuals cannot be required to leave the country (s 42 of the Foreigners Act):

- foreign nationals who do not fall under the Foreigners Act (s 2 I of the Foreigners Act);
- EU citizens provided they do not need to obtain residence permits according to section 8 of the EU Residence Act (Aufenthaltsgesetz/EU);
- foreigners without nationality (s 12 of the Act on the Legal Status of Foreigners in Germany (Gesetz über die Rechtsstellung heimatloser Ausländer im Bundesgebiet);
- asylum seekers who obtained a residence allowance;
- foreign nationals who have filed their applications for residence permits according to section 69 III of the Foreigners Act.

Foreign nationals can be required to leave Germany by operation of law or due to an act of a competent authority terminating the right to stay.

(i) Obligation to leave by operation of law

According to section 42 II of the Foreigners Act a foreign national is required to leave Germany by operation of law if:

- he or she entered Germany without permission (s 58 I of the Foreigners Act);
- his or her residence permit expired and he or she has not yet applied for an extension or a different residence permit; or
- he or she has not yet applied for a residence permit for the first time and the application period (s 9 VI of the Foreigners Act Directive), which is usually three months, has expired.

(ii) Obligation to leave due to an act of a competent authority

Instead of or in addition to the obligation to leave Germany by operation of law such obligation can be forced upon the foreign national by an act (Verwaltungsakt) of the foreigners office. Such acts can be:

- expulsion (Ausweisung) (ss 45 *et seq* of the Foreigners Act);
- temporal limitation of the residence permit according to section 3 V of the Foreigners Act;
- Denial of grant or of extension of residence permit (*cf* ss 69 III, 96 II of the Foreigners Act);
- subsequent temporal limitation of residence permit according to section 12 II or 24 II of the Foreigners Act);
- revocation (Widerruf) of residence permit according to section 43 of the Foreigners Act;
- withdrawal (Rücknahme) of residence permit according to section 43 of the Act on Administrative Procedure (Verwaltungsverfahrensordnung);
- condition subsequent (auflösende Bedingung) according to section 3 V or 14 I of the Foreigners Act.

(iii) Execution of obligation to leave Germany

In case the foreign national does not comply with his or her obligation to leave Germany voluntarily the German authorities will enforce this obligation. The means available to enforce the obligation to leave are:

- instruction not to enter (Zurückweisung) according to section 60 of the Foreigners Act;
- instruction to leave (Zurückschiebung) according to section 61 of the Foreigners Act;
- deportation (Abschiebung) according to section 49 of the Foreigners Act.

Instruction not to enter

A foreign national who intends to enter Germany illegally will be instructed not to enter. Usually the foreign national will be instructed to go back to the country from where he or she came. A foreign national who applies for asylum may not be instructed not to enter Germany.

Instruction to leave

A foreign national may be instructed to leave Germany according to section 61 of the Foreigners Act, provided that:

- he or she entered Germany illegally according to section 58 I of the Foreigners Act; and
- since the foreign national crossed Germany's border, six months have not passed.

Deportation

Deportation is the most important and widely used means of enforcing the obligation of the foreign national to leave Germany. Particular restrictions concerning deportation apply to asylum seekers.

Before a foreign national can be deported, he or she shall be given a last chance to leave voluntarily. Therefore he or she shall be asked to leave within a certain time frame to be set by the foreigners office.

In order to secure compliance of the foreign national with the deportation he or she can be arrested (Abschiebungshaft; s 57 of the Foreigners Act). However, this requires a ruling of a judge.

The foreign national is liable for the payment of the costs of deportation, which are usually very high (s 82 of the Foreigners Act).

11. Tax and social security

Foreign nationals who come to Germany are required to pay German income tax and contribute to German social security insurance funds. Although a detailed survey of such laws is beyond the scope of this study, some practical and useful guidelines should be taken into consideration, such as tax and social security insurance rates.

(a) Income tax

German law requires that the employer deduct the employee's income tax from the employee's monthly salary.

There is no flat income tax rate. Instead, the income tax rate rises as salaries increase. Although the actual calculation of income tax is complex, a basic formula (s 32a of the Income Tax Act, as amended in 1996) may serve as a rough guide:

Annual income (DM)	*Calculation*
Up to 12,095	no income tax
12,096–55,727	$(86.63 * y + 2590) * y$
55,728–120,041	$(151.91 * z + 3346) * y$
over 120,042	$0.53 \cdot x - 22{,}842$

x is defined as the rounded-down taxable income.

y is defined as a ten-thousandth of the rounded-down taxable income exceeding DM 12,042.

z is defined as a ten-thousandth of the rounded-down taxable income exceeding DM 55,674.

(b) Social security

There are four general types of mandatory social security insurance in Germany: health insurance, care insurance, unemployment insurance, and pension insurance.

Only employees are required to contribute to these social security insurance funds. Self-employed foreign nationals are not required to contribute.

If the employee's monthly salary exceeds DM 8,000 (as of January 1996) he or she is also exempt from the requirement to contribute to unemployment and pension insurances. If the employee's salary exceeds DM 6,000 he or she is exempt from contributing to health insurance.

As of January 1996 social security insurance rates as a percentage of gross income are as follows:

Health insurance (former West Germany)	13.3%
Care insurance (introduced July 1996)	1.7%
Unemployment insurance	6.5%
Pension insurance	19.2%

Health insurance rates vary slightly from these rates depending upon the insurance company. All insurance companies within the social security insurances are publicly controlled and limited in number. Private insurance companies exist only for individuals exempt from the requirement to contribute to the mandatory health insurance.

12. Domestic considerations

(a) Civil registration

Each foreign national arriving in Germany is required to register with the local registration office (Einwohnermeldeamt) without undue delay. The foreign national must register in the area in which he or she resides. If the foreign national has a temporary residence only, he or she must register there and after his or her move to a permanent residence he or she is required to reregister in that area.

Such registration is required before an application for a residence and work permit can be filed.

(b) Housing

Germany is a heavily populated country. In particular, in bigger cities it may prove difficult to find a place to live. The situation is much better in smaller towns and rural areas.

Any foreign national should start looking for accommodation well before his or her entry into Germany. German real estate brokers (Makler) may be contacted. However, such brokers usually charge two months' rent for their services. Customarily the tenant/buyer and not the owner of the house or apartment pays this fee.

Placing an advertisement in a local newspaper is one way to find a home. However, usually the feedback of such advertisements is limited due to the undersupply of reasonable housing facilities. Therefore a foreign national should – well before he leaves his or her home country – search the local newspapers of the place where he or she intends to stay, for advertisements concerning houses and apartments. It may be advisable to call the tourist office (Fremdenverkehrsamt) in major cities or simply the Mayor's office in smaller cities and towns to find out the name and address of the local newspaper.

It is difficult to give an indication of the monthly rents payable for housing in Germany because this varies considerably depending upon where the residence is located. However, the rent in medium-sized cities is in the area of DM 10 per square meter. In bigger cities like Hamburg, Berlin, Frankfurt, Stuttgart or Munich the rates may be as high as DM 20 per square meter.

Basically, no restrictions apply to the purchase of German real property by foreign nationals. Contracts for the purchase of real property must be notarised by a German notary public (Notar), and the transfer of ownership, any encumbrance and other specific information must be registered in the land register (Grundbuch). Any contract for the purchase of real property which is not notarised is null and void. The transfer of ownership is effective only after it has been properly registered in the land register.

The transfer of real property is subject to real estate purchase tax (Grunderwerbssteuer), at a rate of 2% of the purchase price.

Owners of real property in Germany are subject to estate tax (Grundsteuer) each year, which rate varies in each community.

(c) Employment

Labour law in Germany has developed over the years into a very specialised field of practice. German labour law is complex, and law suits must be carried out before special labour courts (Arbeitsgerichte). German employees are solidly protected. Therefore, it is strongly recommended that a foreign national should contact a labour law specialist (and not a general practitioner) concerning problems in this field of law.

Sometimes difficult to understand for foreign employers but typical of German labour law is the protection against unlawful dismissal of an employee.

In general, an employee can be dismissed for cause only. The burden is on the employer to prove that he or she had cause to terminate the employment contract. If the employer had no cause, the termination is null and void and the employment contract continues to be in full force and effect. The employee has a right to work and cannot – unless for cause – be instructed to stay home, even if the employer continues to pay his or her salary.

Over and above the termination for cause, particular notice periods must be complied with. The length of the notice periods varies from two weeks to six months depending upon the term of the employment contract and the overall time the employee has been employed by the employer.

(d) Business entities (GmbH)

There is a wide range of forms of legal entities available in Germany as a vehicle to do business. The most commonly used form is the company with limited liability (Gesellschaft mit begrenzter Haftung, GmbH) and for bigger enterprises, the stock company (Aktiengesellschaft, AG). Both forms provide for limited liability of the shareholders.

The formation of a GmbH is relatively straightforward and inexpensive (approximately DM 2,000 for a standard formation). However, the formal requirements are a little cumbersome to comply with, in particular for a foreign corporation.

The required minimum capital of a GmbH is DM 50,000. The GmbH can be formed with a single shareholder and has no mandatory board of directors. The chief executive officer of the GmbH is the Geschäftsführer.

The statutes of a GmbH must be notarised. The GmbH is legally existent only after its entry into the local commercial register (Handelsregister). All individuals acting on behalf of the GmbH before registration are personally liable.

13. Statutory material and sample forms

Appendix I: Foreigners Act Directive, Annex I

Andorra	Brazil
Argentina	Brunei
Australia	
as well as the Coconut Island, the	
Norfolk Island, Christmas Island	Canada
Austria	Chile
	Colombia
Belgium	Costa Rica
Benin	Cyprus
Bolivia	Czech Republic

Denmark

Ecuador
El Salvador

Finland
France
   including French Guayana, French
   Polynesia, Guadeloupe, Martinique,
   New Caledonia, Réunion, St Pierre
   and Miquelon

Greece
Guatemala

Honduras
Hungary

Iceland
Ireland
Israel
Italy
Ivory Coast

Jamaica
Japan

Kenya
Korea (Republic of Korea)
Kroatia

Luxembourg

Malawi
Malaysia
Malta
Mexico
Monaco

Nepal
Netherlands
   including The Dutch Antilles
New Zealand
   including the Cook Island, Niue,
   Tokelau
Niger
Norway

Panama
Paraguay
Peru
Portugal
   including Macau

San Marino
Singapore
Slovakian Republic
Spain
   including the Spanish territories of
   state in North Africa (with Ceuta,
   Melilla)
Sweden
Switzerland and Lichtenstein

Togo

United Kingdom
   and Northern Ireland as well as the
   Channel Islands and the Isle of Man
United States of America
   including the American Virgin
   islands, American Samoa, Guam,
   Puerto Rica
Uruguay

Venezuela

Appendix II: Foreigners Act Directive, Annex II

A visa is not mandatory for
1. holders of passports from:
   El Salvador
   Ghana
   Korea (Republic of Korea)
   Pakistan
   Phillipines
   Senegal
   Thailand
   Turkey
   Tschad

2. and holders of diplomatic passports from:
   Bulgaria
   India
   Morocco

Appendix III: Foreigners Act Directive, Annex III

Afghanistan
Angola
Bangladesh
Bulgaria
Ethiopia
(The) Gambia
Ghana
Iran

Iraq
Jordan
Lebanon
Nigeria
Romania
Somalia
Sri Lanka
Syria

Brandi Dröge Piltz & Heuer, Rechtsanwälte, Hochstrasse 19, D-33332 Gütersloh.
tel.: (49) 524158886. telefax: (49) 524158881

Sample form for residence permit application*

Antrag auf Erteilung einer Aufenthaltsgenehmigung in Form einer

Application for a residence permit in the form of a / Şeklinde oturma müsaadesi verilmesine ilişkin Dilekçe / Molba za davanje odobrenja za boravak u vidu / Podanie o udzielenie zezwolenia na pobyt w formie / Заявление о получении разрешения на проживание в форме

☐ **Aufenthaltserlaubnis** (§§ 15, 17 ff AuslG)
Residence Permit (§§ 15, 17 Alien law) / **Oturma izni** (Yab. Kan. 15, 17 ve sonrası maddeleri) / **Dozvole za boravak** (čl. 15, 17 ff Zakon o strancima) / **Pozwolenia na pobyt** (§§ 15, 17 i dalsze AuslG) / **Разрешения на проживание** (§§ 15, 17 и т. д. Закона о статусе иностранных граждан)

☐ **Aufenthaltsberechtigung** (§ 27 AuslG)
Residence Entitlement (§ 27 Alien law) / **Oturma hakkı** (Yab. Kan. 27 nci maddesi) / **Prava na boravak** (čl. 27 Zakon o strancima) / **Uprawnienia do pobytu** (§ 27 AuslG) / **Права на проживание** (§§ 27 Закона о статусе иностранных граждан)

☐ **Aufenthaltsbewilligung** (§§ 28, 29 AuslG)
Residence Approval (§§ 28, 29 Alien law) / **Oturma kabulü** (Yab. Kan. 28, 29 ncu maddeleri) / **Pristanka za boravak** (čl. 28, 29 Zakon o strancima) / **Zgody na pobyt** (§§ 28, 29 AuslG) / **Согласия на проживание** (§§ 28, 29 Закона о статусе иностранных граждан)

☐ **Aufenthaltsbefugnis** (§§ 30, 31 AuslG)
Residence Authorization (§§ 30, 31 Alien law) / **Oturma yetkisi** (Yab. Kan. 30, 31 nci maddeleri) / **Ovlašćenja za boravak** (čl. 30, 31 Zakon o strancima) / **Upoważnienia do pobytu** (§§ 30, 31 AuslG) / **Полномочия на проживание** (§§ 30, 31 Закона о статусе иностранных граждан)

☐ **Aufenthaltserlaubnis – EG** (§ 2 Abs. 2 AuslG)
EEC Residence Permit (§ 2 para 2 Alien law) / **AT oturma izni** (Yab. Kan. 2 nci madde 2 nci fıkrası) / **Dozvole za boravak – EZ** (čl. 2 stav 2 Zakon o strancima) / **Pozwolenia na pobyt dla obywateli krajów EWG** (§ 2 ustęp 2 AuslG) (AuslG = "Ustawa o cudzoziemcach") / **Разрешения на проживание – ЕС** (§ 2, абз. 2 Закона о статусе иностранных граждан)

1. Familienname / Surname / Soyadı / Prezime / Nazwisko / Фамилия

   ggf. Geburtsname / for women: maiden name / Kadınlarda: Kızlık soyadı / kod žena i devojačko prezime / u kobiet: nazwisko panieńskie / у женщин: девичья фамилия

2. Vorname(n) / Christian name(s) / Adı (Adları) / Ime(na) / Imię (imiona) / Имя (имена)

3. Tag der Geburt / Date of birth / Doğum tarihi / Datum rodjenja / Data urodzenia / Дата рождения

4. Geburtsort / Place of birth / Doğum yeri / Mesto rodjenja / Miejsce urodzenia / Место рождения

5. Staatsangehörigkeit(en) bei mehreren Staatsangehörigkeiten sind alle anzugeben / Nationality (by multiple nationalities enter all / Tabiiyeti (Tabiiyetleri) (Bir taneden fazla tabiiyeti olanlar hepsini yazacak) / Državljanstvo kod više državljanstava treba navesti sve / Obywatelstwo (w przypadku posiadania więcej niż jednego obywatelstwa podać wszystkie) / Гражданство (при множественном гражданстве указать каждое гражданство в отдельности)

   a) jetzige / Present / Şimdiki / sadašnje / obecne / настоящее гражданство

   b) frühere / Previous / Eski / ranije / wcześniejsze / бывшее гражданство

6. Familienstand / Marital status / Medeni hali / Bračno stanje / Stan cywilny / Семейное положение

   ☐ ledig / single / Bekar / neož./ neud. / kawaler/panna / не женат/не замужем
   ☐ verheiratet / married / Evli / ož./udata / żonaty/mężatka / женат/замужем — seit / since / 'den beri / od / od / с
   ☐ geschieden / divorced / Boşanmış / razv. / rozwodnik/rozwódka / разведен/а — seit / since / 'den beri / od / od / с
   ☐ verwitwet / widowed / Dul / udov. / wdowiec/wdowa / вдов/а — seit / since / 'den beri / od / od / с

7. Ehegatte*) / Spouse*) / Eşi*) / Bračni drug*) / Małżonka/małżonek*) / Супруг/супруга*)

   Name / Name / Soyadı / Prezime / Nazwisko / Фамилия

   ggf. Geburtsname / Maiden name (for women) / Kızlık soyadı (kadınlarda) / Devojačko prezime (kod žena) / Nazwisko panieńskie (u kobiet) / Девичья фамилия (у женщин)

   Vornamen / Christian name(s) / Adı (Adları) / Ime(na) / Imiona / Имя/имена

   Tag der Geburt / Date of birth / Doğum tarihi / Datum rodj. / Data urodzenia / Дата рождения

   Geburtsort / Place of birth / Doğum yeri / Mesto rodj. / Miejsce urodzenia / Место рождения

   Staatsangehörigkeit / Nationality / Tabiiyeti / Državljanstvo / Obywatelstwo / Гражданство

   Wohnort / Domicile / İkamet ettiği yer / Prebivalište / Miejsce zamieszkania / Место жительства

8. Kinder*) Name Children*) Surname Çocukları*) Soyadı Deca*) Prezime Nazwisko dziecka*) Дети*) фамилия	Vorname(n) Christian name(s) Adları Ime(na) imię (imiona) Имя / имена	männl. Masculine Erkek M chłopiec мужск. пол	weibl. Feminine Kız Ž dziewczynka женск. пол	Geburtstag u. -ort Date and place of birth Doğum tarihi / Doğum yeri Datum i mesto rodj. dzień oraz miejsce urodzenia Дата / место рождения	Staatsangehörigk. Nationality Tabiiyeti Državljanstvo obywatelstwo Гражданство	Wohnort Domicile İkamet yeri Prebivalište miejsce zamieszkania Место жительства
		☐	☐			
		☐	☐			
		☐	☐			

*) Angaben sind auch erforderlich, wenn diese Personen im Ausland verbleiben. / Details necessary even if these persons are living abroad. / Bu şahıslar yurtdışında yaşasa bile bu soruların cevaplandırılması gerekir. / Podaci su potrebni i onda, kada te osobe ostanu u inostranstvu. / Dane te należy podać także wówczas gdy osoby te przebywają za granicą. / Указать эти данные также в том случае, если эти лица проживают за границей.

Nachdruck, Nachahmung, Kopieren und elektronische Speicherung verboten!

134/8000 — Deutscher Gemeindeverlag — (91090)
115.11/00 - 0 — Formularverlag W. Kohlhammer
in den Sprachen deutsch, englisch, türkisch, serbokroatisch, polnisch, russisch

* Reprinted with permission of Deutscher Gemeindeverlag, Köln (Form No 134/8000). No uniform forms are used in Germany.

Sample form for work permit application[*]

Antrag auf Arbeitserlaubnis	Application for a work permit Demande de permis de travail Zahtev za izdavanje odobrenja za rad Çalişma müsaadesi dilekçesi	Bitte Hinweise auf der Rückseite beachten.

Angaben zum ausländischen Arbeitnehmer:

1 Name	5 Versicherungsnummer
Vorname	6 ggf. Geburtsname
2 bei Firma	7 Wohnung in der Bundesrepublik Deutschland, soweit nicht nebenstehend angegeben
3 Straße, Hausnummer	
4 Postleitzahl, Ort	

Please note remarks on the reverse.

Faites attention aux indications mentionnées au verso.

8 Geburtsdatum	9 Geschlecht männl. weibl.	10 Staatsangehörigkeit
11 anerkannter ausl. Flüchtling/Asylberechtigter ja ☐ nein ☐	12 verheiratet ja ☐ nein ☐	13 Staatsangehörigkeit des Ehegatten
14 Name und Anschrift des letzten Arbeitgebers		15 letzte Arbeitserlaubnis erteilt vom Arbeitsamt
16 Aufenthaltsgenehmigung erteilt ☐ beantragt ☐	17 durch/bei Ausländerbehörde	18 Aufenthaltsgenehmigung/Duldung bis

Uzmite u obzir napomene na poledjini.

Arbeitserlaubnis wird beantragt

19 von bis	20 als (Art der auszuübenden Beschäftigung)
21 bei (Name und Anschrift des Beschäftigungsbetriebes)	22 Betriebsnummer des Beschäftigungsbetriebes
23 Beschäftigungsort/-gebiet	24 Fortsetzung der bisherigen Beschäftigung ja ☐ nein ☐
26 Es wird bestätigt, daß der Arbeitnehmer entsprechend dem Antrag beschäftigt werden soll Unterschrift des Arbeitgebers	25 Mehrfachbeschäftigter ja ☐ nein ☐
	27 Unterschrift des Arbeitnehmers
	28 Datum

Lütfen arka sahifedeki hususlara dikkat ediniz.

(Wird vom Arbeitsamt ausgefüllt)

⚠ Bundesanstalt für Arbeit	**Arbeitserlaubnis**

Dem obengenannten Arbeitnehmer wird hiermit eine Arbeitserlaubnis nach § 19 des Arbeitsförderungsgesetzes (AFG) vom 25.6.1969 (BGBl. I S. 582) in der jeweils geltenden Fassung in Verbindung mit der Arbeitserlaubnisverordnung (AEVO) erteilt.

Diese Arbeits- erlaubnis gilt für	eine berufliche Tätigkeit nach Ziff. 20 nur bei dem unter Ziff. 21 genannten Betrieb	(§ 1 Abs. 1 Nr. 1 AEVO)
	eine berufliche Tätigkeit als _____	(§ 1 Abs. 1 Nr. 2 AEVO)
	jede berufliche Tätigkeit bei dem unter Ziff. 21 genannten Betrieb	(§ 1 Abs. 1 Nr. 2 AEVO)
	eine berufliche Tätigkeit jeder Art	(§ 19 Abs. 6 AFG/§ 2 AEVO)
	den Zeitraum von bis	
	Geltungsbereich/Beschäftigungsort	

Diese Arbeitserlaubnis wird unter dem Vorbehalt des Widerrufs aus Gründen des Arbeitsmarktes gemäß § 7 Abs. 2 AEVO erteilt. Der Widerrufsvorbehalt gilt nicht, sofern diese Arbeitserlaubnis für länger als 3 Jahre oder unbefristet erteilt ist. Die Arbeitserlaubnis gemäß § 1 Abs. 1 Nr. 1 und § 1 Abs. 1 Nr. 2 AEVO gilt nicht für eine Beschäftigung als Leiharbeitnehmer.

Arbeitsamt	im Auftrag Datum	Dienststempel

BA – Ausl. Nr. 1 1.94 (Blatt 1)   Ausfertigung für den Arbeitnehmer   ✪ Bundesdruckerei

---

[*] Reprinted with permission of Bundesanstalt für Arbeit, Nürnberg.

Contents of Chapter 9

GREECE

Chapter 9

GREECE

Laoura Limberopoulou

1. Country characteristics and general principles

Greece is located in the southern area of the Balkan Peninsula in the Eastern Mediterranean. It has an area of 132,000 square kilometres (51,000 square miles) and consists of the mainland and the islands which occupy approximately 20% of its total area. Athens is the capital of the country. In 1994 Greece had a population of 10.6 million, with an average density of 74 inhabitants per square kilometre. About 43% of the total population lives in the six major cities of Athens, Thessaloniki, Patras, Heraklion, Volos and Larissa, while 31% of the total population inhabits the Athens' area.

The country has a temperate Mediterranean climate, with mild winters and warm summers. The lowest temperatures occur between December and February and the highest in July and August.

The country's language is Greek. Foreign languages, especially English, French and German, are taught in schools and are widely spoken and understood in cities and tourist resort areas.

Greece has been a member of the European Union since 1981. Greece is also a member of NATO, the Council of Europe, the United Nations and the Western European Union, and subscribes to the Charter of Human Rights.

The country's currency is the drachma (Dr). The Greek economy is characterised by structural imbalances and large deficits of the public sector. However, the negative inclinations of the past few years have been reversed. The targets of the economic policy are the diminution of the public deficit and of inflation, in order to achieve an increase in investments and the development of the country's economy.

Visitors from most countries must obtain an entry visa from a Greek embassy or consulate. No visa is required for citizens of the Member States of the European Union, nor is a visa required for citizens of countries which have signed reciprocity Treaties with Greece.

To work in Greece foreign nationals, other than EU nationals, must have work and residence permits. EU nationals can work freely in Greece. Nevertheless, they must register with the authorities and obtain residence permits, which are given automatically once certain formalities are met.

2. Employment and inter-company transfers

(a) Employment

Any national of a non-EU country entering Greece to work as an employee must have obtained prior approval for the necessary work permit. For this purpose, the employer files an application together with all the required supporting documents with the competent Greek authorities before the foreigner enters Greece.

Such prior approval is granted by the Ministry of Foreign Affairs, authorising the consulate of the area where the foreigner resides to provide him or her with a consulate employment visa.

The maximum number of work permits to be granted to foreigners (by nationality, profession and term for various areas of the country) is stipulated on a yearly basis by Ministerial Decision.

Exceptionally no prior work permit approval is required for:

- foreign employees of commercial, industrial or shipping companies which have no branch or subsidiary in Greece, but are established in Greece under a special status only for the purpose of managing their business transactions out of Greece (Law 89/1967 and 378/1988 (offshore companies);

- foreign technicians with special scientific or technical skills, who cannot be replaced by Greek employees with an equivalent background and knowledge, and are employed in industries or mines for a period of three months maximum, in order to repair machinery or other installations urgently;

- foreign athletes, who are employed by sports associations or clubs, under the special terms and conditions expressly provided by Greek law with regard to the maximum number of foreign athletes which such associations are allowed to employ;

- foreigners who are characterised as refugees;

- foreigners married to Greeks, as long as the couple is living together and more than two years from the marriage have lapsed, or foreigners who are parents of a Greek child under 18 years of age;

- foreign coach drivers who are hired by sports associations or clubs according to the provisions and restrictions expressly provided by Greek law;

- one foreign employee per tourist agency, on the condition that the agency does not employ other foreigners, it brings an important number of tourists to Greece and it contributes to the national economy, as certified by the National Tourism Organisation;

- directors of foreign airline companies and their deputies, on the condition that the Civil Aviation Authority consents thereto;

- tour leaders, on the condition that the National Tourism Organisation consents thereto.

Work permits are granted for a specific job, area, time period and employer. Work permits are issued only when it is estimated that the relevant position cannot be covered by unemployed persons already residing in Greece (Greek nationals, foreigners of Greek ancestry, or refugees living permanently in Greece).

(i) Exceptions on grounds of Greek ancestry
Any foreigner, claiming to be of Greek ancestry, must make a declaration to the immigration police authorities and submit the relevant supporting documents.

The conditions, terms and procedure of granting an entrance, residence and work permit to foreign nationals of Greek ancestry are regulated by Ministerial Decision. The Ministerial Decision currently in effect provides for the maximum number of work permits to be granted to foreigners during 1995, but exempts from this restriction work permits to foreign nationals of Greek ancestry.

In general, there are many exceptions from the restrictions applying to work permits of public or private employees, as well as those of professionals, in favour of foreign nationals of Greek ancestry.

(ii) Permit-free employment
No work permit is required for:

- foreign press correspondents who are legally accredited in Greece and have obtained a certificate from the Ministry of Presidency on their capacity;

- members of artistic groups entering Greece in the frame of cultural exchange activities, supervised by the Ministry of Culture and the organisations of local administration, on the condition that they apply to the Ministries of Foreign Affairs and Public Order at least 20 days prior to the beginning of the performance.

Nevertheless, these persons require entrance visas and residence permits, pursuant to the general applicable provisions.

(iii) Trainees
There are no special provisions regulating the status of trainees.

Work and residence permits of trainees would fall under the general requirements for work and residence permits, or under the provisions of short-term residence, depending on the specific circumstances of each case.

(iv) Doctors and dentists

In principle no licence is granted to foreign doctors and dentists, other than EU nationals, to practice their profession in Greece.

Exceptionally, a licence can be granted to foreign doctors or dentists where reciprocity exists between Greece and their country of origin.

Further, foreign nationals of Greek ancestry can exceptionally be granted a licence to practice medicine or dental medicine in Greece, if they already have a legal residence and work permit.

(v) Journalists and broadcasters

Foreign press correspondents, who are legally accredited in Greece and have obtained a certificate from the Ministry of Presidency, do not need a work permit, but only an entrance visa and residence permit pursuant to the general applicable rules.

Further, journalists and broadcasters would fall under the general requirements for work and residence permits.

(b) Inter-company transfers

A Greek company wishing to employee a foreign staff member of another company which belongs to the same group must follow the general rules applying to employment, and seek the issuance of a prior work permit approval and subsequent work and residence permit, for the employee to work in Greece. Highly qualified managers, as well as persons of specialised professions, would not have difficulty in obtaining a work and residence permit in Greece.

(i) Representatives and employees of off-shore companies

Foreign companies dealing exclusively with commercial business whose object lies outside Greece can be established in Greece following a special permit granted by decision of the Minister of National Economy (for commercial and industrial companies, under Law 89/1967), or by joint decision of the Ministers of National Economy and of Mercantile Marine (for foreign shipping companies, under Law 378/1988). These companies must meet their local expenses by importing foreign currency amounting to US $50,000 minimum yearly.

The company's representative in Greece, if a foreigner, as well as the foreigners employed by it, are granted work and residence permits.

3. Business

Foreigners, other than EU nationals, wishing either to work as professionals or to establish a personal business or a company in Greece, must apply to the Greek consulate in their country of residence for the prior approval of a work permit.

The application and supporting documents are sent by the Greek consulate to the Ministry of Labour, together with a report of the commercial attaché in respect of the business credit and the business activities of the applicant. The prior approval of a work permit is granted by the Ministry of Labour after taking into consideration the kind of business and the funds to be invested in the country.

Within one month of entering Greece, any foreign professional or business-man/woman must appear before the police department of the area where he or she is staying and file the necessary documents to obtain a work permit, among which is a certificate of the Bank of Greece concerning the amount of foreign currency imported in Greece and converted into dracmas. A work permit is granted for one year and may be renewed, as long as the foreigner's professional activities are considered profitable for the Greek economy.

4. Retired persons of independent means/investors

(a) Retired persons of independent means

Retired persons of independent means are only entitled to a residence permit in Greece if they are EU nationals. Their spouses, children, parents and parents-in-law are also granted residence permits irrespective of their nationality.

(b) Investors

In general there are no investment restrictions on foreign investors. A foreign investor may do business in Greece by establishing (or by participating in) any type of company provided for by Greek law, or by establishing a branch of a company constituted under foreign legislation.

(i) Types of companies under Greek law

There are four types of company provided for under Greek law:

- the corporation (Societe Anonyme) which requires at least two founders, persons or legal entities and a minimum capital of DR 10 million. The Board of Directors of a corporation must consist of at least three members, who do not need to be Greek nationals or reside in Greece. However, the managing director of a corporation must be resident in Greece and must have residence and work permits;

- the limited liability company, which, in principle, has two founders, persons or legal entities, but can be set up by one founder, and requires a minimum capital of DR 3 million. The administrator(s) of a limited liability company must be resident in Greece and must have a residence and work permit in Greece;

- the general partnership, in which all the partners are liable with all their assets for the company debts, and fall under the requirements of residence and work permits for businessmen;

- the limited partnership, in which some of the partners are liable with all their assets for the company debts, and which fall under the requirements for residence and work permits for businessmen. The other partner(s) whose liability is limited to the amount of their contribution in the company's capital, and who have, in principle, a financing role, may require a residence and work permit depending on the specific circumstances in each case.

(ii) Branches of foreign companies

A foreign corporation, or a foreign limited company may open a branch in Greece upon authorisation of the Ministry of Commerce and only where reciprocity exists between Greece and the country in which the foreign company is based.

(iii) Non-trading branches of foreign companies

A foreign (commercial, industrial or shipping) company may establish an office in Greece which operates as an off-shore company, provided it carries out its activities outside Greece (see chapter 2 part 8).

(c) Property investment

In certain areas of Greece, which are characterised as "border areas", it is, in general, forbidden for reasons of national defence for foreign nationals to purchase property or acquire property rights. The restrictions apply both to direct and indirect acquisition of property, through the purchase of shares or parts of a company owning a border area property. In addition, where the purchaser is a legal entity the nationality of its shareholders/partners, as well as the origin of the capital invested, are examined.

5. Spouses and children

No prior work permit approval is required for the foreign spouse of a Greek national, on the condition that the couple lives together and the marriage has lasted for at least two years, or that they are parents of a minor (child under 18 years of age) having Greek nationality.

A foreigner who has been granted a work and residence permit and has already legally resided in Greece for five years, may request that his or her family members are permitted to reside in Greece, for the purpose of family reunion. In this case the foreigner's family members are entitled to a residence permit of equal duration to that granted to the foreigner.

If the foreigner has legally resided in Greece for a shorter time period, he or she may apply to the Ministry of Public Order for his or her family members to be granted residence permits, but it is at the discretion of the Ministry to grant them, after having examined the specific circumstances.

Family members are considered to be the spouse (husband/wife), the unmarried children under 18 years of age, and the parents on the condition that they were living with and were supported by the foreigner before his or her coming to Greece.

A member of the foreigner's family may obtain a separate residence permit after becoming an adult, following an approval of the Ministry of Public Order, on the condition that such individual has sufficient funds to support himself or herself and cover his or her housing needs. Nevertheless, even in this case the term of the residence permit granted to the foreigner's family member is the same as that granted to the foreigner himself or herself.

6. Temporary stays

(a) Students

Foreigners entering Greece to study in local schools are granted a one-year residence permit, which is renewed annually until graduation.

Students' residence permits are issued and renewed after taking into consideration their progress, the duration of studies for each academic year, and the availability of sufficient means for living and studying expenses and medical care. In addition, no important objections on the grounds of public order, security or public health should exist.

(b) Visitors

Foreigners can enter Greece provided they have a valid passport, or other equivalent document recognised by international Treaties, and have obtained a visa, if required. They can stay provisionally in the country for up to three months without any further permit from the authorities. If a visa is required, it cannot exceed a three-month term.

(c) Short-term residence

Foreigners over 18 years of age having entered Greece for tourism or for any other purpose (other than employment, studies, or as family members of a foreign employee) and who wish to stay in Greece for a short period, must appear personally before the police authorities of the area where they are staying at least 15 days before the expiration of their three-month provisional stay permit, and apply for an extension.

The provisional stay permit cannot be extended for more than a three-month period. Before granting a short-term residence permit, the police authorities take into consideration the purpose for further residing in Greece, the existence of satisfactory means of living, the validity and term of the applicant's passport or other equivalent documents, if there is any guarantee that the foreigner can re-enter his or her country of origin, the intention of long-term residence in Greece and other reasons regarding public health and the social or public interest in general.

7. Permanent residence and nationality

(a) Permanent residence

In order to apply for a permanent residence permit a foreigner must have legally resided in Greece for a total period of 15 years and must have been insured with a "main" social security fund for at least 120 months. Any period of study in any school in Greece, as well as any term of imprisonment, are not counted for the calculation of the time period during which the foreigner must have resided in Greece.

(b) Nationality

Greek nationality is acquired:

- by birth;
- by legitimation;
- by adoption;
- by naturalisation.

A foreigner of non-Greek ancestry is qualified to apply for Greek nationality by naturalisation after having resided in Greece for at least 10 years in total within the 12-year period preceding the date on which the relevant application is filed, or for a period of five years thereafter. Only when these conditions are met, as evidenced by the foreigner's passport, can Greek nationality be granted. The period during which a foreigner has resided in Greece in his or her capacity as a diplomatic or administrative employee of a foreign country does not count for the calculation of the required duration of stay.

The above-mentioned conditions are not required for persons who were born and live in Greece.

The children of a foreigner who acquires Greek nationality also obtain Greek nationality if they are under 18 years of age and unmarried.

Marriage does not have any effect on either obtaining or losing Greek nationality.

8. Refugees and political asylum

Political asylum in Greece can be granted to foreigners "coming directly from a country where their life or freedom are in danger in the sense of Article 1 of the 1951 Geneva Convention"..Asylum claims must be made at the borders upon arrival in the country, or at the nearest public authority in case of illegal entry.

Asylum claims also apply to the refugees' family members, who have entered the country with him or her.

Asylum claims which are made for immigration purposes, or in order to avoid leaving the country upon legal request of the authorities, are rejected. If asylum is refused an appeal can be filed against the relevant decision. In case an asylum claim is irrevocably rejected, the Minister of Public Order can exceptionally and for special humanitarian reasons allow the foreigner to stay in Greece for a six-month period until he or she is able to leave the country. However, this exceptional permit is not a recognition of refugee status.

Foreigners who are recognised as refugees are given a special identity, pursuant to the Geneva Convention, and are granted a one-year residence permit, which can be renewed.

9. Government discretion

The restrictions provided for by Greek immigration law can often be waived by Ministerial Decision exceptionally and for serious reasons, such as public interest, *force majeure*, humanitarian reasons etc. On the other hand, licences and permits granted under Greek immigration law can be cancelled or revoked for reasons such as the protection of public health, public order, public interest, etc, or when the foreigner is found to have exercised his or her rights in an abusive way.

Therefore, the exercise of ministerial discretion is provided for directly by the law and, in practice, the individual circumstances of each foreigner are taken into account.

10. Sanctions

A foreigner is liable to deportation if he or she:

- has been convicted and given a prison sentence by the Greek court;
- violates Greek immigration legislation regarding the obligation of foreigners to obtain work and residence permits;
- by being present in Greece is considered a danger to public order or health, or to the security of the country;
- appears before the Greek authorities with different nationalities.

Foreigners staying in Greece for more than 30 days after the expiration of their residence permit or their permit of provisional stay, are liable to pay at departure an amount equal to fee payable for the issuance of a residence permit.

Foreigners who have illegally stayed in Greece for more than 30 days are liable to a fine of DR 50,000–200,000.

Any person violating the immigration law provisions is liable to imprisonment of up to six months, or to a fine, or to both, according to the Greek Penal Code.

11. Tax and social security

(a) Tax

Principal taxes in Greece are:

- income tax;
- capital gains tax;
- value added tax (VAT);
- inheritance and gift taxes;
- immovable property transfer tax;
- tax on ships.

(i) Income tax

Taxation of individuals

Persons (foreigners or Greeks) residing in Greece are subject to income tax on their annual income worldwide, whether or not remitted to Greece. Tax proved to have been paid outside Greece on non-Greek sources of income is deductible from the amount of tax payable in Greece on the same income.

In addition, persons (foreigners or Greeks) residing out of Greece, as well as persons who are temporary residents in Greece, are taxed on their annual income arising in Greece. These general rules are subject to the specific terms of any applicable Treaties for the avoidance of double taxation.

Taxation on legal entities

Greek legal entities are subject to income tax on their annual income worldwide, whether or not remitted to Greece.

Foreign legal entities are taxed only on income deriving from a "permanent establishment" in Greece. Subject to any applicable bilateral Treaties for the avoidance of double taxation, which prevail over national tax law, foreign legal entities are deemed to have permanent residence in Greece if:

- they maintain an office or a branch, or a warehouse or other place of operation, or other processing facility in Greece;
- they are engaged in manufacturing activities in Greece;

- they carry on business, or provide services through a representative (agent) in Greece, and in case the services rendered are of a technical or scientific nature, even when provided without an agent;
- they maintain stocks of goods in Greece, from which they fill orders;
- they participate in a personal company (general partnership, limited partnership) or in a limited liability company established in Greece.

In case bilateral Treaties for the avoidance of double taxation are applicable, the term of permanent establishment is defined in each Treaty in a different way, usually resulting in a preferential taxation of the legal entities covered by it, compared to national tax law.

Exceptionally, companies operating under Law 89/1967 and 578/1988 (offshore companies) are not subject to income tax in Greece.

(b) Social security

The social security system in Greece is administrated by a number of "social security funds" which cover specific occupations or professions. Social insurance is compulsory for workers and employees. In general, employed persons are covered by the Social Insurance Institute (IKA) which is financed by contributions from both employers and employees, calculated on the monthly salary of the employees. IKA benefits include medical treatment, pharmaceutical care and pensions.

12. Domestic considerations

(a) Civil registration

Foreigners who entered Greece after obtaining a prior work permit approval (as well as intended employees who do not need one) have to appear before the authorities within five days of arrival, in order to be sent to a Greek hospital for blood tests.

Further they must apply to the immigration police authorities, together with their Greek employer, within one month of arrival (in case of artists within three days), for work and residence permits and submit the appropriate documents.

(b) Housing

Accommodation in Greece is privately owned. A large variety of houses and apartments is available for rent in all major cities. Real estate transfers are subject to 9% or 11% tax (for urban areas) on the value of the property, as designated by the tax authorities, or any higher price agreed, up to DR 4 million and to 11% and 13% tax (for urban areas) on sale prices in excess of that amount.

Real estate agencies are available to assist foreigners in buying or renting property.

(c) Employment

In principle, a five-day, forty-hour working week applies to employees of both the private and the public sector.

Salaries are agreed on a monthly basis and employees are entitled to 14 salaries per year, including Christmas and Easter bonuses and annual leave allowances. In principle a written employment agreement is required.

(d) Schooling

Education is compulsory from the age of six to 16, including six years' elementary school and three years' gymnasium. Education in secondary schools is completed by another three-year study in "lyceum" (general or technical). Schools operated by the State are free. A number of private schools, as well as foreign schools, are also available. Universities are operated by the State and university studies are free.

(e) Health care

In principle, persons covered by social security as well as their dependants are entitled to free health (hospital and pharmaceutical) care.

Private medical services are also available through hospitals, clinics and independent professionals.

Messrs. Vgenopoulos & Partners, 15 Kolonaki Square, Athens 10673.
tel.: (30) 17221832/7217803/7220149. telefax: (30) 17231462

Contents of Chapter 10

IRELAND

Chapter 10

IRELAND

David Cantrell

1. Introduction

The guidelines contained in this chapter concerning the rights of aliens to reside, work and/or establish a business in Ireland should be viewed with full cognisance of Ireland's inherent features. These features include:

- Ireland's geographical position on the periphery of the European Union;
- economic climate;
- historical emigration trends;
- implementation of aliens legislation;
- European Community obligations.

2. Minister for Justice

The Minister for Justice has the sole responsibility for implementing legislation on aliens. The Minister is given wide discretion concerning all matters of the entry, residence and employment of aliens. There is no appeal against any decision and/or condition the Minister may make or impose as he thinks appropriate to the entry, residency and employment of an alien. However, all such decisions are subject to judicial review by the High Court and Supreme Court of Ireland which is a procedure that deals with the decision-making process as opposed to the decision on/or condition of entry, residency and employment.

The definition of aliens does not include persons born in Great Britain or Northern Ireland and, accordingly, such nationals are treated in the same way as Irish nationals. There exists a common travel area between the two jurisdictions and there is no passport control in respect of persons travelling to and from each country. Nationals of Great Britain and Northern Ireland are therefore not subject to:

- visa requirements;
- work permits;
- business permits; or
- registration of aliens.

3. Legislation

All persons who are not citizens of Ireland are described as "aliens". The Aliens Act 1935 and Aliens Orders 1946 to 1994 regulate the position of aliens wishing to enter, reside, work or establish a business in Ireland.

4. General principles applicable to permanent and temporary immigrants

(a) Visa requirements

The current legislation obliges certain aliens to obtain from the Department of Justice a valid visa prior to presenting himself or herself at a port of entry.

Unless an alien is a citizen of a State specified in Appendix I (at the end of this Chapter), a valid Irish visa shall be required.

Any alien to whom the visa requirements apply and who proposes to take up employment or establish himself or herself within the State must specify his or her intention in a visa application, which application should be supported by relevant documentation, such as an application for a work permit and/or a grant of work permit. If an alien requiring a visa proposes to establish a business in Ireland, details of the business venture, together with a business plan and evidence of available finance, should be referred to in the visa application. The alien must specify the purposes of travel to Ireland as a visa is only valid for that purpose, and if an alien wishes to change his or her immigration status while in Ireland it is the Government's stated policy to request the alien to leave the jurisdiction and reapply for a new visa.

Certain aliens may be obliged to obtain a transit visa for the purposes of transiting the State.

Any visa secured by false and misleading information is invalid, and the holder may be liable to prosecution and/or subject to deportation.

(b) Leave to land/entry

At the port of entry an immigration officer has extensive powers to refuse leave to land to an alien coming from a place outside the State other than Great Britain and Northern Ireland (see **7** below).

An alien arriving into the State from Great Britain or Northern Ireland who is not a national of a country specified in Appendix I (at the end of this Chapter) must have a valid Irish visa issued for the purpose of the travel.

An alien entering Ireland from Great Britain or Northern Ireland who proposes to engage in employment or establish himself or herself in business is required to report to the registration officer of the district in which he or she intends to reside within seven days of arrival in the State and produce valid identity documentation establishing his or her nationality. In addition, an alien, if intending to establish a business in the State, must not remain in the State for longer than one month without the written permission of the Minister for Justice.

Any other alien entering the country from Great Britain or Northern Ireland who does not propose to engage in employment or establish himself or herself in business must not remain in the State for longer than a three-month period without completing registration and obtaining the written permission of the Minister to remain.

(c) Registration permission to remain

Every alien subject to the immigration laws must register after three months his or her presence in the jurisdiction with the registration officer for the district in which the alien resides.

On registration, an alien will obtain a registration book and will be given permission to remain in the jurisdiction for a limited period (usually one year), after which registration and permission must be renewed.

The obligation to register with the registration authority and/or possession of valid documentation does not apply to aliens under the age of 16.

(d) Permanent immigrants

(i) Employment
Employees granted work permits
The Department of Enterprise and Employment has the responsibility for issuing work permits to alien nationals and has as its aim preservation of jobs for Irish/EU nationals.

Every non-EU national is obliged to obtain a work permit prior to arrival in Ireland, which application is processed by the prospective employer. Work permits will only be issued where the employer can satisfy the Department of Enterprise and Employment that there is no Irish/EU national with the appropriate professional or technical skills required for the particular job. Usually, the employer must prove that attempts were made to recruit from local/EU markets by advertising locally, nationally and with Sedoc recruiting offices in Europe.

Applications will usually receive a favourable consideration from the Minister for Enterprise and Employment if it can be shown that the granting of a work permit will create job opportunities for Irish/EU nationals in the short or long term.

An alien engaged in employment in the State, having entered the State with a valid work permit in respect of that employment, and who wishes to take up different employment may, depending on the particular circumstances, be required to leave the country and re-enter having received, prior to re-entry, a valid work permit in respect of new proposed employment. A similar provision also applies in the case of an alien who is solely residing in Ireland and who subsequently wishes to take up employment within the State. In both cases the Department of Justice and the Department of Enterprise and Employment should be consulted to ascertain whether such departure will, in fact, be necessary or whether it will be possible for the alien to continue residing in the State during this transition period. The current legislation is silent on this issue. However, practice and policy dictates that an alien wishing to change his or her immigration status can be required to leave the State.

The work permit relates to a specific employee, a specific job and a specific employer.

The work permit requirement is universal and applies to all aliens no matter how short the duration of stay. Performing artists, such as musicians and actors, also require work permits. Such applications are usually granted automatically. In the case of musicians, "group permits" may be issued to cover all members of the band on tour.

Exceptions on the grounds of Irish ancestry

Only non-Irish and non-EU nationals require work permits. Persons of Irish descent, though not born in Ireland as defined by the Irish Nationality of Citizenship Acts 1956 to 1994, do not require work permits.

Trainees

No distinction is made in the governing legislation and regulations between trainees and those engaged in full, gainful employment. All aliens who propose to work in Ireland, however short the duration or purpose, are obliged to apply for work permits. Exceptions to this general rule have been made in cases where trainees are transferred by a foreign-based parent company which continues to pay the salary of the transferee.

Sole representatives of overseas firms

Sole representatives of overseas firms are also subject to the work permit provisions. However, there are usually cogent arguments for granting such representatives permits on grounds of prospective investment and/or employment for Irish/EU nationals. Further, it is accepted that persons with prior knowledge of a particular skill and knowledge of company policy will be granted permits where they are seen as necessary and essential to an overseas firm setting up a branch business in Ireland (often referred to as "key personnel").

(ii) Business

Business men/women

All non-EU business persons wishing to establish a business in Ireland must obtain a business permit from the Minister for Justice. Any non-European Economic Area national (EEA) (15 members of the European Union, plus

Norway, Iceland and Liechtenstein) who wishes to pursue a business activity, other than as an employed person for whom an employer would have to obtain a work permit, must obtain a business permission.

The permission will allow a person or group of persons to engage and become established in a business in the State for a defined period.

To succeed, the applicant(s) must show, inter alia, that the granting of the permission would:

(1) result in the transfer to the State of substantial assets and capital in the minimum sum of £300,000; and

(2) create employment for two EU nationals in a new project, or maintain existing employment in an existing business.

There are a number of stated exceptions to the £300,000 limit, in particular writers and artists, who may make a separate application to the Minister.

To apply for a business permission the applicant should provide, inter alia, (a) a detailed business plan which will satisfy (1) and (2) above; (b) a statement of character from the police authorities of each country where the applicant has resided in excess of six months for the last 10 years.

A decision should issue from the Minister's office within one month from the date of receipt of the application.

Any appeal following a refusal must be lodged within one month of the date of refusal.

A business permission is renewable before the expiry date of the permission. If the applicant can satisfy the Minister that the criteria on foot of which the original permission was granted have been met, the Minister may extend the permission for a further five years.

Residency permission will be granted to the applicant, his or her spouse, and dependent children under 18 years of age for the duration of the permission.

(iii) Persons of independent means/investors

The current legislation does not create a special category of persons of independent means/investors (but see **5(d)** below). Any alien who does not wish to take up employment and/or establish a business but who wishes to stay in Ireland in excess of three months will be obliged to register and obtain the written permission of the Minister for Justice to remain. The immigration official will satisfy himself/herself that the person has sufficient means to support himself or herself and, where appropriate, any necessary dependants. The Minister has a very wide discretion in all matters concerning the entry, residence and/or employment of aliens.

(iv) Dependants and family

The current legislation and alien orders relate to all aliens. There is no absolute right for dependants to accompany an alien, although such permission will normally be granted once an alien can satisfy the immigration officer at the port of entry and the Department of Justice that he or she is in a position to support each dependant so that they will not become a burden on the State.

Registration requirements and the requirement to obtain permission to remain in the State apply equally to such dependants (see also **4(d)(ii)** above).

Marriage

Aliens married to Irish nationals will, subject to fulfilling certain requirements, be entitled to Irish Citizenship after a period of three years. In the intervening period the provisions relating to registration and obtaining work permits apply. Leave to land will generally be granted. However, an immigration officer may refuse entry on the grounds that the purpose of entry to Ireland is primarily to obtain admission to the United Kingdom, and is satisfied that the alien would not qualify for admission to the United Kingdom if entering from a place other than Ireland.

Children born in Ireland

Pursuant to the Irish Nationality and Citizenship Acts 1956 to 1994 every person born in Ireland is an Irish citizen from birth.

Other children

Children under the age of 16 are not obliged to comply with registration requirements described above, and their admission with alien parents will be automatic.

Adopted children

Once an adoption order has been made in favour of the parents who are Irish nationals, the child is accorded the same equal rights as those accorded to the parent's natural issue. Where a child is adopted by a married couple and either spouse is an Irish citizen, the adopted child, if not already an Irish citizen, will be an Irish citizen.

Exceptions for UK nationals

As explained above, aliens legislation does not apply to persons born in Great Britain and/or Northern Ireland. Such persons are effectively treated as Irish nationals and there is no restriction on their movement in or out of Ireland.

(e) Temporary immigrants

(i) Visitors

A visitor, although not defined, is clearly understood to mean a person who does not intend to remain in the State in excess of three months. Thereafter, the procedure outlined above with regard to registration and applying for permission to remain will apply. The term is usually associated with tourists and holiday-makers and, unless an immigration officer at point of entry is not satisfied as to the purpose of travel, or the appropriate visas have not been obtained, such persons receive little attention.

(ii) Business visits
Persons entering Ireland to transact business or attend conferences are treated liberally by immigration officers. Persons may be asked to provide some proof of the purpose of the visit.

(iii) Students
Aliens wishing to study in the State must provide the immigration officer at the port of entry with proof of:

- enrolment on a particular course;
- payment of fees;
- financial support for the course period;
- valid passport and/or visa.

The immigration officer must be satisfied that the course is full time, bona fide, and that the proposed student will not become a burden on the State.

(iv) Prospective students
An alien who wishes to change his or her immigration status from that of a visitor to a student or worker may be required to leave the State and reapply for a student visa or work permit.

(v) Au pairs
Au pairs do not fall into any official category, though, generally, it is usual that the sponsoring family will not need to apply for a work permit.

(vi) Working holiday-makers
United States' and Canadian students may obtain temporary holiday work visas on a reciprocal basis as is afforded Irish nationals by the US and Canadian authorities. The students must prove that they are in full-time education and that they propose to return to it after the maximum period of four months.

5. Naturalisation and citizenship

(a) Citizenship by birth and descent

Every person born in Ireland is an Irish citizen from birth. Every person is an Irish citizen if his or her father or mother was an Irish citizen at the time of his or her birth. In certain circumstances, a person may acquire Irish citizenship through an Irish-born grandparent and, in certain circumstances, through an Irish born great-grandparent. Irish citizenship may also be acquired by marriage to an Irish citizen.

(b) Northern Ireland

A person born in Northern Ireland on or after 6 December 1922 may declare himself or herself to be an Irish citizen, in which case Irish citizenship will apply to him or her from birth.

(c) Naturalisation

The Minister for Justice has absolute discretion to confer Irish citizenship on an alien by means of a certificate of naturalisation. There are two separate sections under which citizenship may be conferred. The first relates to fulfilling certain residence criteria, and the second relates to the power of the Minister to dispense with such conditions of naturalisation.

In the first instance, if the Minister is satisfied, inter alia, that the applicant is of full age and of good character, has a period of five years' legal residence in the state and intends in good faith to continue to reside in the State after naturalisation, a certificate of naturalisation will be issued.

The Minister has an absolute discretion to dispense with the conditions of naturalisation if he is satisfied that the applicant is of Irish descent or of Irish association.

(d) Irish association and business-linked naturalisation

A practice has developed in the State whereby the Minister may exercise discretion to grant naturalisation based on investment. In October 1994, the Minister indicated that this practice would continue and would be put on a statutory basis. While, to date, it has yet to achieve statutory status, its key terms (which are subject to change) are as follows.

Any applicant seeking to secure naturalisation through "business-linked naturalisation" will be obliged to comply with the following conditions:

- There must be a net investment of IR£1 million per applicant and per application.
- The basis of the investment must be job creation and job maintenance in Ireland. The investment may be in the form of a low interest loan for a period of seven years, in which case the interest rate will approximate the return on a government bond. Further, the loan arrangement must be transparent and may not be factored or sold on, and must not be secured by the assets of the company receiving the investment.
- Where the investment is not by way of a loan, its duration in an operation should be for at least five years. The investment must go towards the creation of jobs, and the number of jobs must be readily quantifiable and arise only from the investment.
- A substantial residence in Ireland must be purchased and retained by the applicant for a period of five years.

- The applicant is required to undertake to reside in Ireland for a minimum period of 60 days in the two years following naturalisation.

These are the very broad terms upon which the scheme is operated and all applications are vetted by a body representing various departments of the Government.

The scheme encourages inward investment and has the effect of securing an investment which may not otherwise have occurred.

The acquisition of Irish citizenship by a person does not of itself confer Irish citizenship on his or her spouse.

6. Refugees and political asylum

Ireland is a signatory to the United Nations Convention relating to the Status of Refugees and Stateless persons of 1951 and the 1977 Protocol relating to the status of refugees. Neither the Convention nor the Protocol have been made part of domestic law of the State. However, the procedure for the determination of refugee status in Ireland has been established by an informal agreement between the Department of Justice and the United Nations High Commission for Refugees (UNHCR). It was held in a recent Supreme Court decision that the Minister is obliged to apply the agreement to appropriate cases, and that the decision-making process would be subject to judicial review. Thus, this agreement is legally binding.

(a) Procedure

An application for refugee status and asylum may be made by the individual to the immigration officer on arrival, or directly to the Department of Justice if the individual is already in the country. Application may also be made to an Irish consul abroad.

The following is an extract of a letter from the Department of Justice to the UNHCR which is the basis of the aforementioned agreement, and outlines the procedure for determination of refugee status in Ireland in general terms:

2. Immigration officers have been provided with written guidelines which indicate clearly that a person should not be returned to a country to which he is unable or unwilling to go owing to a well-founded fear of persecution for reasons of race, religion, nationality, membership of a social group or political opinion, nor should be returned to a country where his personal safety might be seriously threatened as a result of political situation prevailing there.

3. Whenever it appears to an immigration officer as a result of claim or information given by an individual that he might be an asylum seeker, his case will be referred immediately to the Department of Justice, Dublin, for a decision. Immigration officers have been instructed that it is not necessary for an individual to use the term "refugee" or "asylum" in order to be an asylum seeker. Whether or

not an individual is an asylum seeker is a matter of fact to be decided in the light of all the circumstances of the particular case, as well as guidelines which may be issued from time to time by the Department. In case of doubt, the immigration officer shall refer to the Department of Justice.

4. Such an individual will not be refused entry or removed until he has been given an opportunity to present his case fully, his application has been properly examined, and a decision reached on it.

5. The asylum application will be examined by the Department in accordance with the 1951 Convention and the 1967 Protocol on the Status of Refugees. This shall not preclude the taking into account of humanitarian situations which might justify the grant of leave to remain in the State.

6. The applicant will be given the necessary facilities for submitting his case to the Department. If he is not proficient in English, the services of a competent interpreter will be made available when he is interviewed. He will be informed of the procedure to be followed and will be given the opportunity, of which he will be informed, to contact the UNHCR representative or a local representative of his choice. An applicant will be given this information in a language which he understands. It should be noted that there is no office for UNHCR in Ireland.

7. All applicants will be interviewed in person. Interviews will be conducted, as far as possible, by officials of the Department who understand asylum procedures and the application of refugee criteria, and are informed on human rights situations in the countries of origin. Where interviews cannot be undertaken by the Department, for example because the asylum seeker is outside Dublin, adequate guidance will be provided by the Department to the local immigration officials to ensure that all relevant information has been obtained and forwarded to the Department.

8. In line with the supervisory role of the UNHCR under the 1951 Convention and the 1967 Protocol on the Status of Refugees, the Department may seek the views of the UNHCR on any case prior to reaching a decision, or the UNHCR may make representations on the situation of the specific individual case or group of asylum seekers.

9. In any case where refusal of the application is proposed or an immediate positive decision is not possible, the Department of Justice will consult with the UNHCR representative accredited to the Republic of Ireland, before reaching a final decision and before taking steps to remove the applicant from Ireland, provided that the representative is available at the time.

10. If the applicant is recognised as a refugee, he will be informed accordingly and issued in due course with documentation certifying his refugee status and with the travel document, if he needs one. If the applicant is not recognised, he will be informed, in writing, of the negative decision and the reason for refusal.

The aforementioned procedure may take up to one year.

In the event of a negative decision, an asylum seeker has 28 days within which to initiate an appeal to the Interim Appeals Authority. This authority was set up by the Minister for Justice in November 1993. It must be noted that the authority has no statutory basis. In the event of such an appeal being refused, an asylum seeker may then apply to remain in the country on humanitarian grounds.

There is currently proposed legislation before the Irish legislature dealing with the matter of refugees and asylum seekers. The Bill, inter alia, proposes to give the power to make decisions in relation to refugees and asylum seekers to a refugee board. It must be noted that this is merely proposed legislation.

In the past, there was a certain amount of conflict as to whether or not the judiciary could interfere with a decision of the Minister in relation to political asylum and other matters. However, as a result of the recent aforementioned Supreme Court decision, it would appear to be the case that decisions of the Minister in this area are subject to judicial review. Where all domestic appeal mechanisms have been exhausted, it may be the case that an individual would have rights under the European Convention on Human Rights or the International Covenant on Civil and Political Rights.

In the event that an individual is detained by order of the Minister for Justice or an immigration official, that individual may invoke the habeas corpus procedure, alleging that his or her detention is unlawful. It has been held that where discretion exists, it must be exercised in accordance with the law.

7. Sanctions

(a) Refusal to grant leave to land

At the port of entry, an immigration officer has extensive powers to refuse leave to land to an alien coming from a place outside the State, other than Great Britain and Northern Ireland. The grounds upon which an immigration officer can rely vary, depending on whether the alien is an EU national.

Generally, an EU national may not be refused leave to land unless:

- he or she is suffering from certain specified diseases or disabilities; or

- his or her personal conduct has been such that it would be contrary to public policy or would endanger public security to grant him or her leave to land.

In the case of a non-EU national, an immigration officer may refuse leave to land to an alien where the immigration officer is satisfied that the alien:

- is not in a position to support himself or herself and any accompanying dependants;

- although wishing to take up employment in the State, is not in possession of a valid permit for such employment;

- is suffering from certain specified diseases or disabilities;

- has been convicted (whether in the State or otherwise) of an offence punishable under the law of the place of conviction by imprisonment for a maximum period of at least one year;

- does not hold a valid Irish visa;

- is the subject of a deportation order;

- has been specifically prohibited from landing in or entering into Ireland by ministerial order;
- belongs to a class of aliens prohibited from landing in or entering into Ireland by ministerial order;
- is not in possession of a valid passport or other document which establishes his or her nationality and identity;
- intends to travel to Great Britain or Northern Ireland, and the immigration officer is satisfied that the alien would not qualify for admission to Great Britain or Northern Ireland.

Where an immigration officer refuses leave to land, he or she is obliged to inform the alien in writing of the ground or grounds on which leave to land has been refused.

Where an alien has been refused leave to land, he or she may be arrested by an immigration officer or by a member of the Garda Siochana and detained in a specified place. An alien detained in such a manner may only be detained until such time (being as soon as practicable) as he or she is removed from the State.

(b) Deportation

The Minister may make an order requiring an alien to leave and remain out of the State for the duration of such an order where he deems it to be conducive to the public good. An alien with respect to whom a deportation order has been made may be detained in such a manner as may be directed by the Minister. The Minister may, if he thinks fit, apply any money or property of an alien in payment of the expenses incurred to transport the alien from the State.

(c) Exclusion

The Minister may, wherever he thinks proper, by order provide for the exclusion of an alien from the State. The power is not used frequently – only one such order has been made in the last five years.

(d) Sanctions operating against third parties

Where an individual is obliged to register or report as an alien and is lodging with, or living as, a member of the household of any other person, it is the duty of that person to take steps to secure compliance with any such registration or reporting obligations. Proprietors of hotel premises are obliged to keep a register of all persons staying at such premises. It is the duty of every such proprietor to preserve every register kept by him or her for a period of two years after the date of the last entry.

Where an individual fails to comply with these obligations, he or she may be taken into custody without warrant by an immigration officer or a member of the Garda Siochana. Furthermore, such an individual may be imprisoned for a period of up to six months or fined up to £100 (this applies to any contravention of the Aliens Orders).

(e) Detention

Where an alien is refused leave to land, he or she may be arrested by an immigration officer or by a member of the Garda Siochana and detained in one of the places specified in the regulations.

An alien, in respect of whom a deportation order is made or a recommendation is made by a court with a view to the making of a deportation order, may be detained in such a manner as may be directed by the Minister.

Any person acting in contravention of the Aliens Orders may be taken into custody without warrant by an immigration officer or by a member of the Garda Siochana.

8. Domestic considerations

(a) Foreign investment

The Minister for Finance has power to make orders which restrict financial transfers between Ireland and other countries. It appears that this is to enable the Minister to impose financial sanctions on countries on foot of, for example, coordinated action of the European Community or United Nations Resolutions. To date, the Minister has imposed restrictions in respect of nationals of Iraq, the Federal Republic of Yugoslavia (Serbia and Montenegro), Haiti and Libya.

In general terms, there are no restrictions on foreign investment in Ireland. The Industrial Development Authority (IDA) is empowered to provide grants and other incentives, on such terms and conditions as it thinks fit, to industrial undertakings that meet certain eligibility criteria laid down by statute. The actual level of grant and other incentives will depend on how attractive the project appears to the IDA. There are percentage limits on the amounts of grants and other incentives which can be given by the IDA.

Recently, there has been increased foreign investment in the area of financial services. This has been assisted by the Irish Government, which was responsible for the launching of the International Financial Services Centre (IFSC), which is based in Dublin. The IDA is charged with the responsibility for marketing the IFSC. Companies licensed to operate from the IFSC qualify for a range of benefits. Examples of such benefits are as follows:

- significantly reduced corporation tax (38% to 10%). In order to benefit from this reduced corporation tax, it is necessary to obtain a tax certificate from the Minister for Finance;
- a number of property-based allowances/reliefs;

- allowances for plant and machinery used or to be used in the IFSC. In order to obtain such allowances, an operation must be covered by a tax certificate;

- preferential value added tax rates;

- access to in excess of 20 double taxation agreements.

The IDA has a specialist department – the International Financial Services Department – which will provide extensive assistance to potential applicants in developing a proposal for the establishment of an operation in the IFSC and in obtaining a tax certificate under the programme.

(b) Business entities

The three most common ways in which business is carried on in the Republic of Ireland is by means of:

- a company.

- in partnership; and

- as a sole trader.

(i) Company

The company may be public or private and have limited or unlimited liability. By far the most common of these is the private limited liability company, generally having liability limited by shares.

A company may be incorporated with limited liability. The liability of the members for the debts and wrongs of the company may be limited to the amount unpaid on the shares which they own in the company (a company limited by shares) or to the amount which they undertake to pay in the event of the company ceasing to exist (a company limited by guarantee). The company is a legal entity distinct from its members. The shares in a company are freely transferable unless the constitution of the company provides otherwise. A person who acquires shares becomes a member with all the rights of the person who transferred the shares to him or her. The affairs of a company are managed by its directors and not by the members.

Some fundamental distinctions may be drawn between public and private companies. A private company is the most likely vehicle in the case of a small to medium-sized business, while a public company is appropriate in the case of a large business. A private company must have at least one and not more than 50 members. In the case of a public company, the minimum number of members is seven, with no maximum. In the case of a private company, there must be a restriction on the right to transfer shares and a prohibition on any invitation to the public to subscribe for shares or debentures of the company. A public company normally invites members of the public to subscribe for shares by means of a prospectus. There are strict regulations governing this. In addition, before the company's shares can be quoted or dealt in on the stock exchange, the company must comply with the rules of the Stock Exchange on the *Admission of Securities to Listing*. There is no requirement for a minimum share capital in the case of a private limited company. However, it is normally the case that such a company will have a nominal share capital of IR£2 divided equally into two shares of IR£1 each. A public limited company, on the other hand, is required to have a minimum share capital of IR£30,000.

A company may be formed which is limited neither by shares nor by guarantee. In such a case, it is known as an unlimited company.

(ii) Partnership

Partnerships are an important feature of Irish life, particularly in the field of the professions. The principal difference between a company and a partnership is that, generally speaking, a partnership will not be afforded the possibility of limited liability, as is the case with a company. Limited liability is only available to partnerships in very restricted circumstances. Thus, partners are liable for the debts and wrongs of the partnership.

Each partner is entitled to participate in all the partnership activities. A partnership is not obliged to file accounts in the same way as a company.

(iii) Sole traders

Sole traders are likely to arise in cases of particularly small businesses. The only obligation which arises where an individual is trading as a sole trader is that the individual registers the name under which he or she trades, where that name is not his or her own name.

(iv) Other business entities

It should be noted that the aforementioned only represents the more common business entities encountered in Ireland. In recent times, the growth of the international financial services sector has required the legislature to provide for business entities appropriate to that market. Examples of such entities are:

- undertakings of collective investments in transferable securities;
- unit trust companies;
- investment limited partnerships; and
- variable capital companies.

(c) Employment

The employer-employee relationship in Ireland is essentially based on contract law. However, legislation has been enacted over the years, particularly since Ireland's accession to the EEC in 1973, which limits the extent to which parties to an employment contract may negotiate the terms of that contract. Employees in Ireland today have many statutory entitlements.

The following is a broad overview of the legislation most pertinent to the current discussion.

(i) Minimum Notice and Terms of Employment Act 1973

Within one month of commencement of employment, an employee is entitled to a written statement of the terms of his employment outlining the following:

- the date of commencement of employment;
- the rate or method of calculation of remuneration;
- the intervals of the remuneration paid (weekly, monthly or otherwise);
- any terms or conditions relating to overtime;
- any terms or conditions relating to:
  - holidays and holiday pay,
  - incapacity for work due to sickness or injury, and
  - pension schemes;
- any period of notice which the employee is required to give and, in the case of a fixed-term contract, the date upon which the contract expires.

There is currently draft legislation before the Dail which provides for the repeal of the current obligations in relation to notice of terms of employment and for their replacement, with more extensive obligations arising on the part of the employer.

(ii) Anti-Discrimination Pay Act 1974 and Employment Equality Act 1977

The employment equality legislation deals with equal pay and anti-discrimination. It is an implied term of the contract under which the female employee is employed in any place of employment that she is entitled to the same rate of remuneration as her male counterpart employed in like work. The reverse is also true. It is also prohibited to discriminate on grounds of sex or marital status in relation to:

- recruitment;
- conditions;
- training; or
- promotion.

(iii) Holidays (Employees) Acts 1973 and 1991

Employees are entitled to a minimum annual leave of three working weeks, although this may shortly be increased to four working weeks in addition to nine days' public holidays.

(iv) Maternity Protection of Employees Acts 1981 and 1991

Generally speaking, a female employee who works for 18 hours or more per week has the right:

- to take up to 18 weeks' maternity leave;
- to return to work after such leave;

- to take reasonable time off both before and after the birth; and
- to protection of her job.

(v) Minimum Notice and Terms of Employment Act 1973
Where an employer wishes to terminate the contract of employment of an employee who has been in the employer's continuous service for at least 13 weeks, the employer is obliged to give certain minimum notice. These minimum notice periods are as follows:

- length of service: 13 weeks to two years – minimum notice one week;
- length of service: two years to five years – minimum notice two weeks;
- length of service: five years to 10 years – minimum notice four weeks;
- length of service: 10 years to 15 years – minimum notice six weeks;
- length of service: more than 15 years – minimum notice eight weeks.

These statutory periods may not be replaced by shorter periods of notice. However, parties may agree longer periods of notice.

(vi) Unfair Dismissals Act 1977 and Unfair Dismissals (Amendment) Act 1993
There is also provision to protect employees from unfair dismissal. Where an employee has been unfairly dismissed, his or her redress may take the form of:

- reinstatement (re-employment on identical terms);
- re-engagement (re-employment of the employee although not on identical terms);
- financial compensation.

(vii) Redundancy Payments Acts 1967 to 1991
Where an employee is dismissed for reasons of redundancy, that employee will be entitled to a minimum redundancy payment. An employee qualifying for redundancy payment is entitled to a lump sum made up as follows:

one week's normal remuneration and one half week's pay for each year of employment between the ages of 16 and 41 years and one week's pay for every year of employment over the age of 61.

This payment is subject to a ceiling of IR£300 per week.

(viii) Worker Protection (Regular, Part-Time Employees) Act 1991
Most of the aforementioned statutory benefits now extend to "a regular part-time employee", who is defined as an employee who has been in continuous service of the employer for at least 13 weeks and is normally expected to work at least eight hours a week.

(d) Taxes

The principal taxes in Ireland are levied by Central Government and include the following:

- stamp duty;
- value added tax (VAT);
- income tax;
- corporation tax;
- capital gains tax;
- capital acquisitions tax;
- pay related social insurance (PRSI).

(i) Stamp duty

Stamp duties are taxes on legal instruments. The most common transactions giving rise to stamp duties are transfers of property, transfer of shares in an Irish company and the creation of mortgages and debentures charged on properties situated in Ireland.

Stamp duty is payable on the purchase of freehold property at a rate determined by the purchase price. The rates chargeable range from 1% of an amount exceeding IR£5,000 and not exceeding IR£10,000, to 6% of an amount exceeding £60,000. The duty is payable to the Irish Revenue Commissioners by the purchaser of the property within 30 days of the completion of the purchase of any interest in the property.

On the conveyance or transfer on sale of any stock or marketable securities, stamp duty is payable at the rate of 1% of the consideration. It should also be noted that on the allotment of shares in companies, capital duty of 1% of the consideration is payable.

In the case of a mortgage which is a security for the payment or repayment of money which is a charge or encumbrance upon property situated in Ireland, the rate of stamp duty is 0.1% of the amount secured (where the amount secured exceeds £20,000), subject to a maximum duty of £500.

(ii) Value added tax

Value added tax is chargeable on supplies of goods and services and the development and supply of land and buildings. The rates vary from 0% to 21%.

(iii) Income tax

Income tax is assessed on individuals on a sliding scale according to the level of income of that individual. The current maximum rate is 48%. In general, income which arises in Ireland is subject to income tax irrespective of the nationality, domicile or residence of the recipient. Foreign income is normally subject to Irish tax if the recipient is resident in Ireland. In cases where tax

Treaties exist between Ireland and other countries, credit will usually be given for taxes paid in another country.

(iv) Corporation tax

All companies resident in Ireland and all non-resident companies which carry on a trade in Ireland through a branch or agency subject to specific exceptions are liable to corporation tax. Companies resident in Ireland are liable to corporation tax on all profits wherever these arise. The standard corporation tax (as of September 1995) is 38%.

In the assessment of corporation tax, many reliefs and allowances are available and some of the more important of these are set out as follows.

Manufacturing companies tax rate

A reduced rate of corporation tax applies to manufacturing companies in respect of income arising in the period from 1 January 1981 to 31 December 2010 from the sale of goods manufactured in Ireland. The relief reduces the liability of a qualifying company to corporation tax to 10%. In addition to conventional manufacturing, certain activities specified in the legislation also qualify for the 10% manufacturing relief. These include computer services, certain construction design services, ship repair and certain shipping activities.

Urban renewal relief

The Urban Renewal Relief Act 1986 and the Finance Act 1986 contain tax incentives to encourage development in certain urban areas in Dublin and other cities throughout the country. Certain areas in Dublin were designated under the legislation to qualify for reliefs, one of which was the Custom House Dock area. The Finance Act 1987 introduced the concept of the International Financial Services Centre (IFSC) which is located in the Custom House Dock area. The incentives available to a company located in the area are as follows:

- allowances against income in respect of capital expenditure incurred in the construction or reconstruction of commercial buildings and for capital improvements to existing buildings;

- a deduction for double the amount of rent actually paid for commercial or industrial buildings for set-off against trade income of companies located in the Custom House Dock area; and

- a full remission of rates for 10 years on new buildings and also on newly enlarged or improved buildings.

As well as the benefits outlined above, the Finance Act 1987 extended the 10% rate of corporation tax to certain trading operations carried out in the IFSC. Examples of trading operations which attract the 10% rate are the supplying of financial services to persons not ordinarily resident in Ireland and insurance and related activities.

To qualify for relief, the company must obtain a certificate from the Minister of Finance that the company is engaging in qualifying activities and that it will contribute to the overall development of the IFSC. The relief is available from the date specified in the certificate until 31 December 2005 unless the certificate is, for some reason, revoked before that date.

Because of these substantial benefits, the IFSC has attracted considerable international interest and, since September 1995, 437 companies have been approved for operation of financial service from the IFSC, 366 of which are active. Applications for certificates are made to the Industrial Development Agency, which has been appointed by the Government as the marketing agency for the programme.

Capital allowances

No deduction is allowed for capital expenditure or depreciation in computing the adjusted profits of a trade. However, the tax legislation provides specific allowances for capital expenditure, which are known as capital allowances. The allowances are available in respect of two main types of assets, namely industrial buildings and plant and machinery.

(v) Capital gains tax

Capital gains tax is imposed on persons or companies making a capital profit on the disposal of any assets. In the computation of the tax liability, allowance is made for the effects of inflation on the original acquisition cost of the asset. In the case of the disposal of an asset for a sum in excess of IR£100,000 a purchaser must pay to the Revenue Commissioners a sum equal to 15% of the purchase price of the asset, unless a certificate has been produced to the purchaser by the vendor from the Revenue Commissioners indicating that it is not necessary for the purchaser to make such a deduction. A certificate to that effect will generally not be issued in the case of a non-Irish resident disposing of an asset in Ireland.

(vi) Capital acquisitions tax

Capital acquisitions tax is imposed on the disposal of assets by an individual either by gift during his or her lifetime or upon death. The tax is charged at progressive rates on a slice system, with different threshold amounts for different classes of beneficiary depending on their relationship to the person from whom the gift or inheritance is received. There is a territorial limit to the extent to which gifts and inheritances are taxable. The entire property comprised in the gift or inheritance is taxable where, at the time of the gift or inheritance, the disponer is domiciled in Ireland or where the proper law of the disposition is the law of Ireland. If neither of these criteria applies, only so much of the gift or inheritance as is situated in Ireland at the date of the gift is liable to tax. It is important that a purchaser of property from such a donee obtains from the donee a certificate from the Revenue Commissioners confirming that any duties payable on the receipt of the property by the donee have been fully discharged. Unpaid capital acquisition tax is a charge on property from such a donee. Without obtaining such a certificate, a purchaser could be acquiring a property with tax liability attached.

(vii) Pay-related social insurance

Strictly speaking this is not a tax, but all persons who are defined as employees under the Social Welfare (Consolidation) Act 1981 are required to have paid a contribution for the purpose of a social insurance. There are two elements to the payments – the employee's and the employer's contributions. An employee's contribution is deducted from his or her salary and the employer adds his or her contribution to this. Currently, an employee's contribution is 7.75% of reckonable earnings. The employer's contribution is 12.20%. There are earnings ceilings on these figures.

9. EU Nationals/Citizens of the European Economic Area (EEA)

Nationals of EU Member States must be treated in the same way as Irish nationals. Such nationals (with minor exceptions) do not require work or business permits, but must comply with certain registration requirements described below.

(a) Right of entry

Pursuant to regulations, a national of a Member State who:

(1) is established or wishes to become established in Ireland,
(2) is coming to provide or receive a service in Ireland,
(3) is coming to take up or pursue an activity as an employed person in Ireland,
(4) is a dependant of a person referred to in (1), (2) or (3),

cannot be refused to land on production of a valid national identity card or passport. No visa or equivalent document can be demanded.

(b) Refusal of leave to land

Leave to land may only be refused where the national of the Member State or his or her dependant is suffering for a specified disease or disability, or his or her personal conduct has been such that it would be contrary to public policy or would endanger public security to permit entry. The Minister must notify the national or dependant of the reasons for refusal of leave to land and enter.

(c) Right of residence (residence permit)

A national of a Member State who:

(a) has established himself in the State;

(b) is supplying or receiving a service in the State,

(c) is in employment in the State,

may apply for a residence permit to the registration officer in the district in which he or she is resident. The Minister must provide, on production of sufficient documentation, a residence permit to an EU national as proof of residence. It is the practice in Ireland that EU nationals applying for a residence permit will be required to prove that they are qualified persons pursuant to the Regulations.

(d) Validity, duration and issuance

Residency permits are valid throughout the State, and their issuance and renewal are free of charge. The permit issues within six months of application and is valid for a five-year period of residency as opposed to the more limited version of permission to remain, which is usually granted for a period of one year. Nationals of Member States are not obliged to apply for a residence permit prior to the expiration of three months after entry into Ireland. Application for renewal of the five-year residency permit can be made before the expiration of the five-year period for a further five years free of charge, and so on, indefinitely.

An EU national supplying or receiving a service in Ireland will be issued with a residence permit for the duration of the service, and such residence permit will, subject to certain conditions, be renewed automatically where the national is continuing to provide or receive the service.

An EU national who is in employment in the State and holds a post for more than three months, but less than one year, will be issued with a temporary residence permit limited to the duration of his employment.

A break not exceeding six consecutive months will not affect the validity of a residence permit, nor will absence on military service.

An EU national holding a residence permit is entitled to remain in the State during the validity of the permit. Seasonal workers in the State or a person who, while in employment in another Member State, has a residence in the State to which he or she returns weekly, has a right of residence.

(e) Members of a worker's family and dependants

Dependants of persons referred to at (a), (b) and (c) above who are also EU nationals may apply for a residence permit to the registration officer where such dependants ordinarily reside. The period of validity is the same as that of the residence permit issued to the EU national on whom he or she is dependent. A dependant who is not an EU national may apply for a residence document to the registration office of the registration district where he or she is resident.

Therefore, the right of residence must also be granted to members of a worker's family on production of the document of entry and proof of relationship and, in the case of dependency, proof thereof from a competent authority of the State of origin.

Dependants will also be granted a five-year residency permit once the primary applicant can satisfy the Department of Justice that he or she can adequately support his or her dependants so that they do not become a burden on the State.

(f) Rights of EU nationals to remain permanently in Ireland

Generally, any EU national who has been in employment in Ireland or who has pursued an activity in Ireland as a self-employed person may remain permanently in the State on cessation of such activity if:

- at the time of cessation he or she has reached a pensionable age and has pursued that activity in the State for the previous 12 months and has resided continuously in the State for more than three years;
- having resided continuously in the State for more than two years, he or she ceases to pursue the activity in the State as a result of permanent incapacity for work; or
- he or she has been incapacitated for work as a result of either an accident at work or an occupational illness entitling him or her to a pension which is payable in whole or in part by the State.

(g) Departure

The right to reside terminates when the purpose for which such right was granted expires. The loss of the right to reside may also be lost by reason of departure and absence for more than six months from the jurisdiction (other than on military service).

(h) Refusal of residence permit

A residence permit which is valid cannot be withdrawn from a person solely on the grounds that he or she is no longer in employment if this unemployment is caused by his or her being temporarily incapable for work as a result of illness, accident or otherwise involuntarily. In addition, where a person has been involuntarily unemployed for a continuous period of more than 12 months, the renewal of his or her residence permit may be limited to 12 months and if, after the expiration of that period, the person is still unemployed, the renewal may be refused.

The first residence permit may be refused and the applicant requested to depart when the applicant fails to undergo a medical examination for the purposes of ascertaining whether or not he or she is suffering from any specified disease or disability or the applicant fails to satisfy the Minister that he or she is a person to whom the Regulations apply.

A residence permit may be refused and the applicant requested to depart if the Minister is satisfied that the conduct of the person concerned has been such that it would be contrary to public policy or would endanger public security to permit him or her to remain in the State. However, any EU national holding a residence permit may not be refused renewal or may not be required to leave the State before his or her case has been considered by an authority appointed pursuant to the Regulations before whom the person may appear to be heard and represented by a legal advisor. A person who does not hold a residence permit and who has been refused leave to land having been notified that he or she is obliged to depart the State may on request, have his or her case referred to the authority appointed pursuant to the Regulations before whom he or she may appear in person.

10. Appendix

The European Communities – Rights of Residence for Non-Economically Active Person (Regulations 1993), extend the general principles enunciated above at (9) to Students, Retired Persons, or other economically non-active persons and their accompanying dependants.

List of countries whose passport holders do not need visas to enter Ireland

Andorra	Guatemala	Norway
Argentina	Honduras	Panama
Australia	Hungary	Paraguay
Austria	Iceland	Poland
Bahamas	Israel	Portugal
Barbados	Italy	San Marino
Belgium	Jamaica	Singapore
Botswana	Japan	Slovakia
Brazil	Korea (Rep of South)	Slovenia
Canada	Latvia	South Africa
Chile	Lesotho	Spain
Czech Republic	Liechtenstein	Swaziland
Costa Rica	Lithuania	Sweden
Cyprus	Luxembourg	Switzerland
Denmark	Malawi	Trinidad & Tobago
Ecuador	Malaysia	Tonga
El Salvador	Malta	United Kingdom & Colonies*
Estonia	Mexico	United States
Finland	Monaco	Uruguay
France	Nauru	Vatican City
Germany	Netherlands	Venezuela
Greece	New Zealand	Western Samoa
Grenada	Nicaragua	Zimbabwe

* British dependent territories (colonies)

Anguilla, Bermuda, British Antarctic Territory (South Georgia, South Sandwich Islands), British Indian Ocean Territory (Chagos Archipelago, Peros Banos, Diego Garcia, Danger Island), Cayman Islands, Falkland Islands and dependencies, Gibraltar, Hong Kong*, Montserrat, Pitcairn (Henderson, Ducie and Oneno Islands), St Helena and dependencies (Ascension Island, Tristan Da Cunha), the Sovereign Base areas of Akrotiri and Dhekelia, Turks and Caicos Islands, British Virgin Islands.

Transit visas
Foreigners from the following countries require transit visas: Albania, Bulgaria, Cuba, Iran, Iraq, Romania, Lebanon, Moldova, Montenegro, Serbia, Somalia, Sri Lanka.

* A person in possession of a Hong Kong Certificate of Identity requires an entry visa for Ireland.

Messrs. Eugene F. Collins, 61 Fitzwilliam Square, Dublin 2.
tel.: (353) 1 6761924. telefax: (353) 1 6618906

Contents of Chapter 11

ITALY

Chapter 11

ITALY

Mario Giovanazzi/Susanne Pelzel

1. Country characteristics

Italy is a country of 311,255 square kilometres, shaped in a peninsula, with two main islands, Sicily and Sardinia, situated in the South of Europe, surrounded by five seas (Ligurian, Tyrrhenian, Ionian, Adriatic, and Mediterranean). France, Switzerland, Austria and former Yugoslavia are its border countries. The territory is made up of mountains (35.2%) hills (41.7%) and lowlands (23.1%).

A 1991 census indicated a population of 56,778,031, while an estimate dated 1992 indicated a population of approximately 56,930,300.

The present national economic growth rate (PIL) is approximately 2.6%, the inflation rate is around 5.6%, and the jobless rate is 11% (ISTAT: Italian National Statistics Institute).

The Italian monetary unit is the lira, and the exchange rate is approximately US$1 = Lira 1600.

Since 1948, Italy has been a parliamentary republic.

A Referendum held after the Second World War, brought Italy into the republican system.

Rome is the capital city of Italy. Within Rome is the independent Vatican State, seat of the Pope, who is the head of the Catholic Church.

Italy was a founder member of the European Community for Steel and Coal in 1951, and the European Community for Atomic Energy, which led to the European Union, following the European Economic Community (1957). Italy was also a founder member of the Council of Europe in 1949.

2. General principles according to the provisions of Law No 39/90

Article 2 of Law No 39/90 states that foreign, non-EU nationals are allowed to enter Italy for reasons of tourism, study, employment, self-employment, medical treatment, religion and family.

In order to gain admittance, foreign, non-EU nationals must present a valid passport or document recognised by the Italian authorities, and a visa, namely an authorisation issued by the Italian embassy or consulate of the State where that person is a resident. A visa is required according to a list of countries provided by the Italian Minister of Foreign Affairs, approved by the Minister of the Interior.

The list of countries from which visas are required is revised every year within the context of bilateral and multilateral agreements.

Non-EU citizens coming from countries not appearing on the list are exempted from the requirement to hold a valid visa, but only regarding visas issued for purposes of tourism, which are valid for a maximum period of three months. Citizens from Switzerland and San Marino are also exempted. The visa will specify the reason for entry, length of stay and the number of entries into Italian territory (when applicable).

Border officials must place a dated entry stamp on the passport of non-EU nationals who enter the country.

The data of non-EU nationals must also be collected by the frontier police and sent to the database of the Ministry of the Interior. Foreign nationals who do not fulfil this requirement will not be accepted by the frontier police.

Border officials must also refuse those visa holders who have previously been expelled, have been identified as a danger to the security of the State, who belong to criminal, drug-trafficking or terrorist organisations, or are connected to the Mafia.

Refusal of entry must be given in writing. This decision can be appealed to the regional administrative tribunal.

Foreign nationals who are without any visible means of support are also refused entry unless they can provide proof of support, including documents of property in Italy or regular income from employment.

A religious body, an association or a private person can "sponsor" and guarantee financial support and take upon themselves the responsibility to provide for the immigrant's financial needs. In order to do so, they must obtain a certificate of guarantee from the competent police headquarter (the Questura) and deliver the certificate to the immigrant.

3. Historical evolution

Italy has been a country of emigration, especially to the most industrialised countries, from the date of Italian unification in 1861, until the 1970s.

Immigration into Italy, however, began in the 1970s, since when the number of non-EC immigrants has greatly increased over the years.

A 1971 census indicated an immigrant population of 121,116, while recent statistics taken in the past few years revealed 862,977 immigrants in 1991, 952,171 in 1992 and 987,405 in 1993, with the rate of increase slowing from 10.4% in 1991, to 7.2% in 1992, and 6.7% in 1993.

In 1993 the non-EC component was high, at 834,451 (84.5%), compared with 152,954 (15.4%) EC nationals.

Immigrants come mainly from Morocco (97,604), followed by the former Yugoslavia (72,377), the United States (63,960), the Philippines (46,332), Tunisia (44,505), Albania (30,317), Senegal (29,368), Egypt (24,555), China (22,875) and Brazil (21,037) (Eurostat).

The Italian Constitution clearly states that the status of foreign nationals is governed by international Treaties. Civil rights are granted to foreign nationals on a reciprocal basis.

The first law on entry, stay and expulsion relating to immigrants arriving from outside the European Community was issued only in 1990 (Decree No 416/89 – Law No 39/90). Before this law was introduced, the status of non-EC immigrants was regulated by the general principles contained in the Italian Constitution, article 10 § 2, which enacted the relevant provisions of international Conventions, and the provisions relating to public security, which took into consideration the presence of non-EC citizens from a mere "public order" point of view (R Decree No 777/31 and its executive regulation).

Law No 943, in 1986, dealt with the specific problem of the employment of non-EC citizens present in Italy, and applied the principle of equal treatment between national and non-national workers, as contained in ILO Convention No 143/75. In 1988, an internal measure of the Italian Ministry of the Interior (Circolare 559/443/1863/5/11/1/I) was issued to specify the conditions to be satisfied in order to achieve family reunification of non-EC citizens.

Law 39/90 contains an "act of indemnity" or "amnesty", for those already illegally present in Italy.

A Ministry for Immigration was set up in 1992, but owing to the political crisis it was dropped the following year.

At present all decisions on matters regarding immigration are taken by various branches of the administration. However, illegal immigration has been an increasing phenomenon: for example, in 1993, 54,274 immigrants were lodged on police records for a variety of offences; 20,497 of these were arrested and 49,000 were threatened with expulsion.

The presence of illegal immigrants is a serious problem. The lack of efficiency of the system of controls over immigrants can be explained for two reasons. First, it is almost impossible to patrol the entire borders of Italy, which has 7,456 kilometres of coastline; secondly, the system of expulsion of non-EC citizens illegally present in Italy, laid down by Law No 39/90, allows a waiting period of (normally) 15 days following an order of expulsion before its execution. This is a sufficient period of time to evade the law and disappear. As a consequence, of the 190,000 ordered expulsions since 1991, only 24,000 have actually been enforced – a figure which represents less than 15%.

Following the arrival and entry into force of the Schengen Agreement (1990) providing for the abolition of internal frontiers between the signatory States (and not signed by the United Kingdom, Ireland or Denmark), Italy's European partners expected efficient controls on external borders. The introduction of

Law No 38/90 was, therefore, welcomed for the restrictive approach it adopted towards non-EC immigration. It also allowed Italy to became a signatory of the Agreement. However, when the Schengen Agreement entered into force in 1995, Italy was excluded, and the inefficiency, in practice, of the Italian external border controls was just one of the reasons for that exclusion.

With Decree M 376 of 16 July 1996 sanctions will be imposed on anyone who helps a non-EC citizen to enter Italy in violation of the existing provisions, and fines imposed on carriers who do not inform the national authorities of the presence of illegal immigrants in their vessels or planes, will also be increased.

Other relevant aspects of the Decree concern seasonal work, the fact that any employer offering employment to non-EC citizens in violation of the existing provisions will commit a crime, and the reduction of the possibilities for family reunification – except in relation to spouses and children (not including grand-parents), provided the non-EC immigrant already present in the Italian terri-tory, has accommodation in which to lodge his or her relatives, and can supply evidence of economic means at least equivalent to five or six times the state pension, and or a 2 year labour contract of his/her spouse.

4. Visitors

All non-nationals, whether or not citizens of the European Union, must obtain from the office for non-nationals or Questura in the province in which they are domiciled, a residence permit within eight days of their arrival. The Questura then issues the permit, within eight days from the date of request, displaying all relevant information, including the visitor's reasons for staying in Italy (as appear on his or her visa). A residence period of three months is normally granted.

For some specific countries a visa is required in order to obtain a residence permit. However, an exception can be made for short stays.

The granting of a residence permit may be refused when the provisions of the law on entry and stay have been broken, or for reasons of security, public order or health. As a consequence, instructions may be given to the person con-cerned to leave the territory within a specified time, usually 15 days, or a decree of immediate expulsion from Italian territory can be issued.

A residence permit issued for reasons of tourism is normally valid for the same period as the visa (three months).

In other cases a permit generally expires after two years, but is, in principle, renewable, unless the permit expressly states the contrary. The request for renewal must be presented to the Questura of residence or domicile, and in case of first renewal the applicant is required to supply evidence of economic means of support. After the first renewal, an extended residence permit normally lasts for twice as long as the original permit.

Once the residence permit expires and is not renewed, the immigrant must leave the country and hand the expired document to border officials.

Reasons for refusing or renewing a residence permit must be in writing, in a language comprehensible to the person concerned (English, French or Spanish). Either decision may be appealed, within 30 days of notification, to the Administrative Regional Tribunal (TAR).

If a decree of expulsion follows the decision to refuse, grant or renew a residence permit, and an appeal is presented within 15 days of notification, the effectiveness of the decision is automatically suspended. The applicant may remain in Italy pending the hearing. If the tribunal voids the decision, the petitioner may remain in Italy; if it does not, the petitioner must leave the country.

Non-EC nationals holding a residence permit can leave Italy and return, without the need to request a new entry visa from the Italian diplomatic office abroad, provided that he or she has obtained a specific re-entry stamp on his or her passport from the competent Questura. This does not apply, however, to holders of tourist visas.

A non-EC national who marries an Italian citizen is entitled to an unlimited residence permit after living in Italy for three years.

5. Obligations for residence permit holders

EC nationals holding residence permits are subject to the following obligations: to keep their travel documents up to date; to avoid activities not permitted by the residence permit; and to report to the Questura any change of habitual residence within 15 days (except those already in receipt of a registered residence in an Italian town, or those who move for reasons of tourism). Duties are also imposed on Italian citizens who supply lodging or accommodation, or who employ non-EC nationals, who must communicate the details of the person concerned within 24 hours to the Questura or to the mayor. Violation of this obligation is punishable with a fine.

6. Employment

Work permits are issued by the Head of Police (Questore). A specific visa is required and a certificate from the Labour Office (UPLMO) must be obtained by the employer while the prospective employee is still abroad.

Employers must explain in detail the exceptional reasons why the prospective employee is to be hired, and adequate living arrangements must also be guaranteed.

Unemployed persons on labour office lists, who meet the employers' requirements, are informed by the labour office, and have the right to be interviewed.

A labour office certificate will only be issued for board level executives, senior managers, highly skilled professionals or personnel with rare technical skills, nurses or private domestics.

Extensions can be obtained by proving that the same circumstances exist as at the time of the original application.

In general, the above dispositions apply to temporary workers.

(a) Exceptions on grounds of Italian ancestry

Former nationals who have lost Italian citizenship within five years from the date of Law No 39/90 can obtain a work permit without a specific visa. It is possible to reclaim citizenship on grounds of *ius sanguinis* (see **14** below).

(b) Employees of a branch company in Italy

It is necessary to prove that the company pays the employee in the foreign country. The length of the period of employment in Italy must be declared either for employment or self-employment. A specific inter-company transfer visa is mandatory. If the company wishes to extend employment for a further two years, it must confirm the employee's duties and the period for which the employment will last.

(c) Self-employment

For the self-employed it is mandatory to have a visa before entering Italy. Reciprocity between the foreign nationals' State and Italy, and evidence that the foreign national intends to work as a self-employed person in Italy, are essential conditions for grant of a visa.

It is necessary to obtain a licence from the local chamber of commerce and/or to be accepted by the national professional category council in order to work as a self-employed person, especially in the areas of trade, business or investment activities. Procedures for obtaining licences from the chamber of commerce or authorisation by the national professional category councils are very detailed and require the applicant to undertake a period of training and/or courses organised by the chamber of commerce.

A specific college diploma is required.

Residence permits will be granted for the purpose of attending the chamber of commerce courses if the foreign national holds a working visa.

Professionals, such as architects, lawyers, dentists, etc do not need to register with the chamber of commerce, but must meet the requirements of their professional category council in order to carry out their professions in Italy.

Work permits for physicians are now being monitored, and very few such visas are issued.

In some cases, a company might act as a sponsor.

It is possible to modify the permit of stay obtained with a work permit for employment into a permit for self-employment work or vice versa.

There are no restrictions on switching from self-employment to employment.

As regards switching from employment to self-employment, reciprocity between Italy and the country of foreign national is to be considered. In doubtful cases the Questura has discretionary authority to evaluate the case.

(d) Artists and athletes

Artists must obtain visas and certificates from the employment office (show-business department). A 90-day extension can be granted once only.

Athletes are required to supply documentation from the sport federation to which they belong. The foreign national sport federation must be recognised by the National Olympic Committee (CONI).

7. Business and foreign investment

Investment of foreign capital in Italy is governed by law, and is very welcome. In addition to complying with legal provisions concerning specific types of foreign investments, a company must register at the "Registro delle Imprese" in order to carry out business.

With some exceptions, corporations may be controlled or owned by foreign nationals and there is no limitation, in principle, on foreign nationals being directors or officers of a company, or on the amount of capital which may be subscribed to by foreign nationals.

In addition to companies which have limited and unlimited liability of their partners, there are also limited and unlimited companies.

(a) "Società per azioni"

The "Società per azioni" (Spa) has many similarities to US corporations. The company must be incorporated by public deed, and the memorandum and articles of association must be executed before a notary public and ratified by the district tribunal. The capital subscribed by the shareholders cannot be less than 200 million lira, and shares are nominal.

Incorporators are required to pay at least 30% of the subscribed capital when the company is formed. Each shareholder's liability is limited to shares subscribed by him or her unless he or she is a sole shareholder.

(b) "Società a responsabilità limitata"

The "Società a responsabilità limitata" (Srl) is very similar to the German Gmbh, and the setting-up procedure is almost identical to the Italian Spa. Shareholders have limited liability, and stock must be worth not less than 20 million lira.

A certificate of share is called a "quota", which can be negotiated through assignments in the company's books. Quota shares are not transferable.

For SRLs, a board of auditors is only required if a company's stock is worth 100 million lira or more.

(c) **Other types of companies**

Partners of the "società in accomandita per azioni" or "società in accomandita semplice" have different kinds of liabilities, which are limited or unlimited according to their investors or managing role.

There are also different kinds of companies in which partners have full and unlimited liability.

Foreign corporations must carry out their business in Italy in compliance with the provision of Italian law.

8. Tax

There are direct and indirect taxes in Italy. Examples of direct taxes are personal income tax (IRPEF), and legal entities income tax (ILOR). IRPEF is imposed on all net income deriving from any source, produced in Italy by non-residents or produced anywhere else by Italian residents.

Foreigners who stay in Italy for more than six months are obliged to pay taxes. Tax rates vary from 10% to 51%, which also applies to foreigners.

ILOR is imposed on net aggregate incomes, corporations and other private or public legal entities. IRPEG is also imposed on capital gains.

Examples of indirect taxes are value added tax, inheritance donation tax, and registration tax. There are different anti-double taxation Treaties between Italy and the majority of the world's nations. However, the Italian income tax consolidated text specifically states that "if more favourable to the taxpayer, the provisions of this Text shall be applied even though in contrast with international agreements against double taxation".

9. Families

In order for families of foreigners to enter Italy, an entry visa is required. A family residence permit will not be granted on a tourist's visa. A marriage certificate or proof of married status obtained from the consulate must be produced to the Italian authorities. After three years of effective legal residence, if a foreigner is married to an Italian citizen a residence permit will be granted for family reasons for an unlimited period. A foreign national married to an Italian is permitted to work. If he or she is married to a foreign national, he or she will be allowed to work following one year of effective residence in Italy.

(a) **Cohabitation**

A residence permit will not be normally granted on the basis of cohabitation. Only in the most exceptional circumstances can discretion be exercised in favour of a couple seeking a residence permit on cohabitation grounds. Even if a residence permit was granted, this would not permit the couple (or either of them) to apply for a work permit.

(b) Children and minors

A person's parental status must be proved by a passport or birth certificate from the competent consulate in order to register children on the residence permits of parents. A specific visa must be obtained from the Italian embassy in the resident country before children are permitted to enter Italy.

10. Retirement

A visa for "family reasons" is required. In cases where the foreign national does not hold a specific visa, the Officer has discretionary authority to evaluate the application. Pensions and means of support are taken into consideration.

11. Students

Students require a specific visa. Evidence of university enrolment, insurance and a consular statement for admission to universities are all required. If a student is attending high school rather than university, the consular statement for admission to school is not required. The consular authority will grant a study visa to applicants wishing to attend courses in State and private schools and universities, polytechnics, art academies, music conservatories, professional courses, specialist and post-graduate schools and State-operated elementary schools.

A university study visa will be granted according to the number of positions available for foreign students, which is determined by the conference of praetors of Italian universities.

12. Religion

A specific visa from an Italian consular authority abroad is mandatory. The applicant must produce a statement from the congregation to which he or she has been invited.

13. Medical treatment

If medical treatment in Italy is being sought, a statement concerning the need for therapy in Italy must be produced to the Italian consular authority.

14. Citizenship

Citizenship is granted by decree of the Minister of the Interior, upon request by the interested person to the mayor of the town of residence or the competent consular authority. The leading principles are *ius sanguinis* and *ius soli*.

Ius sanguinis provides that any child born from one parent, whether the father or mother, who is an Italian citizen, qualifies for Italian citizenship.

Adopted children automatically acquire Italian citizenship by virtue of *ius soli*, which may only be evoked in extraordinary circumstances, *i.e.* in the case of a child born of unknown or stateless parents; a child whose parents are citizens of a country which does not grant the child that citizenship; and a child who is born of unknown parents, who has been found on Italian territory and whose nationality is impossible to establish.

A foreign national who marries an Italian citizen may assume, upon application, Italian citizenship after six months if he or she resides legally in Italy, or after three years of marriage provided that the couple has not divorced or become judicially separated.

Foreign nationals or stateless persons whose parents or direct ancestors were Italian citizens can obtain citizenship in the following circumstances:

- he or she enters military service and states that he or she wishes to assume Italian citizenship;
- he or she accepts employment for the Italian Government abroad and states his or her intention to assume Italian citizenship;
- in becoming 18 he or she resides legally for at least two years in Italy and declares his or her intention within one year.

The same rights apply to foreign nationals, born in Italy and residing legally and without interruption up to the age of 18 who do not declare an intention to preserve their former citizenship. Citizenship may be denied if the applicant has been sentenced to imprisonment for felonies (Law No 91 of 5 February 1992).

Citizenship may be granted by Presidential decree on the favourable opinion of the State Council to the following persons:

- foreign nationals residing for at least three years in Italy, either of whose parents or whose direct ancestors were citizens by birth, or if the foreign national was born in Italy;
- adopted foreign nationals who have been legally resident in Italy for five years after adoption;
- foreign nationals who have been in the government service in Italy or abroad for five years;
- citizens in a Member State of the European Union who have lived in Italy for four years;

- stateless persons who have lived in Italy for at least five years;
- foreign nationals who have resided legally in Italy for 10 years.

By Presidential decree, citizenship may be granted to persons who render special services to Italy or for any other exceptional reasons in the interests of the State. Foreign nationals to whom citizenship is granted must take oath within six months of Decree before the Consular authority of the competent Italian official.

15. Refugees and political asylum

Article 10, paragraph 3 of the Italian Constitution recognises the right to political asylum for anyone not allowed to practise in his or her own country those democratic freedoms listed in the Constitution itself.

This provision is relevant for two reasons. First, it declares a right to enter Italy for the asylum seeker, and not merely a legitimate interest, which is the usual position applicable to non-EC citizens applying for entry into Italy. Secondly, the provision could, in theory, be invoked by a wider range of refugees than those covered by the definition of the Geneva Convention on the Status of Refugees (1951), as interpreted by the Member States. In particular, under the provisions contained in the Italian Constitution, it is not necessary that any persecution be specifically directed to the individual applicant (the so-called "well-founded fear of persecution"). Nor is it necessary to particularise the grounds of the persecution in terms of the Geneva Convention (*i.e.* "for reasons of race, religion, political opinion, nationality, or membership of a particular social group").

"Displaced persons" who are obliged to leave their country for reasons of war, generalised acts of violence and violations of human rights can also benefit from the right of asylum stated in article 10, paragraph 3. However, in the absence of a law executing this right and clarifying the procedures and conditions precedent to a grant of asylum, the constitutional right remains a largely theoretical one. In practice, the much stricter criteria of refugee definition contained in the Geneva Convention, ratified by the Italian State under Law No 722/54, are applied.

In 1989, refugee and asylum matters were regulated for the first time by Decree No 416/89 (Law No 39/90). However, the provisions of article 10, paragraph 3 of the Constitution have not been implemented; Law No 39/90 recites the definition of "refugee" contained in Article 1 of the Geneva Convention, and does not recognise the competence of ordinary judges of asylum cases, which would otherwise have followed from a reading of Article 10, paragraph 3, according the status of the "right" to political asylum. Law No 39/90 merely removed the existing geographic restriction of the effects of the Geneva Convention, which had previously been limited to persons coming from European countries.

Special provisions have been issued on an extraordinary basis relating to displaced persons forced to move from their countries of origin for reasons of war. For those fleeing from the territory of former Yugoslavia, who belong to an Italian national minority group, Law No 423/91 provides for an extraordinary permit to reside in Italy for one year (but renewable) and to work as an employed and self-employed person (including commercial and professional activities) which would otherwise require special registration.

Other residence permits, with a validity of three months, have been issued to those from the former Yugoslavia who do not belong to an Italian minority group. Exceptional residence permits similar to those issued to Italian minorities from the former Yugoslavia have also been issued to Somalian citizens, who have left their State because of war. However, the reaction of the Italian authorities to the significant numbers of arrivals from Albania has changed over time. During the initial phase, many extraordinary residence permits were issued. This policy has since been replaced by stricter rules, as the numbers arriving have increased.

The "humanitarian asylum" granted to the citizens of the former Yugoslavia has recently been reorganised by Decree No 350/92 (Law No 390/92) which provides for a special residence permit for reasons of work and study on a general basis, without discrimination on the grounds of religion or ethnic origin.

An Executive Directive of the President of the Council of Ministers of 14 April 1994 specifies the conditions precedent for obtaining the benefit of the new provisions. According to Law No 39/90, at the port of entry the asylum seeker must present a written and reasoned application to the border officials. If he or she is already present on Italian territory, the request for protection must be presented to the relevant Questura.

Following an interview, the border officials may refuse entry if it is evident that the person has been convicted of one of the crimes listed in article 380 of the Italian Procedural Penal Code or represents a danger to State security. In addition, border officials may refuse entry if the applicant is a member of a terrorist or Mafia-connected organisation, or is involved in the illicit traffic of drugs (art 1, para 4 of Law No 39/90).

Border officials may also refuse entry on the grounds listed in Article 1(f), subparagraph (c) of the Geneva Convention, as well as in circumstances where a State of "first asylum" has already been established, namely a country where the applicant's status as a refugee has already been recognised within the meaning of the Convention, or where the person resided for a short time, but could have asked for protection. The "country of first asylum" principle has been confirmed by the EU Member States at a supranational level, at the Dublin Convention (1990), on the State responsible for examining an asylum application and the relevant provisions of the Schengen Agreement (1990).

A decision refusing entry by border officials is open to appeal to the regional administrative tribunal, but the appeal does not suspend its effects. This means, in practice, that the applicant has no right to stay in Italy pending the hearing.

When entrance is granted, both in the case of an asylum application produced at the port of entry and at any later stage, the person concerned must subsequently appear in front of the competent Questura to record his or her application. He or she must then supply all relevant details concerning the persecution already suffered in his or her country or origin or habitual residence, or the grounds on which he or she fears to return.

Once the statements of the applicant have been recorded, the Questura will issue a residence permit valid for a period of three months (renewable), with the result that, pending the hearing, the person concerned can remain in Italy. This permit does not accord a right to work, but if the applicant does not have sufficient economic means, a request may be made for an allowance of 25,000 lira per day, granted for a maximum of 45 days according to Decree No 237/90.

After having registered at the Questura of elected domicile, the applicant is free to move to another place provided that the police are previously informed, so that they are at all times able to locate him or her, and communicate to him or her the date for the hearing of the case in front of the Central Committee.

If refugee status has been recognised, the applicant will receive a specific document certifying this decision, and on the basis of this document the Questura can issue a residence and work permit. Law No 39/90 does not specify the duration of this permit, but it should be presumed valid for two years (renewable) by analogy with the normal duration of a first residence permit for non-EC immigrants.

A negative decision by the Central Committee may be appealed to the regional administrative tribunal within 30 days of its notification.

If a decree of expulsion has been issued by the Prefect against the applicant, he or she may also appeal against this act if he or she is willing to remain in Italy pending the final hearing. However, if the asylum seeker does not appeal a negative decision of the Central Committee, or following an unsuccessful appeal to the regional administrative tribunal, a decree of expulsion will be issued against the person concerned, who must then leave the country. It must be noted, however, that the preclusion to expulsion contained in Article 6, paragraph 6, and in paragraph 10 of Law No 39/90, according to which expulsion is not permitted when the asylum seeker would be sent to a country where he or she may suffer persecution, also applies in these circumstances.

According to provisions of the Geneva Convention, refugees whose status has been recognised and, as a consequence, enjoy a right to reside in Italy, also enjoy, apart from the right to be free from persecution, all the economic, social and cultural rights to which contracting parties commit themselves. These rights include:

- rights relating to freedom of religion, social security, primary education, public and administrative assistance, access to justice, taxation, transfer of property and industrial and intellectual property;
- rights relating to employed activities and the right of association;

- rights relating to freedom of movement, housing, self-employment, and all cases not falling within the above two categories.

Refugees who have been residing in Italy for at least three years will be exempted from reciprocity clauses under Article 7 of the Geneva Convention. In addition, according to Article 28 of the Geneva Convention, the competent Questura must issue a travel document to allow the recognised refugee to leave the country and return without the need for a re-entry visa. This document also allows the refugee to travel in all the States of the Council of Europe without a visa according to the European Agreement on the Abolition of Visa for Refugees of 20 April 1959, and in all the other States with a visa. This travel document is normally considered to be valid in all the countries which have been recognised by the Italian State, with the exception of the refugee's state of origin.

Once their status has been recognised, refugees who are lawfully resident in Italy become subject to the same obligations as Italian citizens, namely to respect Italian laws and regulations and other acts issued for public order purposes.

Refugees are free to express their beliefs and to be politically active, with the single exception applicable to the national measures adopted by the State for public order purposes.

In any event, violation of these duties is governed by existing provisions concerning non-nationals in general, and a serious violation could result in expulsion of the refugee under Article 32 of the Geneva Convention.

16. Sanctions

Aiding a non-EC national to enter Italy in violation of the above provisions is punishable with imprisonment for a period up to five years and a fine of 10 million lira.

These sanctions are increased to a maximum period of 12 years and a maximum fine of 100 million lira, if the above-mentioned crime have been committed to make money, or there is complicity of at least three persons.

A fine is also imposed on carriers who do not inform the authorities of the presence of illegal immigrants on their vessels or planes. A duty is imposed on such carriers to take non-EC nationals who have been rejected at the border for not being in possession of the correct documentation back to their State of origin.

Expulsion and deportations are prescribed for illegal residence in Italy which violates the Penal Code norms and provisions relating to laws of entry and sojourn in Italy.

Studio Legale Astoli, Corso di Porta Vittoria 14, 20122 Milano.
tel.: (39) 255183100. telefax: (39) 25466743

Contents of Chapter 12

LUXEMBOURG

Chapter 12

LUXEMBOURG

Patrick Weinhacht

Introduction

The Grand-Duchy of Luxembourg is a country which has the most important proportion of foreigners on its territory compared to the rest of Europe. To this impressive number of foreigners residing in Luxembourg, there must be added the numerous cross-frontier workers who transit Luxembourg's borders each day to exercise their profession in the Grand-Duchy. This special situation of immigrating into Luxembourg began with the arrival of Italians at the beginning of the twentieth century and has continued during the whole century. As a result, Luxembourg's legislation concerning foreigners is liberal.

1. Entry and temporary residence of foreigners

The Law of 28 March 1972 applies to the:

- entry and residence of foreigners;
- medical control of foreigners;
- employment of foreign workers.

(a) General dispositions on entry and temporary residence of foreigners

(i) General dispositions concerning foreigners

Every foreigner who wants to stay more than three months in Luxembourg must inform the local authority of the place where he or she wants to stay within a period of eight days following his or her arrival. The foreigner who wants to change residence must inform the local authority of his or her new residence.

This registration concerns every foreigner living in the household, including servants.

However, for foreigners who reside less than three months in Luxembourg without wishing to carry out a profitable activity, registration in the hotel registers replaces the information of the local authority.

A foreigner above the age of 15, who wishes to stay in Luxembourg for more than 30 days, must inform the competent local authority within eight days following his or her arrival or the day he or she turns 15. He or she must apply for a foreigner's identity card.

The requirements of the arrival declaration
The person concerned must:

- present the travel documents which have allowed him or her to cross the border;
- have enough means of maintenance or a possibility to get these means in a legal manner;
- present a medical certificate;
- submit three photographs;
- give information concerning his or her person;
- present a certificate delivered by the registry office which proves the payment of a charge of LUF 1,000;
- present an extract from any criminal record. If the original country does not deliver these extracts he or she must present a certificate of integrity delivered by the competent authority of his or her last residence.

This information is provided in a form, of which five copies are produced. They are signed by the person representing the local authority and by the foreigner concerned.

Furthermore, a foreigner who wishes to reside in Luxembourg for more than three months must undertake a medical examination within the eight days following his or her arrival in Luxembourg. This medical examination is supervised by the Ministry of Health and is executed by doctors acknowledged by the Ministry of Health. The examination includes an X-ray examination of the lungs and is meant to discover contagious diseases and infirmities such as drug addiction, significant mental disorders, and obvious psychosis leading to agitation, hallucination or confusion.

If the foreigner is not an EC national and intends to have a remunerated activity he or she should not suffer from illness or physical or mental infirmity which would prohibit the exercise of his or her profession or which would present a risk of resulting in long hospitalisation.

(ii) Granting the identity card
The principle
A foreigner who has declared his or her arrival is granted an identity card valid

for five years. However, in certain circumstances the period of its validity can be shorter. The application for renewal must be made within one month following its expiration, and must be made to the authority competent to receive the declaration at arrival.

The identity card loses its validity and is withdrawn if the foreigner ceases to reside in Luxembourg for a period of at least six months.

The competent local authority must validate the identity card if the foreigner changes residence. This validation must be made within eight days following the change of residence.

Exceptions

If a foreign worker is employed by a foreign firm which must carry out a job in Luxembourg, which will be finished within one year, he or she is not obliged to apply for a foreigner's identity card. However, he or she must fill in a declaration of arrival and get a certificate from the employer which proves that he or she is working only temporarily in Luxembourg. The employee receives a copy of the certificate which will replace the temporary residence permit.

A foreigner who does not have a job in Luxembourg and who wants to stay in Luxembourg for a period of less than one year does not need to apply for a foreigner's identity card. However, this exception exists only if his or her main residence is in another country.

He or she must apply at the Ministry of Justice for a temporary residence permit, with proof that he or she is in possession of financial means securing his or her maintenance during the stay. He or she must also provide information concerning the purpose of the visit.

The identity card granted can be withdrawn or the renewal of the identity card can be refused if:

- the behaviour of the foreigner endangers public peace and order, public safety and health;
- the foreigner is no longer in possession of the means to secure his or her maintenance;
- he or she does not respect the conditions of residence imposed on him or her;
- he or she manufactures, imitates, changes or counterfeits the identity card or uses another identity card than the one delivered to him or her or gives the card to another person to use.

The foreigner must leave Luxembourg within a fixed period if permission to remain is refused, if he or she is not granted a foreigner's identity card or if the card has been withdrawn or not renewed.

The Ministry of Justice makes the expulsion order after the Government's deliberation. The order must contain the reason for the expulsion. This decision is subject to a juridical remedy which must be introduced within one month of the notification of the decision. Furthermore, a consultative committee concerning the foreigners' police has been created.

Entry and residence in Luxembourg can be refused to a foreigner who:

- is not in possession of an identity card or visa requested;

- endangers public peace and order, public safety and health by his or her behaviour;

- is not in possession of sufficient means to finance the return to his or her country of origin and stay in Luxembourg.

Furthermore, the residence permit can be refused if the foreigner:

- intends to carry out an economic activity without being in possession of the required authorisations unless an international Convention excepts him or her from these obligations;

- is prosecuted or sentenced in another country for a crime which, according to the law or international Conventions, allows the extradition;

- does not respect his or her legal obligations towards his or her family;

- has given false information concerning former residences, civil status or criminal records to the competent authorities;

- refuses to take a medical examination or who has given false information concerning his or her health to the authority charged with this examination.

(b) Exceptions to the conditions of entry concerning certain categories of foreigners subject to international conventions

(i) EC nationals

EC nationals above the age of 15 who wish to reside in Luxembourg for a period of less than three months can do so legally with the documents which have allowed them to cross the border. However, they must inform the local authority of their place of residence, and must comply with the rules which must be respected by all foreigners residing in Luxembourg.

Persons above the age of 15, who intend to live in Luxembourg for more than three months, may receive a definite authorisation by obtaining a permit of residence for EC Member State nationals.

A permit of residence granted to relatives who are not EC Member State nationals has the same validity as the permit of the EC Member State national on whom they are dependent.

The permit of residence loses its validity if its holder ceased to reside in Luxembourg for more than six months. However, an absence motivated by medical reasons, even for a period of more than six months, does not have any influence on the validity of the permit.

The permit of residence, which may be renewed automatically, is valid for five years upon the first delivery. After the first renewal, the permit is valid for 10 years.

For students, however, the residence permit has a validity limited to the duration of their studies or their professional training. Students must apply for a permit to the competent local authority, and must attach the following to the application:

- cross-border documents;

- a certificate of medical examination;

- documents proving that he or she belongs to one of the categories covered by the Regulations applying to EC nationals.

The residence permit can be refused or withdrawn only if the EC national is considered a danger to public peace, health or security. This condition is also necessary for an expulsion from Luxembourg.

These dispositions apply to EC nationals who:

- have a remunerated activity in Luxembourg;

- have a non-remunerated activity in Luxembourg;

- without intending to stay in Luxembourg offer as independent workers services defined by Article 60 of the Treaty or Rome or who want to profit from such services;

- are studying in Luxembourg;

- were exercising an activity within the European Community, remunerated or not, and who benefit from an invalidity pension, an old age pension or an early retirement, a working accident pension or a working illness pension granting them an income of an amount which is at least equal to the guaranteed minimum income;

- are not granted a residence permit by the application of other EC Regulations. In this case they have to prove that they have subscribed to an illness insurance for themselves and their family and that they have an income of an amount which is at least that equal to the guaranteed minimum income.

The present regulations are also applicable to spouses, descendants, ascendants and to EC nationals who have a remunerated job in Luxembourg but who do not have their main residence there. The last category of persons must return to their main residence every day or at least once a week.

(ii) Nationals from the Netherlands and Belgium

Belgian and Dutch nationals are allowed to cross the border with identity cards. A residence permit is granted if they are able to prove that they have means of maintenance.

Belgian nationals who have a residence permit of one of the EC Member States can only be expelled if they endanger public order or security.

(iii) Refugees and stateless persons

The Geneva Convention of 21 July 1951 concerning refugees and the New York Convention of 28 September 1954 concerning stateless persons are applied to grant or refuse these persons a foreigner's identity card. Once such a card is granted, the refugees or stateless persons can only be expelled for reasons of public order or security.

(iv) Pupils and students

There is particular legislation concerning the admission of foreign pupils and students. Hence, the conditions concerning foreigners intending to reside or to work in Luxembourg also apply to them. Students who are nationals of EC Member States are treated in the same way as EC workers.

Students must prove that they have been admitted to a school in order to follow studies or a professional training and that they receive no indemnity. In addition, they must be in possession of illness insurance.

(v) Tourists

Tourist must carry identity papers or travel documents and must fill in a form. According to the Law of 16 August 1975, whoever may lodge a person in a hotel, a house, a hostel, a boarding house, an apartment, an equipped room, on a campsite or in a youth hostel must fill in a form for every person with information about the establishment, the traveller and accompanying persons.

2. Employment of foreigners

The Law of 28 March 1972 concerning the entry and residence of foreigners and medical control also applies to the employment of foreign workers on the territory of Luxembourg.

(a) The work permit

(i) General conditions

A foreign worker can only be employed in Luxembourg as a manual or intellectual worker if he or she has obtained a work permit. Furthermore, he or she cannot change his or her employer or profession without authorisation.

Apprentices and trainees or homeworkers are assimilated to workers.

A foreign worker may only be employed if he or she has been granted a valid work permit. The employer must declare the available job at the "Office National du Travail" (National Office of Labour). This declaration, presented in duplicate and countersigned by the employer, is considered as a request for grant or renewal of a work permit.

This request must be presented before the employee begins work.

There is an exception for foreign workers employed in accordance with an international labour convention or with a previous written agreement by the National Office of Labour. The request must be presented at least three days before the employee begins work.

A certification of the declaration is delivered by the National Office of

Labour. The certification is assimilated to a provisional working permit. If the work permit is refused this provisional work permit is no longer valid.

An employer who wishes to recruit a foreign worker who has already been granted a work permit which authorises a change of employer or which authorises the worker to be employed by several employers, does not need to notify the jobs to be occupied by the new employee to the National Office of Labour.

If all these conditions are respected the foreign worker obtains one of the following working permits.

- Permit A is issued for a period of one year, and is valid for one specific profession and only one employer.
- Permit B is issued for a period of four years, and is valid for one specific profession but any employer.
- Permit C is issued for an undetermined period of time, and is valid for any profession and any employer.
- Permit D is issued to apprentices and trainees, and is valid for the duration of the apprenticeship or the training period.

The individual or collective working permit is issued only if the employer provides evidence of the existence of a bank guarantee at an agreed bank. This guarantee must cover the cost of a possible return journey of the worker for whom the work permit has been requested.

The bank guarantee is fixed by a special committee at an amount which cannot be less than LUF 60,000. The Ministry of Labour can allow an exception to this obligation or adapt the amount. This exception concerns workers who are granted a Permit C, but this is only possible if they are employed for an undetermined period without any trial period.

The granting and the renewal of the work permit can be refused to foreign workers *not* from EU Member States for reasons of situation, evolution and organisation of the labour market, in accordance with the principle of hiring EU nationals or nationals of the Member States of the European Economic Area.

The working permit may be withdrawn in the following situations:

- the foreign worker has used dishonest practices in order to have his or her work permit granted;
- he or she has given false information to the authorities in order to obtain the work permit;
- he or she has been working in a profession which is different from the profession for which the work permit was granted;
- if his or her residence permit has been withdrawn.

(ii) Exceptions

Foreigners who do not need a work permit are:

- the administrative and technical staff of embassies and consulates, at the head of which is a career agent;

- the domestic staff in the service of a diplomatic agent who is accredited in Luxembourg;

- persons occupied in tasks overstepping national limits or persons who benefit from an international charter;

- the staff of fairgrounds, circuses, theatres and other travelling establishments, on the condition that they do not stay for longer than one month in Luxembourg;

- foreign workers working temporarily for a foreign or national employer.

A collective work permit is granted at the request of the employer. The collective work permit is valid for a period of six months and only for those jobs and persons specified in the application for the permit.

Three copies of the application for a collective work permit are addressed to the National Service of Labour and include the name, Christian name, date and place of birth, civil status, nationality and profession of the workers, their residence, the nature of the job and time it will take, and the social insurance which they are affiliated with during their residence in Luxembourg.

Provisions concerning Spanish and Portuguese nationals

In principle the general regulations concerning the employment of foreigners also applied to Spanish and Portuguese nationals until the 31 December 1972, who must respect the Regulation of 12 May 1972 determining the employment of foreign workers in Luxembourg and the Regulation of the same date concerning the medical control of foreigners.

However, by derogation from the Regulation of 12 May 1972 Spanish and Portuguese workers must receive a working Permit E (for Spanish workers) or P (for Portuguese workers).

These working permits are valid for any profession and are not limited in time. However, working Permits E and P, which are issued to seasonal workers who have concluded a labour contract for a period of less than 12 months, are limited to the duration of the working relationship.

Spanish and Portuguese nationals regularly occupying a remunerated job in Luxembourg on 31 December 1995 and by virtue of a permit issued according to the above-mentioned Regulations, have the right to choose, without restriction, a job in Luxembourg from 31 January 1996. To that effect, the Ministry of Labour must deliver a special title before 1 July 1996.

The spouse and children under 21 years of age in the charge of a Spanish or Portuguese worker who has exercised a regular job in Luxembourg have a free choice of jobs and free access to employment on the condition that they have regularly resided with the worker in Luxembourg before 12 June 1995.

Spouses an children who have resided regularly in Luxembourg since 12 June 1995 must have a working permit until 31 December 1995. They have the right to a working Permit E or P after at least three years.

Au pairs

Luxembourg has ratified the European Agreement dated 24 November 1969 concerning the "placement au pair" which came into force on 1 January 1991. The initial placement au pair may not exceed one year, but can be renewed to allow a stay of a maximum of two years. A person who can be placed as an au pair must generally be at least 17 and at most 30 years old, but in exceptional cases the competent authorities of the State can allow derogations. Persons intending to be placed as au pairs must have a medical certificate established less than three months before their placement indicating their general state of health. The two parties must agree on the conditions of employment. This agreement must exist before the person has left his or her original country or at the latest during the first week of his or her arrival. The rights of the au pair are determined by article 8 of the Au Pair Agreement. The person placed as an au pair will receive housing and food from the family. This person should, if possible, be entitled to an individual room. The family must grant sufficient time to pursue linguistic studies and the au pair has the right to one free day a week, which must be a Sunday at least once a month. He or she must also be granted the right to practice his or her religion. Finally, the au pair will receive pocket money, the amount of which is provided in the original contract.

EC nationals and members of their families

Every EC national, wherever he or she resides, has the right to a remunerated activity and to exercise a job in another Member State. He or she has the same advantages as a national. He or she cannot be treated differently from nationals because of his or her nationality. He or she has the same fiscal advantages, can benefit from the education of the professional schools and the rehabilitation centre, and has the right to reside in Luxembourg with his or her spouse and descendants who have not reached the age of 21 or are dependent upon them.

The spouse and the children under 21 years of age or at the charge of an EU national having a remunerated or non-remunerated job in an EU Member State have the right to a remunerated job even if they are not EU nationals. The children of an EU national who has a job in an EU Member State can take up an apprenticeship or professional training.

(b) Commercial activities

A Law of 28 December 1988 regulates the admission to skilled, commercial and certain liberal and industrial professions.

Even if it is the case that it is not his main profession, nobody has the right to exercise any industrial, commercial or skilled profession or work as an architect, engineer, chartered accountant or consultant in intellectual property without written authorisation. Authorisation is granted by the competent minister charged with granting the right of establishment. This right is strictly personal and nobody is allowed to exercise a profession regulated by the above-mentioned law under cover of another person or an intermediary in order to evade the law.

The employment of a qualified manager must be evidenced by the employment contract specifying his or her rights and duties, working hours and the amount of remuneration which may not be less than the minimum remuneration of a qualified employee.

(i) Businessmen and women

As a professional qualification is required in every commercial profession, the person applying for the authorisation must show evidence of this qualification. If he or she is not able to do so he or she must undertake training of at least three years. The condition in which this training takes place are determined by Regulation.

A person who has no certificate of professional qualification must present an equivalent certificate acknowledged by the Minister for Economic Affairs. Persons with high school certificates or equivalent certificates must undertake training for one year. Persons with a university degree must undertake training for three months.

In the hotel business the applicant must present a degree from the State Hotel School or a certificate of his or her professional qualification or an equivalent degree. He or she must undertake training of one to three years.

A person with a certificate of professional qualification as a cook or a waiter must undertake training in hotel management for one or two years.

In the beverage sales business, the applicant must have one of the following certificates:

- a degree from the State Hotel School;
- a certificate and professional qualification in hotel business, cooking and waiting; or
- any equivalent certificate.

In the restaurant business, the same qualifications are required. The applicant must undertake a training programme of one to three years.

Owners of businesses or tourist agencies, organisers of public shows or carriers must be in possession of certificates discussed above.

(ii) Craftsmen

Craftsmen exercising their trade as their main profession and industrial building contractors must have a university degree, or a master craftsman's certificate in this branch.

An applicant who is not in possession of these certificates, but who has enough professional qualifications, can be admitted by the Ministry to all or a part of the profession.

Craftsmen who do not exercise these trades as their main profession must prove their professional qualifications by training for up to three years.

In certain professions, repairing and maintenance can be accomplished by handicapped workers, or persons in possession of a certificate of professional and technical qualification with experience of 20 years or more in the branch on acknowledgement of the competent Minister.

(iii) Independent professions

Architects

The professional qualification of architects must be a university degree or an equivalent degree delivered by a school acknowledged by the State of residence of the school after four years of successful studies.

The professional qualification of an EC national is the possession of a degree, certificate or other document prescribed by the Regulations of the European Council Nos 85384, 85614 and 86017.

Architects or construction engineers having evidenced their professional qualifications are subject to training of one year, which must take place after obtaining the degree or certificate.

Independent engineers

In order to obtain the right of establishment, an independent engineer or an engineer employed by a firm must prove his or her professional qualification by possessing a university degree or an equivalent certificate, achieved after four years of studies.

Chartered accountants

A chartered accountant must hold a certificate of qualification and have undertaken training for a period of three years. Acknowledged certificates are:

- school leaving certificate granted by a State or a university recognised by the State of his or her residence establishing his or her professional qualification as a chartered accountant;
- a university degree granted after at least three years of economic, financial or commercial studies.

Consultants in intellectual property

The professional qualification is based on:

- a certificate granted after passing the European examination of professional qualification created by Article 145 of the Munich Convention dated 5 October 1973 concerning the granting of European patents;
- a certificate of admission as a patent agent issued by an EU Member State governmental office of intellectual property;
- a degree granted by an EU Member State university specialising in intellectual property, after a period of training of 12 months;
- a university degree or equivalent granted after a complete cycle of scientific, technical or law studies of four years and training of 12 months.

Attorneys-at-law

The professional practice of giving legal opinion or drafting legal documents is reserved to attorneys-at-law. The Law of 29 April 1980, modified by the Law of 10 August 1991, regulates activities of attorneys admitted to practise in another EC Member State when such attorneys practise in Luxembourg. These activities are representation, defence in court and before public authority and other professional activities practised by the attorneys registered at the Luxembourg Bar.

Any attorney allowed to practise in another EU Member State can practise in Luxembourg without either having his or her residence there or being registered with the Luxembourg Bar.

For representation and defence in court, the foreign lawyer must be assisted by a local attorney and be introduced to the President of the Jurisdiction and to the President of the Bar.

Attorneys-at-law who are bound to a public or a private enterprise by a contact of service, cannot represent or defend their own enterprise in judicial matters.

An EU national who is in possession of a certificate proving his or her aptitude as an attorney-at-law is allowed to exercise the profession in Luxembourg, on the condition that he or she has passed a qualification examination.

Certificates must be granted by a competent authority of an EU Member State, appointed by law and regulated by the administrative regulation of that State and must provide evidence that the holder of the certificate has successfully completed at least three years of university studies at a university or similar establishment, and has successfully achieved the professional training required after studies.

The certificate must indicate that the holder is qualified as an attorney in the EU Member State. He or she must practise in this condition being realized if the professional education achieved in the European Union or if the holder has a professional experience of three years, certified by the Member State which has acknowledged the certificate delivered in a third State.

The test the EU national must take is essentially meant to verify his or her professional knowledge and ability to practise as an attorney in Luxembourg. The test consists of a written and oral examination, usually in French, although the oral test can also be carried out in German.

Economic advisers

The authorisation to work as an economic adviser, who professionally renders services in economic matters, is granted by the competent minister to persons having a university or similar degree granted after a period of at least three years in the discipline in which the services will be rendered.

Auditors

The profession of an auditor consists in the legal verification of enterprises and other organisations, as well as accomplishing all other tasks entrusted to him or her by law. He or she must not be bound to organisations by an employment contract. In order to be allowed to practise as an auditor the following conditions be fulfilled.

Natural persons must:

- be EC nationals of a State which allows Luxembourg nationals to be auditors, without any distinction between Luxembourg nationals and nationals of that State;
- have evidence of their professional qualification and respectability. The qualification is established by graduate studies of a period of at least three or four years and training of at least three years. The certificates must certify knowledge of fiscal law, Luxembourg corporate law and deontology of auditors;
- have a professional establishment in Luxembourg.

Corporate bodies, in addition to the above-mentioned conditions, must fulfill the following conditions:

- the natural person who executes legal control in the name of the juristic person must have the power to bind the juristic person;
- the majority of administrators or managers must be natural persons fulfilling the conditions above;
- the majority of voting rights of the body's shares must be owned by natural persons fulfilling the conditions above.

Physicians, dentists and veterinarians

Authorisation to exercise these professions in Luxembourg is granted by the Minister of Health following consultation with the Medical Board.

A Luxembourg national or EC national must be in possession of one of the degrees, certificates or another medical title prescribed by EC Directive 75/362 and modifying Directives, a list of which is being issued by the Minister of Health. They must fulfill the conditions of formation as decreed by EC Directive 75/363.

A Luxembourg national who is in possession of a degree, certificate or another medical title of a non-EU Member State must fulfill the conditions prescribed by the law of 18 June 1969 concerning graduate studies and recognition of diplomas.

The applicant must fulfil the conditions of respectability and morality, and of physical and mental health which are necessary to exercise the profession.

Exceptionally, the Medical Board can give a temporary authorisation to a qualified EC national to practise in Luxembourg in order to deputise an established physician.

Rendering of services

Administrative authorisation is not necessary for EC nationals who are not established in Luxembourg but who occasionally come to the country in order to render their services to commercial or independent professions.

Skilled workmen and manufacturers, however, must prove to the competent minister that they are legally authorised to pursue their profession in their State of establishment.

Non-EU nationals, stateless persons and persons without a determined nationality who are not established in Luxembourg, but who occasionally come to Luxembourg to collect purchase orders or to render services, must apply for an authorisation.

3. Citizenship and nationality

Matters of citizenship and nationality are governed by the Law of 22 February 1968 which was modified in 1975, 1977 and 1986 (Loi sur la nationalité Luxembourgeoise, and hereinafter referred to as the "Nationality law").

By virtue of article 1 of this Law, the following persons are considered to be natives of Luxembourg.

- A child who is born in a foreign country from a progenitor of Luxemburgish nationality, if the descent of the child is established before the age of 18 years, and if the progenitor is a Luxembourg national at the moment of the establishment of the descent.

  If the judgment establishing the descent is pronounced only after the death of the father or the mother, the child will be a native of Luxembourg if the progenitor had Luxemburgish nationality at death.

- A child who is born in Luxembourg and whose parents are legally unknown. A child who is found on the Luxembourg territory is presumed to be born in Luxembourg in the absence of evidence of the contrary.

- A child who was born in Luxembourg and who has no other nationality.

According to article 2 of the Nationality Law, the following persons will acquire Luxembourg nationality.

- A child who was adopted by a Luxembourg national by way of a plenary adoption (adoption plénière).

- A child who has not yet reached the age of 18 and who has been adopted by a Luxembourg national by way of a simple adoption (adoption simple), if this child is either stateless or has lost his or her original nationality as a result of this adoption.

- A child who has not yet reached the age of 18 and whose progenitor or adopter voluntarily acquired or recovers Luxembourg nationality.

(a) Naturalisation

The process of naturalistion must be introduced by a written request addressed to the Minister of Justice, who then deliberates with the city council of the foreigner's residence in Luxembourg (arts 9 and 10 of the Nationality Law).

After this, the request will be submitted to Parliament which will have to grant the naturalisation by law (art 13). The foreigner must then accept this naturalisation by a declaration to the civil status officer (art 15).

The naturalisation will be effective four days after the publication of the notice indicating the date of its acceptance in the Official Gazette (*Memorial*), (art 18). Different conditions must, however, be fulfilled by the person in order to benefit from the naturalisation process such as determined by article 6 of the Nationality Law. Specifically, the subject must:

- have reached the age of 18;

- have resided in Luxembourg for at least 10 years, the last five years of which must have been without interruption. The compulsory residence period of 10 years can be reduced to five years in the following situations:
  - if the applicant is stateless;
  - if the applicant was born on Luxembourg territory;
  - if the applicant is a widow or widower of an original Luxembourg national with whom he or she has one or several living children and of whom at least one is established in Luxembourg;
  - if the applicant is a divorced spouse of an original Luxembourg national with whom he or she has one or several living children whose custody has been attributed to him or her and at least one of whom is residing in Luxembourg;
  - if the applicant is a stateless person unless the loss of his or her anterior nationality is the result of his or her express request or the request of his or her legal representative;
  - if the applicant is a refugee recognised as such by virtue of the Geneva Convention on Refugees of 28 July 1951.

Naturalisation can also be granted without satisfying the condition of residence if the applicant has rendered special services to the state of Luxembourg.

The Law of 11 December 1986 modifying the Nationality Law introduced a particular provision in case of marriage. If the applicant is married to a person who fulfils the above-mentioned conditions and who also requests naturalisation, he or she must have his or her residence on Luxembourg territory for three years, and must live in community with his spouse. The condition of age does not have to be fulfilled (art 8 of the Nationality Law).

(b) Option

The process of option (choice) is introduced by a declaration of option to the Minister of Justice who must grant his approval after deliberation with the city council of the foreigner's residence (art 23 of the Nationality Law). The declaration of option comes into effect four days after its publication in the Official Gazette (art 24 of the Nationality Law).

The possibility of a declaration of option exists only in the following situations, listed in article 19 of the Nationality Law:

(1) a child born in Luxembourg from a foreign progenitor;
(2) a child born in a foreign country from a Luxembourg national progenitor;
(3) a foreigner whose spouse is either a Luxembourg national, or who acquires or recovers Luxemburgish nationality;
(4) a child born in a foreign country from a foreign progenitor who has accomplished his or her entire compulsory scholarship in Luxembourg;
(5) a child having been adopted by way of a simple adoption (adoption simple) by a Luxembourg national and who has not lost his or her nationality at the moment of the adoption;
(6) a foreigner having reached the age of 18 and whose progenitor acquires or receives Luxembourg nationality.

By virtue of article 20 of the Nationality Law a person who finds himself or herself in one of the situations (1), (2) or (5), must have been residing in Luxembourg for an uninterrupted period of five years, as well as during the year prior to depositing his or her declaration of option. This declaration must be made between the age of 18 and 25.

The admission of the option in case of situation (3) above depends upon the following double condition; the subject must have been resident in Luxembourg for at least three years, and must live in community with his or her spouse (art 21).

Moreover, the declaration of option can be rejected in different cases listed in article 22 of the Nationality Law, as modified by a Law of 26 June 1975; for example, if the subject does not prove, by way of certificates delivered by the competent authorities, that he or she has lost his or her original nationality or that he or she will automatically lose it by acquiring another nationality (in conformity with the Convention on the reduction of the cases of plurality of nationalities dated 6 May 1963 which came into force on 1 January 1991). Furthermore, the option is refused if the person cannot justify a sufficient adoption.

Particular attention must be paid to the provision concerning married women. Luxembourg has signed and ratified the Convention on the nationality of married women (2 February 1957) which came into force on 1 January 1991. This Convention provides that neither the concluding nor the dissolution of a marriage between a Luxembourg national and a foreigner, nor the change of nationality by the husband during the marriage, can have any effect on the nationality of the wife (art 1 of the Convention).

(c) Technical certificate

A car registered in Luxembourg must pass a technical control.

The check-up at first registration is valid for three years. After three years, this check-up must be carried out once a year.

(d) Insurance

Every car registered and circulating in Luxembourg must be covered by a liability insurance.

(e) Local taxes

Local taxes concerning renting are limited to electricity, gas, television, water and sewage.

(f) Bank facilities

Every foreigner, whether or not established in Luxembourg, can open an bank account in Luxembourg.

4. Conclusion: the National Council for Foreigners

A Law of 27 July 1993 concerning the integration of foreigners in Luxembourg and the social action in favour of foreigners has introduced the National Council for Foreigners.

The National Council for Foreigners is an advisory organ charged to examine, at the request of the Government or at its own initiative, all problems concerning foreigners and their integration in Luxembourg. It gives its opinion on all bills and draft statutory orders relating to the Governments policy on foreigners. It can present to the Government every proposition it considers useful for the improvement of the situation of foreigners.

A Regulation of 29 March 1995 determines:

- the manner in which the representatives at the Council are distributed between the different nationalities;
- which associations can put up candidates;
- the conditions to be fulfilled in order to be a candidate, which are
    - not to be a Luxembourger;
    - to be at least 21 years of age;
    - to be established in Luxembourg;
    - not to be under guardianship.

THE NETHERLANDS

Chapter 13

THE NETHERLANDS

Ted Badoux

1. Country characteristics and general principles

(a) Country characteristics

The Netherlands, commonly known as Holland, is a small and densely populated country. It is situated along the North Sea coast, north of Belgium and west of Germany.

The total area is about 25,000 square kilometres. From Groningen in the north to Maastricht in the south is a distance of 330 kilometres; from Haarlem near the coast to Arnhem at the German border the distance is approximately 190 kilometres.

Over one-third of the country is below sea level; which is why the French call the Netherlands "les Pays Bas".

Holland has a sea climate; the weather is mild and changeable. The country has substantial natural resources; natural gas and oil are commercially exploited both on land and in the North Sea.

The present population is around 15.4 million; 45% of the population live in the western region called "the Randstad". The Randstad is situated between Amsterdam, Utrecht, Rotterdam and The Hague. It is considered to offer the best infrastructure for business establishment. Rotterdam has one of the largest ports in the world.

The working population numbered 6.5 million in 1994; unemployment was at 8.8%.

Holland is a heavily industrialised country. Besides this, it is rich in tradition, culture and fine arts.

The monetary unit is the guilder. The average exchange rate in 1994 was approximately US$1 = f1.70.

The inflation rate in 1994 was 2.8% The GNP (gross national product) for 1994 was f599 billion; the economic growth rate was 2%.

In 1994 the total population earned some ƒ1.797 billion; about 45% was spent on taxes and social security premiums.

The current account balance for 1994 had a surplus of ƒ16.4 billion.

The Netherlands is a constitutional monarchy; since 1980 the sovereign has been Queen Beatrix.

The political system is a parliamentary democracy. Elections in 1994 resulted in a Government of Social Democrats and Liberals for a term of four years, excluding the Christian Democrats from public office for the first time since the end of the Second World War.

Together with Belgium and Luxembourg, the Netherlands is part of the Benelux Economic Union. In 1957 the Benelux entered into the European Economic Community. Today the Netherlands is one of the Member States of the European Community. Since 1994 the countries of the European Community and the European Free Trade Association (except Switzerland) form a European Economic Area (EEA). The following European countries are members: Austria, Belgium, Denmark, Finland, France, Germany, Greece, Iceland, Ireland, Italy, Liechtenstein, Luxembourg, the Netherlands, Norway, Portugal, Spain, Sweden and the United Kingdom. For the purpose of this chapter nationals of these countries are referred to as EEA nationals. They have the right to move freely within the EEA to pursue economic activities and can take up permanent residence for that purpose in any of those countries. They may also stay for study or retirement if proof of sufficient means of subsistence is provided. Non-EEA nationals obtain a dependent status if they have family ties with an EEA national who takes up residence in a European country other than his or her own.

(b) General principles: the Dutch Government's attitude towards immigration and naturalisation

Since the Second World War, migration to the Netherlands has led to the establishment of ethnic minorities, growing at present to over two million. The main groups are Antilleans, Surinammers, Turks and Moroccans, 44% of which are living in the main cities: Amsterdam, Rotterdam, The Hague and Utrecht. Most have become Dutch citizens. Some 780,000 however, are still "aliens": anyone not having Dutch nationality is considered to be an alien under the Dutch Aliens Act 1965. Due to the ever-increasing numbers of asylum seekers at the time, this Act has been thoroughly revised and tightened up by a Bill which entered into force on 1 January 1994. The term "immigrant", being a person who is seeking a new home country for permanent residence, is not used in Dutch aliens law. The Dutch Aliens Act 1965 provides a system of permits for temporary and permanent stay, whereby continued lawful stay on the basis of a temporary residence permit for a period of five years may lead to the obtainment of a permanent residence permit. Immigrants therefore may very well have a temporary residence status. The word "visitor" is used in this chapter in connection with the word "immigrant". An immigrant is any person seeking a new home country for permanent residence; a visitor is regarded as a person seeking temporary stay or residence for a specific purpose.

Surinam nationals enjoyed preferential treatment for some years pursuant to a bilateral agreement which was concluded in connection with Surinam's independence in 1975. Nowadays, the implications of this agreement have diminished considerably. Apart from the admission of elderly members of the family, medical treatment and naturalisation, Surinam nationals are treated in the same way as other aliens.

Recently, it has been reported that, due to migration, the population in the Netherlands has increased more rapidly than had been anticipated. The migration surplus in 1993 was approximately 55,000. However, a sharp decline of the migration surplus was observed in the first half of 1995.

The official policy towards minorities is to promote social integration and to prevent and oppose discrimination, and ethnical and racial hatred. In spite of governmental efforts, high rates of unemployment, scanty knowledge of the Dutch language, poor schooling and the threat of ghetto-formation in the main cities are problems characterising the inferior position of ethnic minorities in the Netherlands today.

Concerns about overpopulation and the critical position of ethnic minorities provide the basis of the Government's attitude toward immigration. As a result, the opportunities for the admission of aliens are limited.

Immigration policies are restrictive in character: aliens, *i.e.* non-nationals, are admitted to the Netherlands pursuant to international obligations or essential Dutch interests, or on humanitarian grounds in cases of severe hardship. In general, policy requirements for admission relate to travel documents, financial means, housing and the public peace. A criminal record will be an impediment to entry or admission. Public peace issues related to immigration are not dealt with in this chapter.

International obligations with a considerable impact on Dutch immigration policies result from the EC and EEA Treaties and the Regulations and Directives of the European Community.

Essential Dutch interests may be economic or cultural. For the discretion as to what is to be considered to serve such interests the Dutch ministry concerned must be consulted. In general, aliens who wish to take up residence to pursue business activities have to overcome protective policies with regard to the Dutch and the European market. Humanitarian grounds are implemented for the admission of asylum seekers, for family reunion, family visitors and so on. Personal relations with persons living in the Netherlands and the inhospitability or absence of a home country may be considered as general humanitarian factors.

From these premises it is obvious that there are no fixed quotas, either by law or by policy, as to the maximum numbers of admissible aliens in the Netherlands.

Policies with regard to naturalisation are relatively generous. Socially integrated aliens, who have become permanent residents and master the basics of Dutch language, can obtain Dutch citizenship by a simple application procedure, which can take up to two years due to the current high numbers of applications. A Bill replacing the Dutch Citizenship Act is currently delayed on account of opposition in Parliament to the proposed concept of double nationality.

2. Employment and inter-company transfers

(a) Visa requirements; entry clearance

A visa is an entry in a passport or other travel document made by an official of a government to indicate that the bearer has been granted authority to enter or re-enter the country concerned.

As immigrants clearly intend to stay in the Netherlands for more than three months, they would generally need to obtain an entry clearance called "machtiging tot voorlopig verblijf" (authorisation of provisional stay). This special visa is an authorisation to enter and apply for a residence permit for a specific purpose.

The "machtiging tot voorlopig verblijf" should be applied for at the Dutch embassy or consulate in the country where the applicant lives or resides. In case of application for reunion with family, spouse or an unmarried "live in" relation, the parent, spouse or "live in" partner in the Netherlands may also see the local immigration police. The visa is issued upon authorisation of the Visa Service, which is a division of the Immigration and Naturalisation Service of the Ministry of Justice, acting on behalf of the Ministry of Foreign Affairs, which is the formal issuing authority of all visas. Legal duties are f81 for each visa sticker.

Most applications are sent to the immigration police for consultation and advice. The processing of a "machtiging tot voorlopig verblijf" generally takes three to five months.

Nationals of the following countries are exempt from the obligation to obtain an entry clearance: Canada, Iceland, Japan, Liechtenstein, Monaco, New Zealand, Norway, Switzerland, the United States and all EC Member States, including Austria, Finland and Sweden, which have been EC Member States since 1 January 1995.

(b) Submitting a residence permit application

Immigrants who apply for a residence permit in the Netherlands at the office of the immigration police in the municipality where they have or intend to take up residence, are generally – with exceptions for such reasons as public peace etc – permitted to stay pending the decision upon their application.

As a rule, applications for a residence permit which are made after unauthorised (*i.e.* illegal) entry are rejected. However, jurisprudence has forced the administration to grant a residence permit in spite of non-compliance with visa formalities if it can be said that all requirements for admission have been met by the time the application of the residence permit is actually made. On account of this jurisprudence, which has recently been brought before the Dutch Supreme Court by the State for a final test, the impact of this visa instrument on restrictive policies has weakened considerably.

(c) Document

A residence permit takes the form of a plastic identity card with a passport photograph in colour. Legal duties for the handling of an application are ƒ235 per person and ƒ50 for minors under the age of 12.

(d) Employment and inter-company transfers

(i) Employers granted work permits

Work permits are issued on the basis of the Aliens Employment Act of 21 December 1994 (Wet Arbeid Vreemdelingen). The issuing authority is the Central Board for the Provision of Labour (CBA: Centraal Bestuur voor de Arbeidsvoorziening) in Rijswijk, which exercises powers delegated by the Department of Social Affairs and Employment. The new Act, which has only been operational since 1 September 1995, replaces the Aliens Employees Act 1978 and imposes further restrictions on employment by aliens. The Dutch Government felt that the need for a new Act was actuated by the growth of the labour market on account of the expansion of the European Community with new Member States and the creation of an European Economic Area of EC and EFTA countries, by the ongoing high unemployment rates and by increased labour migration.

The objectives of the Aliens Employment Act are:

- the restrictive admission of migrant workers;
- the improvement of the allocation of jobs on the labour market;
- to fight illegal employment;
- to warrant freedom of employment to legally residing foreign employees.

(ii) Connection residence permit/work permit

All aliens, not being EEA nationals, who intend to take employment in the Netherlands for more than three months, must obtain a residence permit which qualifies for work. This permit will not be granted until a work permit has been issued. Basically, a work permit is an employer's permit: it authorises the holder to employ a person from outside the EEA to do the job for which the permit was granted, but only if, and as long as, this person is holding a valid residence permit authorised for taking employment. Work permits will be refused for those who are no longer in possession of a valid residence permit. However, pending the application of a residence permit one can apply for a work permit. For temporary workers, seasonal workers and working holiday-makers, who are short-term visitors with the clear intention to work for no more than three months, a visa (if required) or a stamp as proof of registration with the local immigration police would be sufficient to be admissible for application for a work permit. It should be noted, however, that work permits for temporary work will only be granted in case of full compliance with the legal requirements as to reporting vacancies and in case of proven shortage of candidates within the EEA who would be both suitable and available.

(iii) Employer; employee

A work permit must be applied for by the prospective employer. In the context of the Aliens Employment Act an employer would be any person or corporate body, wherever domiciled or established, who in the practise of an office, profession, business or trade intends to employ an alien to do a job on Dutch territory. It includes paid employment as well as the paid provision of services by, *e.g.*, consultants. It also implies, that a new work permit would be necessary in case of a new employer and/or a new job.

The Aliens Employment Act (the New Act) also includes individuals employing people for household or other personal services. Work permits will not, however, be granted for any work involving sexual services.

(iv) Work permit application

Work permits and the extension of work permits are applied for at the local employment bureau (Regionaal Bureau Arbeidsvoorziening). Applications for artists, musicians, professional sportsmen and women and applications for professional sports trainers should be sent to the Central Board for the Provision of Labour (CBA: Centraal Bestuur voor de Arbeidsvoorziening) in Rijswijk.

The legal requirement is to decide on an application within five weeks; in practice the processing of a work permit may take four to six weeks.

The permit states the names of the employer and the employee and defines the employment for which it has been granted. For a new position a new work permit is required.

(v) Work permit term

In general a work permit is granted for the duration of the contract, which can be any number of days up to a maximum of three years. Those who for three consecutive years have had a residence permit qualified for work, become exempt. Under the new Act, work permits can be granted with binding instructions, for instance with regard to future recruitment, internal training facilities or improvement of employment conditions. These permits have a maximum validity of one year. Renewal or new permits can be refused if such instructions are not carried out.

For temporary (seasonal) work, permits are issued up to a maximum of 24 weeks. These permits cannot be extended and are for migrant workers only, *i.e.* those who come and go with the season.

(vi) Assessment; general requirements

The main criterion for granting a work permit is that the prospective employment by a new immigrant will not injure the interests of the registered Dutch workforce. Employers have to show that they cannot fill the vacancy with a Dutch or EEA national, or a legally established immigrant. The vacancy should be offered on conditions of employment which are normal for the line of business concerned. Under the new Act, failing to do this will result in refusal of the work permit. The new Act also denies work permits to new immigrants in jobs below minimum wage level.

Candidates referred to a company by the employment bureau should not be turned down without good reason. Registered job-seekers who would qualify after additional training with the company or with an official training programme, are also considered to have priority.

Furthermore, employers are supposed to have some awareness of the various avenues for filling vacancies outside the recruitment circuit of the employment bureau. Employers might consider training candidates within the company, recruiting temporary staff or contracting the work out to a specialist company in the Netherlands. Upon submitting a work permit application, an employer may be asked to demonstrate that the vacancy was tried out, not only through the employment bureau but also through other appropriate channels.

The vacancy should be notified to the employment bureau five weeks prior to the application. In principle, any vacation should be tried out, not only locally or in the region, but nationwide and in the EEA territory. To facilitate recruitment within the EEA the vacancy can be reported to the European Employment Service (EURES), which is an automatised network of consultants within the employment bureau organisation for recruitment within the EEA. For recruitment in the EEA through EURES a vacancy would have to be reported at least eight weeks before the projected start of the employment. Furthermore, EURES renders its services only for contracts with a minimum duration of six weeks at 38 working hours per week, with wages at branch level and housing and travelling expenses paid. Under the new Act, lack of vacancy notification five weeks prior to the application of the work permit, is imperative for refusal. In addition, recently published policy rules state that a term of three months must be observed for vacancies which are notoriously difficult to fill.

For new immigrants the age requirements for work permits are that the immigrant must be between 18 and 45 for both skilled and unskilled labour. Exceptions can be made for positions, *e.g.* professorships, which are usually taken by elderly persons.

Finally, housing should be available and adequate according to local standards.

(vii) Special categories

Specific policy rules apply for the categories mentioned hereunder.

Inter-company transfers

Companies abroad have to apply for work permits if they intend to have their employees working in the Netherlands. This also applies in cases of inter-company transfers, involving employees who are being moved from a position with a parent or sister company abroad to a position with a parent or sister company in the Netherlands. In the latter case the Dutch company would be obliged to apply for work permits. Policy rules limit the issue of work permits for inter-company transfers to so-called key personnel, *i.e.* senior managers or personnel with specific technical skills which are essential for the company (but rare) in the Netherlands, provided they have already been employed by the company abroad in a similar function for one year. For the benefit of international trade, EEA workforce priority will not be considered in such cases.

Within the EEA territory inter-company transfers of non-EEA staff, which can be considered as key personnel, are warranted by Article 54, section 3 f of the EC Treaty. In such cases work permit applications can only serve purposes of administrative control.

New business activities

Work permit applications for employment resulting from new business activities – *e.g.* starting a subsidiary company or opening a branch office – should be presented with a professionally drawn-up business plan showing the economic feasibility of the new business development.

Employee-shareholder

Having a shareholding in the company of less than 25% does not exempt the employee from the requirement to hold a work permit. Through a shareholding of 25% or more the employee would qualify as being self-employed. In those cases the employee would have to apply for a residence permit for taking self-employment. However, it is important to note in this context that a work permit would be required for employment beyond the scope of the self-employed activities for which the residence permit has been issued.

Actors, artists, musicians and models

Actors, artists, musicians and models who are contracted to perform in the Netherlands also need work permits, even for single performances or a brief tour up to a maximum of four weeks. Applications for theatre and concert hall performances other than accompaniment will be granted in the interest of international cultural exchange; in most cases these permits are granted easily, provided the rewards match market and minimum wage levels.

However, applications in connection with long-term tours and work for national theatre productions will be considered for EEA workforce opportunities, especially if the regular term for human resource planning is more than five weeks. The same applies for shows and performances in the catering industry (restaurants, etc) and for regular employment with a Dutch theatre company or orchestra. The employment bureau will give special consideration to young EEA artists and musicians.

Professional sport

Work permits are not required for incidental participation in sporting games or tournaments not exceeding a term of four weeks. For regular employment in the sports sector (*e.g.* soccer, baseball, basketball, volleyball) work permits are required. Policies, however, are restrictive, and aimed at protecting the EEA workforce. In this connection special consideration is given to amateur sportsmen and women in the EEA pursuing a professional status. As a rule, work permits for professional sport will be refused:

- for employment out of the highest division of the respective sports federation;
- if the financial rewards, taking into account the value of usual transfer fees, are not in line with the market demands;
- if the player concerned cannot demonstrate to have competed thus far at a level equal to the highest division of the respective Dutch sports federation;
- if, except for calamities, the application is filed after the start of the season.

Catering industry

Command of a foreign language cannot be a valid reason for hiring kitchen personnel out of the EEA workforce. Work permits for kitchen and serving staff in Chinese restaurants, pizzerias, grillrooms, coffeeshops, diners etc are refused in favour of registered unskilled job-seekers. Work permit applications for cooks in speciality restaurants will be turned down if EEA candidates would qualify after completion of a short training period, or if the available staff is capable of preparing the speciality dishes as well. Speciality cooks must produce certified diplomas and references proving professional skills which match the level of chefs in the Dutch catering industry.

Special training facilities are available for Chinese and Indonesian speciality cooks; eventual recruitment out of the EEA is carried out exclusively through official channels.

The permitted number of employees in the kitchen of a speciality restaurant is measured by its annual turnover: one employee for every *f* 250,000.

International transport (freight by air, road or water transport)

A work permit is not required if the vacancy cannot be tied to the Netherlands, either through the Dutch domicile of the employee, the Dutch establishment of the company, or through the Dutch registration of the airplane, truck or vessel. In all other cases, work permits are mandatory, even if only part of the driving takes places on on Dutch territory.

Activities related to the exchange of goods

Work permits are granted without notification of the vacancy and without search for local or EEA candidates if it can be shown that the total labour value, in terms of Dutch standard wages, will not exceed the value of the supplied goods. The goods should have been manufactured in the home country of the workers, who should have been employed by the supplier for more than one year previously.

(viii) Illegal employment

An employer who illegally employs a non-EEA national commits an economic offence, punishable with a maximum prison sentence of six months and a maximum fine of ƒ10,000 (ƒ25,000 for corporate bodies) for each offence. In practice the fine is between ƒ2,000 and ƒ5,000 per illegal employee. However, in most cases illegal employment will also be punishable as a criminal offence under the Dutch Criminal Code, which may result in a maximum prison sentence of one year or a maximum fine of ƒ100,000.

Furthermore, the new Act grants the illegal employee an action at law against his employer based on the legal presumption that he or she can lawfully claim regular wages over a maximum period of six months. The employer can also be taxed for this fictitious term: it will be up to the employer to prove that the taxed term of employment should, in fact, be shorter.

Enforcement is carried out by the local police force and the officials of the Labour Inspection Service (Dienst Inspectie Arbeidsverhoudingen: DIA).

The residence permit of an alien who is working without the required work permit can be withdrawn.

(ix) Permit-free employment

The following categories are worth mentioning.

Most legal immigrants are exempted from the work permit requirement as follows:

- EEA nationals who have come to the Netherlands to take employment, including their dependants (spouses, children and other dependent members of the family even if they are non-EEA nationals). EEA nationals carry an E-type residence permit; their non-EEA dependants carry a D-type residence permit with a note at the back that the holder is free to take employment;

- holders of a Convention refugee status or a residence permit by way of asylum, who carry a B-type residence permit;

- holders of a permanent residence permit, who carry an A-type residence permit;

- holders of a dependent residence permit on account of marriage, family life or an unmarried relation with a Dutch national or with a legal immigrant who is free to take employment. These people carry a D-type residence permit;

- those who have had a residence permit qualified for employment for three consecutive years, who carry a D-type residence permit;

- those who have had a conditional residence permit (*i.e.* asylum seekers) for two continuous years, who carry a F3-type residence permit.

All permits mentioned above have a note at the back stating that the holder is free to take employment.

Holders of a residence permit qualified for self-employment do not need work permits. However, for other employment a work permit would be mandatory.

Furthermore, work permits are not required for:

- those who are neither living nor employed in the Netherlands but who work in the Netherlands incidentally or for a maximum period of four weeks, on behalf of a foreign employer or principal, notably: repair and maintenance mechanics, business persons, prop-men for exhibitions, journalists, performers of fine art, household staff of tourists, and sportsmen and women participating in sports events;

- professional drivers of foreign registered vehicles, who are neither living nor employed in the Netherlands;

- foreign seamen on Dutch-registered sea-going vessels who are not living in the Netherlands (foreign seamen who have been working on Dutch ships or drilling platforms for seven years consecutively, who have a good record and who have a job offer ashore, are eligible for a residence permit without reference to the Dutch labour market);

- foreign correspondents despached in the Netherlands for foreign news media.

3. Business and profession

(a) General principles

The policies on the admission of business persons and professionals are neither extensive nor detailed, and jurisprudence on the subject is not abundant. However, in the mid-1990s we see, as part of the ever-increasing globalisation of the world's economy, the merging of a vast and harmonised European market attracting many non-European companies and business professionals, who want to have a stronghold in the European area. In many cases the Netherlands is chosen as the best option because of its location, logistics, infrastructure and tax facilities for investment.

The key requirement is that the intended activities of the applicant in the Netherlands will serve essential Dutch economic interests. Innovative and other added value for the Dutch economy are decisive factors in this respect. Of course the other requirement would be that the applicant will earn a sufficient income in this way.

It is difficult to say which activities may be "essential" in this context and which may not. Many related factors may be relevant, for example the qualifications, expertise and experience of the applicant, the expected profit, the number of Dutch nationals or legal aliens to be employed, the amount of the investment and the extent to which there will be competition with settled business in the Netherlands.

Applications for an entry clearance or a residence permit must be accompanied by a business plan and satisfactory documentation giving details of the expected future turnover and profit. Furthermore, it must be explained why it would be necessary for the applicant to have to reside in the Netherlands rather than to stay temporarily on the basis of a business visa. Applicants over 60 years of age will be rejected.

The exploitation of restaurants and the like is licensed and conditional on professional qualifications. The same applies to most branches of the retail trade, but in some cases exemptions are granted. Professionals such as doctors, pharmacists and craftsmen must have qualifications which match the Dutch standards.

All applications are decided upon by the Immigration and Naturalisation Service of the Ministry of Justice acting upon the advice of the Ministry of Economic Affairs

(b) Special categories

(i) Self-employed writers, artists and musicians

Writers, artists and musicians may obtain a residence permit if their intended activities in the Netherlands can be considered to serve essential Dutch cultural or artistic interests. In many cases it is difficult to predict whether or not someone will meet this requirement; the Aliens Department decides after consultation with the Ministry of Culture. A certain amount of international recognition and support from art experts is helpful. Foreign pictorial artists are not excluded from receiving government grants and subsidies. Strangely enough, these grants are not considered as income for the obtainment or extension of a residence permit.

(ii) American entrepreneurs and traders

The purpose of the American-Dutch Friendship Treaty of 27 March 1956 is to facilitate trade and shipping between the two nations. On account of this Treaty and its Protocol, US citizens can obtain a residence permit in the Netherlands for self-employment related to trade purposes or the conduct of business for which they have or intend to make a considerable investment.

The restrictions of "trade purposes" and "the conduct of business" seem to exclude professionals.

For a one-man business, a partnership, firm or a private limited company policy rules state that an investment of ƒ10,000 is acceptable as a minimum capital. For a limited liability company the minimum investment would need to be ƒ25,000, which is 25% of the legal minimum paid-up capital. The money must come from private capital and not from a loan. The business must be registered in the Commercial Register. Applications must be served with audited financial documentation.

(iii) Foreign seamen

Foreign seamen who have been working on Dutch ships or drilling platforms for seven years consecutively, who have a good record and are still under 60 years of age, are eligible for a residence permit in case of self-employment ashore, without reference to Dutch economic interests.

(iv) Inhibited economic activities

As of January 1994 the Aliens Circular contains a list of self-employment activities for which residence permits will no longer be granted, as follows

Asian restaurants

The number of Asian restaurants in any given municipality has been limited as follows:

- 1:12,500 inhabitants for Chinese and Indonesian restaurants. For tourist areas the number of inhabitants is slightly smaller;
- 1:20,000 inhabitants for other Asian restaurants.

Applications which do not match these limits are not submitted to the Ministry of Economic Affairs for an advisory report, but are rejected immediately.

Other activities in the catering industry

Applications for grillrooms, shoarma and coffeeshops, pizzerias and the like are not submitted to the Ministry of Economic Affairs for an advisory report, but are rejected immediately.

Other economic activities

Applications for Islamic (Halal) butchery businesses, Turkish and Moroccan bakeries and the like, for workshops for ready-made clothing, textile and general trade are not submitted to the Ministry of Economic Affairs for an advisory report, but are rejected immediately.

(c) Formalities

For visa requirements, entry clearance, submitting a residence permit application, document and legal duties, see **2(a)–(c)** above.

4. Persons of independent means/investors

The purchase of real estate (land, houses, industrial complexes), making investments (industrial development, restaurants, shops) or buying shares in domestic companies are not in themselves grounds for granting residence permits. The one exception may be conduct of business by US citizens who have made a considerable investment or intend to do so, as mentioned in Article II of the American-Dutch Friendship Treaty of 27 March 1956 (see **3(b)(ii)** above).

Taking up residence on the basis of investments or for the purpose of retirement is restricted by the "Dutch essential interests" requirement: applicants must show a need for their presence in the public interest. In each case it will be considered whether some essential Dutch interest would require the applicant to stay in the Netherlands for a longer period than would be possible on the basis of a visitors or business visa. This may be particularly difficult for investors who would only want to be involved financially and therefore act through an agent or proxy.

Retirement, to live on one's private means, will only very rarely be considered to serve essential Dutch interests and will generally not constitute compelling humanitarian grounds for granting a residence permit. For policies on the admission of elderly people as a form of extended family reunion, see **5(a)** below.

In the case of US citizens the policies on admission for retirement seem occasionally to be less strict, perhaps on account of the American-Dutch Friendship Treaty, but much depends on the particulars of the application.

(a) Formalities

For visa requirements, entry clearance, submitting a residence permit application, document and legal duties, see **2(a)–(c)** above.

5. Family and private life

Family life is protected both by national and international law. Article 10 of the Dutch Constitution protects everybody's private life, of which family life may well be a part. Article 8 of the European Convention on the Protection of Human Rights (ECHR) and Article 23 of the International Covenant on Civil and Political Rights explicitly protect family life.

Jurisprudence has made Article 8 of the ECHR a cornerstone of Dutch aliens law. Paragraph 1 of Article 8 grants everybody the elementary human right to family life. Paragraph 2 explicitly stipulates non-interference with this right by any public authority "except such as is in accordance with the law and is necessary in a democratic society in the interests of national security, public safety or the economic well-being of the country, for the prevention of disorder or crime, for the protection of health or morals, or the protection of the rights and freedoms of others".

The elements of this clause are frequently used by the Department of Justice for refusing family life applications and turning down petitions for administrative review.

In 1985 the European Court of Justice in Strasburg ruled that family life comprises a relation based on a lawful and sincere marriage, notwithstanding the fact that the spouses are not yet living together. On 2 June 1988 the court ruled in the *Berrehab* (ECHR 21.06.88 Publ. Court A 138) case that the relation of a divorced Moroccan father and his daughter, who were in contact with each other four times a week for a couple of hours, constituted family life notwithstanding the fact that they were not actually living together as members of one family.

Therefore, the criterion appears to be that the alien involved is keeping actual family ties rather than family ties in strict terms of family law. In Dutch jurisprudence several factors are taken into account: the age of the children, the frequency, duration and character of the contacts, whether these contacts have been judicially endorsed, whether the foreign parent supports his or her children financially and, if so, to what demonstrable extent.

There is no interference with family life if the family member(s) in the Netherlands can reasonably be expected to accompany the alien abroad.

The answer to the question whether an infringement of family life is justifiable, results from an evaluation of both the public interest and the interest which the persons involved may have in maintaining and continuing their family life in the Netherlands. Generally speaking, in cases of first admission the national interests of the State with regard to the economic well-being will outweigh the individual interests.

As of 17 September 1993 stricter policy rules on admissions for family or private life are administered. These new rules concern stricter income requirements for Dutch nationals, permanent residents and Convention refugees. Family Reunion should be completed within 3 years once the requirements for admission have been met. Those who have been admitted for family reunion cannot apply themselves for family formation within the first 3 years of their residence in the Netherlands.

Admissions on the basis of family or private life are of three kinds:

(1) family reunion:
- regular;
- partial;
- extended;
(2) family formation:
- getting married;
- taking a foreign foster-child;
(3) unmarried "live in" relationships.

Unmarried "live in" relationships are listed in the Dutch Aliens Circular as a separate category. The European Court has stated that heterosexual relationships are protected by Article 8 of the ECHR as a form of family life, but homosexual relationships are not. However, any "live in" relationship can be considered as a form of private life.

(a) Family reunion

Applications for family reunion must be made within three years once the requirements as regards income and housing have been met. Applications which have been made too late will be turned down for that reason other than in cases of severe hardship. By way of temporary provision children born on or after 1 September 1978 or before 1 September 1981 are exempt.

Holders of a residence permit who intend to be joined by their spouse and children must have sufficient and durable financial means and adequate housing. "Sufficient means" is a net income equal to the social benefit standard for a married couple pursuant to the General Social Security Act (f1,803.16 monthly as at 1 January 1995). Durable income is income which will be earned for at least another year.

Housing should be adequate in the opinion of the municipal housing authorities, *i.e.* acceptable for Dutch families in similar circumstances. Standards can be found in municipal bylaws on buildings.

Dutch nationals, permanent residents and Convention refugees must comply with stricter financial requirements for family reunion since September 1993, but they are still in a better position in comparison with regular residence permit holders. There are two age categories. First, those between 18 and 23 years of age have sufficient income for family reunion:

- in case of gainful employment at least 32 hours per week irrespective of the revenues;
- in case of gainful employment resulting in at least 70% of the net minimum of the social benefit standard for a married couple pursuant to the General Social Security Act (f1803.16 monthly as at 1 January 1995).

Secondly, those of 23 years of age and above have sufficient income for family reunion:

- in case of gainful employment resulting in at least 70% of the net minimum of the social benefit standard for a married couple pursuant to the General Social Security Act (f1803.16 monthly as at 1 January 1995);
- in case of unemployment benefits pursuant to the Unemployment Insurance Act (Werkloosheidswet: WW), which implies an employment record of at least three years during the last five years immediately before the unemployment and a minimum amount of 52 working days per year during that period;
- in case of unemployment benefits pursuant to the Governmental Regulation for Unemployment Benefits (Rijksgroepsregeling voor Werkloze Werknemers: RWW). Qualification for family reunion on the basis of these un employment benefits implies an employment record above the age of 18 of three-fifths of a person's residence in the Netherlands.

Dutch nationals, permanent residents and Convention refugees are exempt from income requirements in the following cases:

- if they are unemployed and 57.5 years of age or over;
- if – in the case of family formation – the application concerns a one-parent family with one child or more children under the age of six;

- if they are permanently disabled for employment and receive benefits pursuant to the General Disability Act (Algemene Arbeidsongeschiktheidswet: AAW) or pursuant to the Disability Insurance Act (Wet op de Arbeidsongeschikheidsverzekering: WAO), eventually with supplementary payments pursuant to the General Social Security Act;

- if they receive benefits pursuant to the General Retirement Pension Act (Algemene Ouderdomswet: AOW), eventually with supplementary payments pursuant to the General Social Security Act.

Dutch nationals and Convention refugees are also exempt from the adequate housing requirement.

"Regular family reunion" is defined as admission on the basis of a marriage which already existed at the time when both spouses were still abroad. It concerns the spouse and children under 18, who are de facto living in the family. Whether children were born in or out of wedlock is irrelevant.

Jurisprudence has accepted that children may have been raised in a family structure different from the regular Western pattern. However, family life is restricted to one spouse and the children born from that relationship. In case of polygamy, the alien must make a choice. A man having an unmarried "live in" relation in the Netherlands cannot be joined by his legal spouse and children.

If one of the children reaches the age of 18 while the head of the family is still awaiting adequate housing, this child will qualify nevertheless if he or she is under 23, not married, was part of the family in the homeland, is dependent on the head of the family and has arrived with the other members of the family whilst the head of the family was registered with the local housing department as a house-hunter by the time he became 18.

"Partial family reunion" with the spouse and/or some of the children, is possible if all requirements for reunion of the whole family have been met. However, the risk for those who may come later is evident. The Immigration and Naturalisation Department may take the view that actual family ties have ceased to exist in the meantime.

Arriving later on account of military service in the homeland will be accepted if the applicant was under 18 at the time the other family members arrived, and who applies to enter the Netherlands within six months after termination of his or her service. The same term applies for the re-admission of those who have to leave their family to perform military services in the homeland.

"Extended family reunion" concerns members of the family other than spouse and children. The requirements are that they were actually part of the family in the homeland, that they are both financially and morally dependent on the head of the family and that it would be disproportionally hard to leave them behind. The Dutch Aliens Circular states in this respect needy parents (in law) and unmarried daughters of age. Student families are not eligible for extended family reunion. Jurisprudence has allowed divorced women who are socially isolated to join their former family in cases of severe hardship.

In November 1991 criteria for the admission of elderly parents and grandparents were published. Applicants of 65 and over may be admitted if:

- they are socially isolated in their homeland;
- (practically) all children live in the Netherlands and are permanent residents or Dutch citizens;
- the children, either one or all together, have sufficient means to keep their parents;
- adequate housing is available: the parents should live with or in the vicinity of the child(ren);
- they do not pose a risk to the public peace.

(b) Family formation

A delay of three years has been introduced for family formation applications (*i.e.* admission on the basis of marriage) of those who were admitted for family reunion after 16 September 1993.

In cases of marriage to residence permit holders the criteria for admission on sufficient means and adequate housing are the same as for regular family re-union. In cases of marriage to Dutch nationals, permanent residents or Convention refugees, the same mitigated requirements as mentioned above are applicable.

The spouses may have been married abroad or in the Netherlands, but in all cases the marriage should be valid according to the rules of Dutch international family law. The spouses should be registered and live at the same address, and should share a common household or, when taking up residence, show the intention to do so.

On 1 November 1994 a Bill opposing sham marriages came into force. The rules pursuant to this Bill concern Dutch weddings involving non-nationals and the Dutch registration of foreign weddings involving non-nationals. A marriage is considered a sham marriage if obtainment of a residence permit would be its sole purpose. The intended foreign spouse is referred to the immigration police department for the issue of a certificate containing personal details, immigrant status and the department's opinion on the eventual sham nature of the intended marriage. The department is obliged to send the certificate to the registrar of marriages; only the registrar can decide not to register the marriage and refuse to perform the wedding ceremony. Official grounds for refusal to register or marry a couple would be insufficient documentation or conflict with public order. Finally, in the interest of public order the Public Prosecutor is authorised to oppose a marriage or demand its nullification.

Fostering a foreign child can be done in two ways. First, there are admissions of foster-children with the explicit intention of adoption according to the rules and procedures of Dutch family law. If a (not necessarily Dutch) couple has satisfied all requirements laid down in the Act on the Adoption of Foreign Foster-Children, admission will be granted. Following adoption the child will automatically become a Dutch citizen if one of the foster-parents is Dutch. Secondly, there are admissions of foreign children who will not be adopted, but who are taken into the family by next of kin because of their parent's inability to care for them. Less prosperous living conditions as such do not constitute "inability"'

(c) Unmarried "live in" relationships

The nature of the relationship, heterosexual or homosexual, is irrelevant. The partner already living in the Netherlands must be either Dutch or an EC national, a permanent resident or a Convention refugee. The specific criteria are as follows. The partners should have a lasting relationship, *i.e.* live together and share a common household. Both partners should be unmarried and have reached the age of 18. The partner of the applicant should have sufficient means to take full financial responsibility for the cost of living and the eventual return of the applicant to the homeland. Finally, housing should be adequate. For unmarried "live in" relationships there is also a maximum term of three years for application once compliance with all requirements has been achieved and a three-year wait for those who were admitted for family reunion themselves.

(d) Formalities

For visa requirements, entry clearance, submitting a residence permit application, document and legal duties, see **2(a)–(c)** above.

6. Temporary stays: visitors, students and temporary workers

(a) Visa requirements for temporary stays up to a maximum of three months

In general, visas are required for short-term stays up to a maximum of three months under article 8 of the Aliens Act. A visa is an entry in a passport or other travel document made by an official of a government to indicate that the bearer has been granted authority to enter or re-enter the country concerned. As of 26 March 1995 the provisions of the Schengen Agreements of 1985 and 1990 have been implemented within the following Schengen States: Belgium, France, Germany, Luxembourg, the Netherlands, Portugal and Spain.

In view of the achievement of a Single European Market whereby the internal European borders have been abolished, the above-mentioned countries have agreed on a common system of controls at the external borders of their territories. The Schengen provisions attend, amongst other things, to a common policy on visas and an uniform visa for the Schengen territory. Travellers who need visas for one or more Schengen States must travel with a "Schengen visa" which is issued by any one of the seven States and is valid for all others.

Travel between these countries will, in principle, be without documentation check at immigration controls, except if travelling to France, where a full document check is performed again from 27 July 1995.

Schengen visas should be obtained prior to arrival in the Schengen territory. Those who wish to travel to the Netherlands can apply for a Schengen visa at the Dutch embassy or consulate abroad. Visa applications may be dealt with at the diplomatic post or may be sent for investigation and instructions to the Visa Service (Visadienst), a division of the Ministry of Justice, acting on behalf of the Ministry of Foreign Affairs in The Hague.

As a consequence of this, visa applications can take anything from a few hours to a few months to process. Schengen visas are issued for a stay up to a maximum of three months. In general, for the issue of a Schengen visa a valid passport or other permitted travel document is required, as well as sufficient funds to finance the intended period of stay and the return journey. In general, Dutch immigration officers will consider ƒ75 per person per day as sufficient means. Furthermore, one should not be registered as an alien, excluded from entry, or pose a risk to public peace, national security or international relations of any of the seven Schengen States. The validity of the visa is linked to the validity of the passport and the return ticket.

A Schengen visa is no guarantee that admission will be granted; the requirements for a Schengen visa, *i.e.* to hold a valid passport and to have sufficient financial means and so on, may be checked upon entry at the border. Possession of a valid return ticket is recommended.

A Schengen visa can be annulled or not extended if a visitor fails to comply with any of the above-mentioned requirements. Holders of a Schengen visa can freely travel between the Schengen States as long as their visas are valid and up to a maximum of three months, counting from the first day of arrival in the Schengen territory. Upon entering one of the other Schengen States, there is a duty to report to the immigration authorities either upon arrival or within three working days from the date of arrival.

A list of countries whose nationals do not require a Schengen visa for short-term stay in one of the Schengen States is set out in the Appendix at the end of this book.

Those who are exempt from the obligation to hold a Schengen visa can travel freely between the Schengen States up to a maximum of three months within a six-month period, counting from the first day of arrival in the Schengen territory.

Upon entering one of the other Schengen States, there is a duty to report to the immigration authorities either upon arrival or within three working days from the date of arrival.

Those in possession of a residence permit or other valid title or permitted long-term stay have a right to enter the Netherlands at all times. They have the right to travel freely between the other Schengen States up to a maximum of three months as long as they have a valid title of permitted long-term stay, possess a valid passport or other permitted travel document and have sufficient funds to finance the intended period of stay and the return journey. Furthermore, they should not pose a risk to public peace, national security or international relations of any of the other Schengen States. Upon entering one of the other Schengen States, they have a duty to report to the immigration authorities either upon arrival or within three working days from the date of arrival.

Those who need to visit the Netherlands frequently for business purposes can obtain a so-called Schengen business visa. This Schengen visa grants multiple entry to the Schengen territory for an uninterrupted stay of a certain amount of days, up to three months within a six-month period. In cases of specific national interest, visas can be granted up to six months within a 12-month period. In exceptional cases visas can even be granted for multiple entry within a period of one to five years. Upon entering one of the other Schengen States, there is a duty to report to the immigration authorities either upon arrival or within three working days from the date of arrival.

The list of charges for visas, *i.e.* legal duties, is detailed. The charge for a one-month Schengen visa for single or multiple entry is currently *f*70. For a three-month Schengen visa *f*86 is charged.

Nationals of the 18 countries of the European Economic Area (EEA) are exempt from Schengen visa requirements under EC law.

(b) Temporary stays exceeding three months; entry clearance

A special visa, called "machtiging tot voorlopig vervlijf" (authorisation of pro-visional stay or entry clearance) is required for temporary stays exceeding three months. It authorises an alien to enter the Netherlands and apply for a residence permit.

An entry clearance should be applied for at the Dutch embassy or consulate in the country where the applicant lives or resides, be it only temporary. The visa is issued upon authorisation of the Visa Service, which is a division of the Immigration and Naturalisation Service of the Ministry of Justice, acting on behalf of the Ministry of Foreign Affairs, which is the formal issuing authority of all visas. Legal duties are *f*81 for each visa sticker.

Most applications are sent to the local immigration police for consultation and advice. The processing of a "machtiging tot voorlopig vervlijf" generally takes three to five months.

Nationals of the following countries are exempt from the obligation to obtain an entry clearance: Canada, Iceland, Japan, Liechtenstein, Monaco, New Zealand, Norway, Switzerland, the United States and all EC Member States, including Austria, Finland and Sweden, which have been EC Member States since 1 January 1995.

Those who apply for a residence permit in the Netherlands at the office of the local immigration police of the municipality where they have resided or intend to take up residence, are generally – with exceptions for such reasons as a threat to public order etc – permitted to stay pending the decision upon their application.

As a rule, applications for a residence permit which are made after unauthor-ised entry, *i.e.* without entry clearance, are rejected. However, jurisprudence has forced the administration to grant a residence permit in spite of non-compliance with visa formalities if it can be said that all requirements for admission have been met by the time the application for the residence permit is actually made. On account of this jurisprudence, the impact of this visa instrument on restrictive policies has been weakened considerably.

(c) Formalities

For submitting a residence permit application, document and legal duties, see 2(a)–(c) above.

(d) Tourists and family visitors

For a tourist or family visit which lasts no longer than three months, a valid passport is required and sufficient funds to finance the intended period of stay and the cost of the return journey.

Immigration officers check funds and return tickets carefully. Visitors, or their guarantors, may be required to deposit funds with the immigration authorities. These funds are returned upon departure.

Problems may be avoided by showing a letter of invitation from a relative or a friend who is willing to act as guarantor for the cost of the intended period of stay and the return journey. It is also advisable to be in possession of a return ticket.

Those entering on a visa are instructed to report to the local immigration police within three days; those exempted from visa obligations also have to report within three days. However, those staying in a hotel are exempt from reporting, as are EEA nationals.

For the application of a Schengen visa, see 6(a) above.

(e) Business visitors

Visitors for business purposes, *i.e.* self-employed persons such as traders and investors, may be admitted for a maximum period of three months for transacting business during their visit.

However, as the occasion arises, they should make clear that the business intended cannot be considered as seeking self-employment with the intention of taking up residence, *i.e.* for a stay of more than three months.

Business persons who have been admitted as short-term stay visitors but who have changed their minds later on and clearly intend to take up residence (*e.g.* by renting an office and registering their business with the Chamber of Commerce) should report to the local immigration police within eight days and apply for a residence permit.

Requirements and policies for admission are set out at 3 above.

(f) Temporary workers

All aliens, not being EEA nationals, who intend to take employment in the Netherlands for more than three months, must obtain a residence permit which qualifies for work. This permit will not be granted until a work permit has been issued. Basically, a work permit is an employer's permit: it authorises the holder to employ a person from outside the EEA to do the job for which it was granted, but only if, and as long as, this person holds a valid residence permit authorised for taking employment. Work permits will be refused for those who are no longer in possession of a valid residence permit. However, pending the application of a residence permit one can apply for a work permit. For temporary workers and seasonal workers, who are short-term visitors with the clear intention to work for no more than three months, a visa (if required) or a passport stamp as proof of registration with the local immigration police would be sufficient to be admissible for application of a work permit.

It should be noted, however, that work permits for temporary work will only be granted in case of full compliance with the legal requirements as to reporting vacancies and in case of proven shortages of candidates within the EEA, who would be both suitable and available (EEA labour force test). The following categories of persons who are neither living nor employed in the Netherlands can be admitted without a work permit to work on a job or a project up to a maximum of four weeks, on behalf of a foreign employer or principal: repair and maintenance mechanics, business persons, prop-men for exhibitions, journalists, performers of fine art, household staff of tourists and sportsmen participating in sports events.

For those who come to the Netherlands in order to practise for the benefit of an intended job in their home country, can obtain work permits up to a maximum of 24 weeks without a vacancy report or EEA labour force test. These practitioners should have had sufficient basic training in their home country, and their employment in the Netherlands should be based on a practice programme agreed between the Dutch company and the company in their home country.

Actors, artists, musicians and models who are contracted to perform in the Netherlands also need work permits, even for single performances or a brief tour up to a maximum of four weeks. Applications for theatre and concert hall performances other than accompaniment will be granted in the interest of international cultural exchange; in most cases these permits are granted easily, provided the rewards match market and minimum wage level.

However, applications in connection with long-term tours and work for national theatre productions will be considered for EEA workforce opportunities, especially if the regular term for human resource planning is more than five weeks. The same applies to shows and performances in restaurants and the like and for regular employment with a Dutch theatre company or orchestra. The employment bureau will give special consideration to young EEA artists and musicians.

(g) Students

For studies up to three months, foreign students must comply with the same requirements as other foreign visitors; they need a valid passport, sufficient funds and, depending on their nationality, a visa.

For studies which take more than three months a foreign student must:

- produce proof of preliminary registration at a university, college or educational institution;
- sign a statement that he or she is aware of the fact that admission has been granted for purposes of study only; and
- have both durable and sufficient funds to finance the cost of the intended study and the cost of living. "Durable" means covering the cost of the year's course, and "sufficient" means matching the monthly budgets, which are allocated twice a year for public scholarships. An adequate bank balance in the name of or in favour of the student will be acceptable. Periodical payments must be secure; in case of doubt it is mandatory that a third party gives a guarantee. Budgets are made up of the cost of living, books and educational appliances, tuition fees and medical insurance. In comparison with students who are living on their own, students who are still living with their parents are assessed on smaller budgets for the cost of living. In recent years, jurisprudence has decided in several cases that foreign students boarded with close relatives must be treated as students living with their parents.

Long-term admission for studies is only granted for full-time educational courses.

Studies at a university or polytechnical college (third degree) can also be intended for employment.

For studies at secondary level and vocational courses the Netherlands should be "the most suitable country". This criterion is vague, but means that the intended study or course should not be available in the student's home country. Furthermore, the intended study or course should enable the student to contribute to the development of his home country. For preparatory studies (*e.g.* language) a residence permit can be obtained up to a maximum of one year. It should be noted that the period of one year for preparatory studies is not counted from the date of application but from the date of entry.

Foreign students holding a residence permit for the purpose of study are not permitted to take employment unless the work can be regarded as practice, and a work permit – if needed – has been granted. However, under the Aliens Employment Act new policy rules have been introduced which make exceptions to this strict exclusion. Work permits can be granted without a vacancy report or EEA labour force priority test:

- for seasonal work by foreign students in June, July and August; and
- for part-time employment up to a maximum of 10 hours per week.

Rewards should match market and minimum wage level. On application for a work permit, a written statement of the student's educational institution must be produced, confirming the student's registration and assuring that the intended employment cannot be expected to jeopardise the progress of his or her studies.

For foreign students who come to the Netherlands to do practise necessary for completion of educational course work, permits up to a maximum of one year can be obtained without a vacancy report, EEA labour market test or minimum wage requirement. They should have had sufficient basic training in their home country, and it should be the last year of their course or the penultimate year. They should submit a written statement of their institute confirming the need to do practise and setting out the practice programme.

A foreign student can be accompanied by his or her spouse and children, who will receive a dependant residence permit. Sufficient funds according to the financial requirements for family reunion should be available. The same also applies to adequate housing. Dutch students, refugee students or students holding a permanent residence permit who apply for admission of a spouse and children must comply with the same conditions and requirements as foreign students.

Permission to stay will cease upon completion or termination of studies or if the study is considered to have taken too long.

(h) Scholars and scientific researchers

As for all aliens in general, the criteria for the admission of foreign scholars depend on the duration and the purpose of the intended stay. Visiting lecturers, for example, may be admitted for a maximum period of three months under the conditions and restrictions of article 8 of the Aliens Act, much like business visitors. For a stay of over three months they would need to apply for a residence permit.

Under the provisions of the new Aliens Employment Act scholars and scientific researchers are no longer exempted from the work permit requirement. Scholars who have come to the Netherlands as visiting lecturers at a Dutch institution for academic education (university etc) need work permits. However, for lecturing up to a maximum of one year, work permits will be granted without a vacancy report or EEA labour force test. A vacancy report and EEA labour force test can also be deleted from the work permit application requirements for assistants and researchers in training at a university institute. The same applies to post-doctorate students who are invited to conduct specific research in an ongoing project for a maximum period of two years and, finally, for highly qualified researchers who are temporarily assigned to research projects on the recommendation of the Royal Academy of Sciences.

As mentioned previously for temporary workers (see **6(f)** above), to be admissible for application of a work permit, scholars who are short-term visitors with the clear intention to work for no longer than three months, would only need a visa (if required) or a passport stamp as proof of registration with the local immigration police.

(i) Au pairs

Residence as an au pair serves a cultural purpose. Young people are given the opportunity to stay with a host family in the Netherlands and gain an introduction to Dutch society in this way. Light household work and child care by an au pair are admissible and exempted from the work permit requirement, but only in as far as these activities are not and do not become the main purpose of the au pair's stay with the family.

An au pair:

- is between the ages of 18 and 26;
- did not enjoy legal residence in the Netherlands previously;
- must sign a statement that he or she is aware of the fact that admission has been granted for au pair purposes only;
- must sign a statement that he or she has no criminal record;
- will be admitted for a maximum period of one year, but can switch to another host family within this year.

The head of the host family must sign a guarantor statement for the cost of living and return to the home country of the au pair. Health insurance is obligatory.

(j) International youth exchange programs

These programs also serve the cultural purpose of gaining an introduction to Dutch society. As the participants are actively involved in some sort of work, work permits are required. Permits for a maximum period of 24 weeks will be granted without a vacancy report, EEA labour force test or minimum wage requirement. For participants of the Netherlands-Australian Working Holiday Scheme and the Canadian-Netherlands Youth Exchange Programme, work permits can be issued under the same conditions up to a maximum of one year.

7. Permanent residence and nationality

(a) Permanent residence

An alien may be entitled to a permanent residence permit after five years' lawful residence in the Netherlands, from the age of eight. The immigration police are instructed to properly inform any alien, who may be entitled to a permanent residence permit, about his or her rights in this respect.

(i) Residence

To have a residence in the Netherlands means to be actually and more or less permanently living in the Netherlands. This may be proven by registration in the population register of a Dutch municipality or by demonstrating that a certain address is frequented regularly. An alien is also considered to have his or her residence in the Netherlands if he or she has a residence permit for employment entirely or partly abroad. If an alien takes up residence abroad, his or her (permanent) residence permit will be withdrawn. Temporary absence on account of military service or detention abroad will not be considered as residence abroad if the alien returns to the Netherlands within six months after dismissal. However, convictions abroad can lead to withdrawal of a (permanent) residence permit.

Periods of temporary absence abroad for a family visit, studies etc will not affect residence, but a (permanent) residence permit will be withdrawn after voluntary absence from the Netherlands for more than nine months within a period of one year. In these cases, it is up to the alien to prove that his or her absence was involuntary.

Timely notification to the immigration police that an intention to stay abroad for not more than nine months is advisable. However, if an alien stays abroad for at least six months yearly, at the beginning of the third year he or she will be considered to have transferred the main part of his or her social activities abroad and will no longer be considered a resident of the Netherlands unless he or she provides evidence to the contrary.

(ii) Option to return

There is no such thing in Dutch aliens law as a right of former immigrants to return once they have given up lawful residence (no matter how long) and have returned to their country of origin. Only rarely, in cases of extreme hardship, is re-admission granted. Inability to adapt in the home country and unquestionably strong ties with Dutch society, especially if there is still family connections, are factors of importance in this respect.

However, the policy rules grant a limited option to return to two groups of former young immigrants who were raised in the Netherlands:

- those who have had lawful residence for at least 10 years between four and 19 years of age and apply for re-admission before the age of 23;
- those who have had lawful residence for at least five years before the age of 19 and apply because they feel that the Netherlands is the most suitable country for them on account of their strong ties with Dutch society.

Factors to be considered are: the reasons for departure, the term of previous residence, their education and employment record and their command of the Dutch language.

In case of re-admission an unrestricted residence permit will be granted to minors and a permanent residence permit to those of age; there are no financial requirements.

(iii) "Lawful"

Within this context "lawful" means "holding a residence permit or a family member status".

(iv) Requirements

The requirements for permanent residence are that the applicant has both sufficient and durable financial means and that he or she poses no serious threat to national security or to public peace.

Sufficient financial means is a net income equal to the minimum income benefit pursuant to the standards of the General Social Security Act: ƒ1,262.21 monthly for single persons over 23 and ƒ1,803.16 monthly for couples over 21 as of 1 January 1995. The Disablement Insurance Act benefits based on full-time employment and an incapacitation percentage of 55 or more, are also considered as sufficient financial means. Financial means must be durable. For this criterion the applicant's job and social benefits record are taken into account. Jobs which started less then one year previously and offer no prospect of lasting for at least a further year are not durable. Unemployment benefits which will last for at least a further three years are considered durable.

Aliens admitted for temporary purposes such as study or medical treatment will generally not qualify for a permanent residence permit, because they will not be able to demonstrate durable income.

Aliens who have been residing lawfully in the Netherlands for five years consecutively and who are living in wedlock or in an unmarried "live in" relationship with a Dutch national or legal alien who is earning a standard family income according to the General Social Security Act are exempted from the financial means criterion. This policy has been adopted in the interest of foreign women who have no job and are living at home.

Second generation aliens, born in the Netherlands or admitted for family life with at least one Dutch parent, are entitled to an unrestricted residence permit and to a permanent residence permit without financial requirements when they become 18 and if they have stayed lawfully in the Netherlands for at least five years.

Lawfully residing aliens who qualified for a permanent residence permit in the past, will also be granted a permit without further financial requirements.

After 10 years of lawful residence any applicant will be exempted from the financial means criterion.

Financial factors cannot lead to withdrawal of a permanent residence permit.

Only a non-suspended prison sentence of more than two years will be an impediment to granting a permanent residence permit. Such penalty would be sufficient ground to withdraw a residence permit and declare the person an undesirable alien.

(v) Document

A permanent residence permit takes the form of a plastic identity card with a passport photograph in colour. Legal duties for the handling of an application are ƒ500.

(b) Dutch nationality

Article 2 of the Dutch Constitution states that the law will determine who is a Dutch citizen. This constitutional order has been carried out in the Dutch Citizenship Act for the Kingdom of 1985 (Rijkswet op het Nederlanderschap). The Dutch Kingdom consists of the Netherlands, the Dutch Antilles and Aruba.

Dutch citizenship may be acquired (a) by descent, (b) by choice (option) and (c) by naturalisation.

(i) Descent

A child of a Dutch father or mother is Dutch by birth. A child who does not have a Dutch parent but who has a Dutch grandmother who was living in the Netherlands at the time the child's parent was born, is also Dutch by birth, provided the parent was living in the Netherlands when the child was born. In those cases, the country of birth of the child is in no way relevant.

(ii) Choice (option)

This option is open to aliens between 18 and 25 who have been living in the Netherlands since they were born, and is obtained by deposition of a simple statement of option at the local town hall, Dutch embassy or consulate.

Women who lost Dutch nationality by marriage before 1 January 1985 can reclaim it by deposition of a statement of option within one year of their divorce or the death of their spouse.

(iii) Naturalisation

Dutch citizenship is granted at the discretion of the Minister of Justice, whose powers to this extent are exercised by the Immigration and Naturalisation Service. Decisions are taken on the basis of the Guidelines for Naturalisation which are published by the Ministry. The decision to grant Dutch citizenship is given in the form of a Royal Decree. An application for Dutch citizenship takes the form of a written petition and documentation in accordance with prescribed rules. As of 1 January 1996, applications must be served in person at the town hall of the applicant's hometown. Legal duties for the processing of an application are ƒ500. The same amount is due for simultaneous applications for a married couple or a couple in a "live in" relationship.

Dutch citizenship will be granted if the applicant has met the following requirements:

- the applicant should be 18 years of age or over;
- there should be no objection to permanent residence in the Netherlands or in the Dutch Antilles; this will generally imply that one should have a permanent residence permit or a residence permit, with the exception of residence permits qualified for temporary purposes only, *e.g.* for study, medical treatment or a long-term family visit;
- the applicant should have lived permanently in the Kingdom (the Netherlands, the Dutch Antilles and Aruba) for a period of five years

immediately prior to the application. The following categories of person are exempted from this requirement:

– former Dutch citizens, such as Surinam nationals who are not required to have lived in the Kingdom for any specific term;

– partners of Dutch spouses or those in an unmarried "live in" relationship with a Dutch national, are required to have lived in the Kingdom for a period of three years instead of five;

• the applicant should have assimilated with Dutch society, which means that he or she should have an acceptable command of the Dutch language and have adapted to Dutch society. There is ample jurisprudence on the language criterion. As of 1 June 1996 a mandatory test on language and civics will be part of the procedure:

• the applicant should pose no danger to public peace or public security. This requirement should be interpreted in accordance with the jurisprudence of the EC Court of Justice which has held that measures taken on the grounds of public policy or public security should be based exclusively on the personal conduct of the individual concerned. A criminal conviction can be taken into account only in so far as the circumstances which gave rise to the conviction are evidence of personal conduct constituting a present threat to the requirements of public policy. Personal conduct constituting a present threat to Dutch public peace should be based on a irrevocable conviction to an unconditional prison sentence on account of a criminal offence. In naturalisation cases any prison sentence, penal labour or fine of f1,000 or more pursuant to an irrevocable conviction on account of a criminal offence within four years from the date of application, would be relevant for eventual refusal. A recent criminal record with regard to drunken driving or other serious traffic offences, for example, can be an impediment to naturalisation pending the probation term.

Until 1992 it was required that a person should have taken all necessary steps to renounce his or her former nationality, unless this was unreasonable (*e.g.* nationals from Greece, Morocco, Tunisia, Iran and East European countries have no legal possibility to renounce their nationality). This policy, adopted in the interest of preventing dual nationality, has been abandoned; under Dutch law it is now possible to have dual nationality. Whether an applicant would lose his or her original nationality by naturalisation in the Netherlands would depend on the national law of his or her country of origin. Children under the age of 18 participate in the naturalisation of either one of their parents. By submitting a statement of abduction Dutch citizens of age can lose Dutch nationality, provided they will still have another effective nationality. Children over the age of 12 are permitted to express their opinion on the petition for naturalisation of their parent(s). As a rule, children living abroad are excluded.

(iv) New Dutch Citizenship Act

A new Dutch Citizenship Act is expected to be enacted in the course of 1996. One of the main changes will concern the five-year domicile requirement.

Under the new Act the five-year period must have been lawful, *i.e.* covered by a lawful title of residence. Furthermore, the possibilities of obtaining Dutch citizenship by option will be widened. The issue of dual nationality is currently still in parliamentary debate.

8. Refugees and political asylum

Dutch policies distinguish between invited refugees and other refugees. Invited refugees are recognised as such by the Dutch Government; they are transferred to the Netherlands on behalf of the Government, in most cases upon the request of the United Nations High Commissioner for Refugees (UNHCR). The number of cases is small and fixed yearly.

Article 15 of the Aliens Act defines a refugee as a person with a well-founded fear of persecution because of religious or political convictions, nationality or as a result of belonging to a certain race or social group. This concept is identical to the one defined in Article 1 A(2) of the Convention Relating to the Status of Refugees: the Refugee Convention of Geneva (1951). Article 33 of the Convention embodies the principle of non-refoulement i.e. the obligation of nations not to effectively send back refugees back to their countries of origin has direct effect in Dutch aliens law: those who claim to be refugees will not be refused entry and will not be deported unless by special leave of the Minister of Justice. Asylum seekers and Convention refugees are protected by this principle. Asylum applications are decided by the Immigration and Naturalisation Service (Immigratie- en Naturalisatiedienst) which is a largely independent agency of the Ministry of Justice staffed with governmental public servants.

In 1994, 52,576 asylum applications were registered.

(a) The asylum application procedure

The procedure, which has been operational since 1992, is designed to bring about an important acceleration in the processing of asylum applications. The main features of this procedure are:

- to refuse entry to and detain asylum seekers reporting at any port of entry at the border;
- to differentiate at an early stage between likely and prospectless asylum applications;
- to grant limited possibilities for legal remedy to those who have been refused and to restrict their freedom of movement until their actual – if necessary forced – departure from the country.

(i) Submitting an application
An asylum seeker is not required to present himself or herself at the port of entry. Immigration officers are obliged to give information about the Dutch asylum application procedure to any alien indicating that upon refusal of entry to or expulsion from the Netherlands he or she would be forced to return to a

country where he or she has a well-founded fear of persecution. There is no precise rule in Dutch law as to the form by which an asylum application should be made. However, to start the official asylum determination procedure an application should be lodged in writing by means of a signed form. If an asylum claim is made verbally, government directives state that the competent authorities should assist the asylum seeker in filing an application in writing. The application comprises recognition and admission as a Convention refugee or admission on the basis of a regular residence permit for humanitarian reasons.

An asylum application should be made at Schiphol Airport (Amsterdam) at the desk of the Immigration- and Naturalisation Service (Immigratie- en Naturalisatie Dienst: IND) or in one of the two so-called "reporting centres" (Aanmeldcentra) in Rijsbergen (at the German border) and Zevenaar (at the Belgian border), where asylum applications are investigated. Asylum seekers who make their asylum claims, either verbally or in writing, at another authority elsewhere are referred to one of these centres. Asylum seekers in reporting centres are registered, receive an identity document and must report regularly to the immigration police.

If an asylum seeker is in possession of a valid travel document (*e.g.* a passport) there is no official time-limit to lodge the application. In practice, however, asylum applications which are lodged several weeks or months after arrival in the Netherlands are considered to be less credible.

If an asylum seeker is not in the possession of a valid travel document, he or she is required by law to make the application "without delay". As this requirement is interpreted quite strictly, it means that an asylum seeker without a travel document should make the application immediately after arrival in the Netherlands, otherwise the asylum application will be declared inadmissible. There have been several court decisions stating that applications of asylum seekers without travelling documents lodged three days after arrival in the Netherlands were not lodged "without delay" and were therefore inadmissible.

In most cases, asylum seekers are granted leave to enter the territory pending their asylum claims. At Schiphol Airport, gate-checks are occasionally held by the border police. If the airplane, on which an asylum seeker has arrived, comes from a Schengen or EC Member State, he or she will not be granted leave to enter and will be returned to the former destination.

Asylum seekers who arrive overland, necessarily travel through Belgium or Germany. According to the provisions of the Schengen Treaty the Dutch authorities are authorised in such cases to shift the responsibility for relief and determination of asylum status to Belgium or Germany and transfer asylum seekers to those neighbouring countries.

(ii) Submitting an asylum application abroad

An asylum application can be made abroad, but only in an indirect way, by means of applying for an entry clearance (machtiging tot voorlopig verblijf) at a Dutch diplomatic post. In assessing the merits of this application the Immigration and Naturalisation Service will also consider possible grounds for asylum. If the applicant is considered to be a refugee eligible for admission, an entry clearance will be issued, which will be replaced by a refugee document after arrival in the Netherlands.

(b) Representation

After arrival in a reporting centre (or at the IND desk at Schiphol Airport) an asylum seeker is interviewed (with the help of a interpreter) within 24 hours by specially trained officials of the IND. Immediately after the interview a first assessment of the application is made by another IND official. If this first assessment is negative a lawyer is assigned to the asylum seeker free of charge. If this lawyer considers the assessment to be incorrect or premature, he will forward this opinion to the IND. According to a convenant between the National Bar Association and the IND this opinion will have a serious impact on the final assessment of the asylum application.

If the final assessment is also negative, the asylum seeker will receive a written refusal and can subsequently be detained awaiting immediate deportation. In all cases he or she will be excluded from all forms of social assistance and housing facilities.

If the provisional assessment is positive the asylum seeker will be transferred to one of the reception centres (Opvangcentra) in the Netherlands pending the further processing of the application. In the reception centres legal aid by qualified lawyers is available, as well as social assistance by professionals and volunteers of the Refugee Aid Council. In the reception centres free board and lodging is available and asylum seekers receive a small sum of "pocket money" weekly.

Second and third interviews of an asylum seeker are normally attended by a qualified lawyer or a staff member of the Refugee Aid Council. A few days are granted for preparation. The applicant will be interviewed about the particulars of the journey to the Netherlands and all relevant facts and circumstances which caused him or her to leave the homeland. It is very important for an asylum seeker to produce documentation to substantiate and account for the credibility of his or her statements. A copy of the report of the interview is given to the asylum seeker and his or her representative. The asylum seeker then has the opportunity to submit addenda or corrections within a period of no less than two days. As a rule, corrections and addenda are made with the help of a staff member of the Refugee Aid Council and/or the lawyer involved.

(c) Interpreters

The right to an interpreter is laid down in the Aliens Circular. Interpreters have to be used by the IND throughout the asylum procedure. The problem is that not all of these interpreters are of good quality, as was reported recently by the National Ombudsman, an institution to whom citizens can complain about the behaviour of governmental bodies.

The use of interpreters is paid for by the IND.

(d) The role of the United Nations High Commissioner for Refugees

The role of the United Nations High Commissioner for Refugees (UNHCR) is very limited. Only in exceptional cases would a representative of UNHCR present his or her views to the court.

(e) Status pending decision

The liberty of freedom of movement of asylum seekers can be restricted pending consideration of the asylum claim.

Under article 17a of the Aliens Act their freedom of movement can be restricted to a certain area (usually a municipality or a reception centre) or they can be obliged to report regularly (daily, weekly) at a specific time and place.

Under article 7a of the Aliens Act the freedom of movement of asylum seekers who have arrived by air or ship can be restricted to a certain area (usually a reception centre or a special room at Schiphol Airport) pending consideration of their claims. If the (border) police suspect that the asylum seeker has the intention of entering the Netherlands unlawfully he or she can be detained on the basis of the same article.

Following refusal of an asylum application, far more restrictive measures, *e.g.* detention, can be imposed.

(f) Civil and political rights

Asylum seekers in the Netherlands whose cases are being considered enjoy the same civil rights as Dutch citizens, except for the right to family reunion, certain rights to social security and education, the right to access to public service and private enterprise, and the right to employment.

Asylum seekers do not have the right to vote and are not eligible for election. These rights are obtained after five years' legal residence. However, an asylum seeker does have the right to freedom of association and freedom of speech and expression and may, as such, demonstrate or found associations, even if they have political goals.

(g) Subsistence and employment rights

Pending the consideration of his or her claim the asylum seeker has a right to housing and to a subsistence income. In the reception centres asylum seekers receive free board and lodging as well as a small amount of pocket money. After some time they are transferred to regular housing in one of the 723 municipalities in the Netherlands. This housing is provided free of charge. In addition, approximately $f400$ per month is granted to cover the cost of living. The allowance is higher for families.

Only children below the age of 16 of asylum seekers have the right to State education during consideration of the asylum seeker's application. However, the Refugee Aid Council organises language courses (Dutch, English) on a large scale for asylum seekers awaiting a decision.

Pending the consideration of their claim asylum seekers have no right to enter the labour market.

(h) Grounds for rejecting an application

(i) Manifestly unfounded applications

An asylum claim may be declared manifestly unfounded if:

- it is not founded on any grounds which could reasonably lead to admission to the Netherlands;
- an asylum seeker has the nationality of a third country, in which adequate protection could be obtained;
- it has become evident that a third country will re-admit the asylum seeker until he or she finds lasting protection elsewhere;
- an asylum seeker has submitted false or forged documents to support the application and maintains that they are authentic and genuine;
- an asylum seeker has submitted false or forged travelling and/or identity documents and maintains that they are his or her own;
- an asylum seeker comes from a country which by ministerial decree has been designated a safe country, *i.e.* where, as a rule, there is no fear of persecution, unless the application is based on exceptional facts and circumstances which could lead to the presumption that there is a well-founded fear of persecution in the individual case contrary to the general situation in that country.

The ministerial decree lists the following countries as "safe countries of origin": Bulgaria, Ghana, Hungary, Poland, Romania, Senegal, Slovakia and Tjechia.

(ii) Inadmissible applications

Asylum applications may be declared inadmissible if:

- another country, party to the Geneva Convention, due to an international agreement (*e.g.* the Schengen Implementation Agreement or the EC Convention of Dublin on determining the State responsible for examining asylum requests) would be responsible for deciding on the application;
- an earlier application on the same grounds has been rejected finally;
- an asylum seeker has lodged a previous asylum application under another name;
- an asylum seeker has not, without good reason, complied with the obligation to make himself or herself available for examination of his or her claim;
- an asylum seeker is already holding a residence permit for other purposes;

- an asylum seeker is not holding (valid) travelling documents, unless he or she has reported for registration as an asylum applicant upon arrival in the Netherlands without delay.

Manifestly ill-founded and inadmissible applications will be rejected with recourse only to the President of the District Court in The Hague, to be addressed within 24 hours, in order to initiate summary proceedings for obtaining an injunction order against deportation pending administrative review. Those asylum seekers will be restricted in their freedom of movement until their actual deportation or voluntary departure, unless of course they would win their case in court.

Rights of appeal are not dealt with in this chapter.

(iii) Inhibition of making an asylum application

By a Law of 2 February 1995 the concept of the "safe third country" was introduced in article 15, paragraph 4 of the Aliens Act. It means that an asylum seeker cannot *de jure* lodge an asylum application if he or she, after leaving the country of origin, has resided in a safe third country. Safe third countries are:

- Member States of the EU and EEA;
- Royal Decree designated States, where compliance with the Geneva Convention on the status of refugees and Protocol of New York, the European Convention on Human Rights and the International Convention on Civil and Political Rights is ensured.

(i) Status; residence permits

Refugees are granted a permanent and unrestricted residence permit; and are entitled to a Convention travel document. Refugee status can be withdrawn if circumstances have changed to the effect that the alien can take up residence outside the Netherlands without risking persecution.

Jurisprudence on asylum upheld the policy by which a special status was created for asylum seekers, who cannot reasonably be expected to return to their home country in view of the prevailing conditions of life there. This so-called C-status can be considered as an implementation of the Dutch Government's humanitarian policies. It takes the form of an unrestricted residence permit.

By a Law of 1 January 1994 a "conditional" residence permit has been introduced in articles 8a, 12a and 12b of the Aliens Act. This permit cannot be applied for but is granted officially to asylum seekers who are not considered to qualify for any type of regular residence permit, but who cannot be deported to their home country in view of the prevailing conditions of life over there (civil war, natural catastrophes etc). The permit can be extended up to three years. In the meantime any procedure pending to obtain a regular title of permitted stay will be suspended. Permit holders are expected to study Dutch and prepare for participation in Dutch society during the first two years; only in the third year are they allowed to enter the labour market and seek employment. If, after three years, the holder of a conditional residence permit still cannot be deported, a C-status will be granted.

(j) Documents

Residence permits for refugees and asylum seekers take the form of a plastic card with a passport photograph in colour. Legal duties for the handling of an application are nil for refugees, for C-status permits *f*125 per person and for minors under the age of 12 *f*50.

9. Discretionary powers

Rules and regulations concerning immigration are enforced by the Royal Dutch Military Police and customs officers at the border, and elsewhere by the local immigration police and by the officials of the Immigration and Naturalisation Service, a largely independent agency of the Ministry of Justice staffed with governmental public servants, headed by the State Secretary of Justice. All have separate responsibilities. The wide discretionary powers, which were given to these authorities in the Aliens Act, are specified and restricted in a set of administrative rules called the Aliens Circular (Vreemdelingen Circulaire). These rules have a certain statutory force resulting from the principle that similar cases should be dealt with similarly. Decisions contrary to the rules laid out in the Aliens Circular are permissible only if they favour the alien.

The Circular on Border Control of 1984 contains administrative rules which have been formulated as instructions from the Minister of Justice to the Royal Dutch Military Police and customs officers.

The general supervision and the final – political – responsibility for the implementation of Dutch aliens law rest with the State Secretary of Justice.

10. Sanctions

(a) Penal sanctions

Aliens are obliged by law to report and inform the local immigration police about things such as a change of address in the Netherlands or final leave abroad, the loss of identity documents (residence permit identity cards and the like) and if they would no longer have permission to stay, *i.e.* in case of illegal stay. Failing to comply with these obligations is punishable as a penal offence with light regime imprisonment up to a maximum of six months or a fine up to a maximum of *f*5,000. Prosecution does occur. In most cases out-of-court settlement is offered by payment of a fine; fines start at *f*110.

(b) Deportation

Deportation may be defined as the involuntary removal of an alien from Dutch territory. Aliens who do not have permission to stay qualify for deportation. Aliens to whom entry has been refused are put back on an aircraft, train or ship which transported the alien to the Netherlands. If removal must be carried out in another way, the costs thereof will be passed on to the transport company.

Those who claim to be refugees are not refused entry and will not be deported unless by special leave of the Minister of Justice.

Deportation is carried out by order of the Minister of Justice or the immigration police. The order is given in writing to the officer or official in charge of the deportation. The legal intention of the order is to warrant a justifiable deportation of aliens who, in some way, have been staying legally in the country.

In cases of illegal entry and/or stay any alien can be deported without a deportation order (with the exception of EC and EEA nationals).

Before carrying out a deportation order, the officer or official in charge must grant the alien a reasonable term (often two weeks) to prepare his or her departure to a country where entry is warranted. The Supreme Court has ruled that this entry does not have to warrant (taking up) residence.

A reasonable term for voluntary departure may be refused in case of illegal entry if there is a well-founded fear that the alien might go into hiding or there are other circumstances which will prevent entry or transit elsewhere if deportation is delayed, or in case of a serious criminal or doubtful political record.

However, all aliens who are deported are free to choose a country of destination; they must demonstrate that entry is warranted and pay for the travel expenses. In other cases the costs of the deportation will be passed on to the alien if he or she has financial means, or to eventual guarantors.

To carry out a deportation order or a remand in custody, border officials and immigration police officers are authorised to search houses and other places with a warrant.

Family members, who qualify for deportation, will be permitted to travel together as far as possible.

The deportation of aliens frequently poses problems to the authorities. In many cases a country prepared to give leave for entry cannot be found, usually because the alien's nationality cannot be verified.

The operation of the Schengen Agreements obliges the Dutch authorities to make arrangements for deportation of aliens out of the Schengen territory. Deportation will not be carried out, as a matter of right or by policy, in the following circumstances:

- the alien is allowed to stay on the basis of a residence title in the Aliens Act;
- a deportation order, if required, is not given;
- the reasonable term for voluntary departure has not expired;
- the deportation should be postponed considering the health of the persons

to be deported;

- criminal prosecution is proceeding or punishment for criminal offences is executed;
- a request for extradition from a foreign authority is anticipated;
- the decision of the District Court in The Hague in a procedure to determine Dutch citizenship is pending;
- either by right or by policy, an application procedure with regard to a residence title, a procedure of administrative review or an appeal to the District Court in The Hague is pending.

Problems may arise if deportation can be carried out only to a country where the alien concerned will be prosecuted or subjected to punishment for criminal offences, while extradition cannot or will not be requested. Where there is no alternative, deportation will be carried out without previous warning to the State of destination or any other contact which might alert them. In 1963 the Supreme Court did not disqualify such deportation as "disguised extradition"; under the circumstances of the case the deportation was considered to be "reasonably necessary" (Dutch Jurisprudence, NJ 1963, 509).

Stay of execution pending applications, review and appeals is, in many cases, the object of a claim in summary proceedings with the President of the District Court in The Hague. By policy, deportation will not be carried out pending the decision of the President.

(c) Detention

Deprivation of liberty under the Aliens Act is permitted in order to carry out an interrogation to assess identity and residence.

An alien can be held in a police station for interrogation for a maximum of six hours, with the exception of the hours between midnight and 9am. On well-founded suspicion of illegal stay, an alien can be held for another 48 hours.

Detention can be executed in the interest of public peace or national security if:

- a deportation order is given;
- a deportation order is likely to be given;
- the application of a residence permit by an illegal alien is likely to be turned down.

Without a deportation order the maximum duration of detention is one month (30 days). For detention based on a deportation order there is no maximum duration fixed by law; according to the jurisprudence of the district courts this form of detention may last up to seven months.

Detention should not be executed or should be stopped if and as soon as the alien concerned expresses his or her will to leave the country and demonstrates actual means to carry out this plan (passport, ticket, money, warranted entry, etc).

A detention order is issued in the name of the Minister of Justice by an immigration police officer with the rank of substitute public prosecutor. The order will not be given without interrogation of the alien concerned. This interrogation is undertaken with several guarantees, both by law and by jurisprudence. The alien has the right to have a lawyer present for assistance and should be informed in good time about this right by the immigration police officer in charge. If necessary, an interpreter should be involved and an official report of the interrogation should be made.

A request to the district court to lift the detention can be made by the alien or his or her lawyer at all times. The court is obliged to hear the alien at least on the first request. The public prosecutor is obliged to inform the court about the detention of any alien which has lasted for 30 days when a request for lifting has not been filed. This notification will be dealt with by the court as if a first request for lifting the order had been made. In case an alien has no lawyer, the court will appoint one.

A request for lifting the order will be granted if the detention is either unlawful or would be – upon consideration of all interests involved – no longer justifiable. If a request is granted, the court may also grant a claim for damages and compensation.

Although the detention of aliens may clearly be of a punitive character, it is defined as a means of administrative control. The legal system of detention was designed to match the requirements of Article 5 of the European Convention for Human Rights.

Detention must be carried out in a house of detention after 10 days. Since 1 January 1994 detentions can be carried out lawfully in police stations, but according to article 84 of the Aliens Decree a detained alien should be transferred to a house of detention "as soon as this would be reasonably possible". On 11 May 1994 the District Court in The Hague ruled, in a principal decision, that detention of aliens in police stations should be limited to a maximum of 10 days. For the detention of juveniles special rules are applicable. For restrictions on the liberty or freedom of movement of asylum seekers pending consideration of their asylum claim, see **8(e)** above.

11. Tax and social security

The information in this section is meant as an overview of some general principles on tax and social security in the Netherlands and should not be used for practical purposes. For individual tax planning, expert assistance is recommended.

(a) Tax

(i) General principles
Personal taxation includes personal income tax, wage-withholding tax, dividend tax and net wealth tax.

Individual taxpayers are classified as either resident or non-resident taxpayers. Resident taxpayers are taxed on their worldwide income. Non-resident taxpayers are taxed on Dutch sources of income only.

For tax purposes a person is regarded as resident in case of durable ties with the Netherlands. Actual personal circumstances determine each case. For example, the area in which a person maintains a house or keeps a (furnished or non-furnished) residence, in which his or her family resides, or where his or her children go to school, or where he or she participates in social life, or the centre is of his or her financial and commercial interests and whether Dutch social benefits are applicable, etc, are all relevant factors to such a determination. In short, a person is fiscally domiciled where he or she has his or her durable centre of personal life, social and economic interests, apparent from external and perceptible circumstances. Therefore, the fiscal domicile may not be an official address.

The Netherlands is party to a number of bilateral tax Treaties which solve cases where double residence would otherwise lead to double taxation. There are agreements with all EC and EEA countries. Furthermore, worth mentioning are, amongst others, agreements with Australia, Brazil, Bulgaria, Canada, China, Czech Republic, Hungary, India, Indonesia, Israel, Japan, Mexico, Netherlands Antilles, New Zealand, Oekraine, Oezbekistan, Pakistan, Phillipines, Poland, Romania, Russian Federation, Singapore, Slovak Republic, South Africa, South Korea, Switzerland, Thailand, Turkey and the United States. The Dutch tax year runs from 1 January to 31 December. If a person is resident in the Netherlands for only part of a calendar year, his or her income gained in that period will be considered as if it were income over a full calendar year. There is no pro-rated restriction of tax-free amounts or grossing-up of income to an annual basis.

Since 1 January 1989 the administration of taxes and social security benefits is computerised on the basis of a code number system. Persons aged 14 and over, who are resident in the Netherlands, are awarded a so-called "Sofi" number automatically. Newcomers, people who become resident when taking up (self-)employment, must apply for a Sofi number at the local tax office, which they will receive upon presentation of a residence permit.

In general, nobody can take up legal employment or receive social security benefits in the Netherlands without having been registered under a Sofi number.

Foreign residents are subject to Dutch income tax on their worldwide net income at progressive rates. This income may come from a trade or business, from labour, from capital – including income from real estate, dividends, interest and life annuities – from periodic receipts such as scholarships and alimony and from gains on the disposal of shares in a company in which a substantial interest was or is held.

Certain items of worldwide income may be subject to double taxation. Resident taxpayers may request relief under a tax Treaty or under Dutch domestic law.

Foreigners who are non-residents are subject to Dutch income tax on income earned from Dutch sources from trade, business and employment in the Netherlands.

Spouses are independently liable to Dutch tax on their income. If both spouses are resident taxpayers, unearned income such as income gained from investment, deductions for medical costs, life insurance premiums and alimony payments, are allocated to the spouse with the highest personal income. The basis for the computation of taxable income is the aggregate amount of net income or profits from the sources mentioned above, less admissible expenses. A tax-free amount is available by way of personal allowance to all taxpayers, residents and non-residents, and is deducted in the computation of taxable income. These standard allowances depend on the personal circumstances of the taxpayer. The basic allowance for 1995 is ƒ6,074; for a married resident whose spouse has no income or income less than ƒ6,074, the exemption is ƒ12,148.

Non-resident taxpayers and individuals who are resident for less than six months in one calendar year are entitled to an allowance of ƒ6,074.

Income is subject to tax at progressive rates in three brackets. The percentage in the first bracket is made up of social security tax and personal income tax. In 1995 the first bracket for residents is 37.65% on the first ƒ44,349; 50% on the next ƒ44,349 and 60% on taxable income over ƒ88,696. For non-residents who are not subject to Dutch social security taxes, the tax rate in the first bracket is 25%.

(ii) Special expatriate tax status; 35% ruling

A so-called expatriate is a foreign employee who has been transferred to the Netherlands to be gainfully employed. As such he or she will become subject to Dutch income tax either as a resident or non-resident taxpayer. The transfer will often bring about considerable additional costs, for example on account of relocation. To promote foreign investment and corporate establishment in the Netherlands, the Dutch tax authorities have issued a tax resolution, called the 35% ruling. Under this resolution expatriates may receive from their employer a tax-free reimbursement for presumed expenses. This reimbursement is limited to 35% of the salary subject to wage-withholding tax. For maximum benefit from this ruling applications must be made within four months after arrival in the Netherlands. To qualify for the ruling the expatriate should be employed with an employer established in the Netherlands or with an employer abroad who has been appointed as an agent for wage-withholding tax in the Netherlands. The key requirement is that the expatriate has special skills or knowledge which is not readily available on the Dutch labour market. This specific professional expertise is accepted for:

- top executives and product specialists;
- middle and top management executives employed with a concern for at least two-and-a-half years, temporarily assigned to an establishment in the Netherlands within the scope of job rotation;
- those who provide special expertise;
- employees with international organisations required to hire employees from EU Member States;
- teachers at international schools.

An expatriate, who would be a resident taxpayer on account of his or her employment in the Netherlands, may opt for treatment as a non-resident for Dutch tax purposes. Whether this option would be more beneficial depends on the sources of his or her income and expenses; for proper assessment expert assistance is indispensable.

The 35% tax-free allowance is granted for a period of 120 months.

Since January 1996, those with a 35% tax benefit can exchange their foreign driving licenses without any test whatsoever. Also see para 12(d) page 284.

(b) Social security

(i) The social security system

The Dutch system of social security is both extensive and compulsory. There is a national social security scheme, for which social security taxes are paid, and a social insurance scheme, for which social insurance premiums are paid. Both schemes provide benefits to "residents". This term, which includes nationals and non-nationals, has approximately the same meaning as the fiscal domicile explained at 11(a) above. Social security covers both working and non-working residents. Most non-residents are covered by the social security scheme if they are employed in the Netherlands and if their employment income is subject to Dutch wage-withholding tax. Social insurance applies only to employees working in the Netherlands.

The national social security scheme is comprised of:

- General Retirement Pension Act (AOW);
- General Widows and Orphans Act (AWW);
- General Family Allowances Act (AKW);
- General Disability Benefits Act (AAW);
- Exceptional Medical Expenses Act (AWBZ).

These Acts provide compulsory insurance for all residents and most non-residents who are subject to Dutch wage-withholding tax. Because of the merged social security and income tax rates, the general disability insurance (under AAW) and special health insurance (under AWBZ) taxes are levied on employees and reimbursed by the employer by means of a compensation allowance. Social security taxes paid by an employee are not deductible from his or her taxable income.

The social insurance scheme is comprised of:

- Health Insurance Act (ZFW);
- Sickness Benefits Act (ZW);
- Unemployment Insurance Act (WW);
- Supplementary Unemployment Benefits Act (WWV);
- Disability Insurance Act (WAO);

- Income Provision Elderly and Partially Disabled Unemployed Persons Act (IOAW).

These Acts provide compulsory insurance for employees performing their activities in the Netherlands or who are living in the Netherlands and have a resident employer. Social premiums are paid by all employees working in the Netherlands and their employers. Some premiums depend on the industry involved. Employers are obliged to collect the social premiums from their employees and pay the total to the social insurance authorities. Non-resident employers have to register with the Dutch social insurance authorities or apply for a ruling allowing a group company in the Netherlands to account for the social premiums.

In general social premiums are not due if:

- activities are performed by a non-resident employee for a non-resident employer for a period up to a maximum of six months;
- a non-resident remains subject to the social security system of his or her home country.

(ii) General Social Security Act

All residents – nationals and those in possession of a residence permit or other proof of permission to stay – who are not able to provide for their own cost of living on account of personal circumstances other than disability for work, may apply for financial support under the provisions of the General Social Security Act.

For aliens it should be noted that, in general, sufficient income is one of the criteria for obtaining or extending a residence permit or other form of permission to stay. Lack of means, apparent from the fact that a person is receiving social benefits under this Act, may result in refusal and termination of (continued) stay.

(iii) Benefits provided

National social security scheme

Under the General Retirement Pension Act, there is a State pension at the age of 65, to be paid in monthly terms. Depending on personal circumstances (married, single, age of partner, children under 18) gross amounts in 1995 ranged from ƒ 993.91 to ƒ 1,937.82; a holiday allowance is added.

Aliens, residents and former residents receive this pension with a reduction for the years of unpaid premiums.

Under the General Widows and Orphans Act there is a State pension similar to the above scheme.

The General Family Allowances Act pays, in general, child allowances to residents and employees working in the Netherlands. Depending on the size of the family, the age of the children and their personal circumstances (living in or outside the family, studying or not, being employed or unemployed) amounts in 1995 varied from ƒ 284.66 to ƒ 763.06 per quarter.

Aliens with children in the home country or abroad are obliged to produce proof of a minimum contribution to the cost of living of f 56 per week for each child.

The General Disability Benefits Act pays minimum income benefits for persons under 65 who are resident or subject to Dutch wage-withholding tax, in case of disability for work over a period of more than 52 weeks. Amounts are similar to the scheme of the General Social Security Act.

The Exceptional Medical Expenses Act covers, for residents and those subject to Dutch wage-withholding tax, expenses for medicines, medical treatment, hospitalisation, nursing and physical rehabilitation which are not covered by private insurance. It provides refunds of the excess amount paid out of pocket.

The General Social Security Act provides minimum income benefits for residents under 65. In 1995, net amounts varied from f 473.81 to f 1,803.16 monthly, depending on personal circumstances (age, living in or outside the family, married or single). A holiday allowance is added.

The social insurance scheme

The Health Insurance Act covers expenses for medical and dental care, hospital nursing and other treatment. By payment of a nominal contribution, the unemployed spouse is also insured, as are children under 18 for whom the employee is entitled to child allowance, children who are studying and disabled children. This type of health insurance is available for employees with a gross wage income up to f 58,950 in 1995: those with a higher income must take out private insurance.

"Health insurance has been fully privatised as of April 1996. Continued payment of wages to employees under 65 years of age during sickness, accident or infirmity is mandatory for a maximum period of 52 weeks.

Most employers have taken out private insurance to cover these risks."

The Unemployment Insurance Act insures employees under 65 against loss of wages on account of involuntary unemployment or redundancy. In 1995 the legal benefit was 70% of the daily gross wages up to a maximum of f 286 for a period of 26 weeks. Extension of the benefit to a maximum of four or five years depends on the employment record of the insured employee. After this extension, the benefit may be continued for a maximum period of one year amounting to 70% of the minimum age.

The Disability Insurance Act insures employees under 65 who are by 15% or more incapacitated for work, after a period of 52 weeks of unemployment due to sickness, accident or infirmity.

For the first 52 weeks, see under the Sickness Benefits Act above. The monthly gross amount of this benefit depends on the former wages and the degree of incapacity of the insured person. The daily gross wages were insured up to a maximum of f 286 in 1995.

The Income Provision Elderly and Partially Disabled Unemployed Persons Act insures a minimum income to elderly, unemployed and disabled persons under 65 who have fully utilised the provisions of the Unemployment Insurance Act.

12. Domestic considerations

In this section some of the practical issues for newcomers to Dutch society are considered. Hiring the services of a local relocation consultant for assistance and practical advice is recommended.

(a) Civil registration

(i) Population register
Pursuant to article 26 of the Municipal Basis Administration Act those who expect to stay in the Netherlands for at least two-thirds of half a year, are obliged to register on the population register (the municipal basis administration) of the municipality where they have their address. It is necessary first to report to the local immigration police. In order to register, the following documents must be submitted:

- proof of registration at the local immigration police. In most cases this would be a sticker stamp in a passport as proof of application of a residence permit;
- deed of purchase of flat/apartment/house, rental agreement, address of hotel or other temporary housing;
- legalised full birth certificate;
- legalised full marriage certificate;
- legalised divorce certificate.

(ii) Legalisation of public documents
For registration purposes at the municipal basis administration, public documents, such as certificates concerning personal details, must be properly legalised. Certificates must bear a stamp and signature from the authority of issue by way of authentication. In general, this authentication would have to be legalised at the Ministry of Foreign Affairs or the Ministry of Justice in the country of origin. Finally, the legalisation of the ministerial authority would have to be legalised at the Dutch embassy or consulate in the country of origin. This route of double legalisation has been simplified for public documents originating in any country which is a party to The Hague Convention Abolishing the Requirement of Legalisation for Foreign Public Documents. These public documents can be legalised at the Ministry of Foreign Affairs or the Ministry of Justice in the country of origin (United States: Secretary of State) by means of affixing a certificate or "apostille" to it.

Parties to the Apostille Treaty are:

Antigua and Barbuda	Hungary	Seychelles
Argentina	Israel	Surinam
Australia	Japan	Swaziland
Bahamas	Lesotho	Tonga
Belarus	Liechtenstein	United Kingdom
Belize	Macedonia	United States
Bosnia-Herzegovina	Malawi	
Botswana	Malta	
Brunei	Marshall Islands	
Fiji	Mauritius	
Finland	Norway	
Greece	Panama	
Hong Kong	Russian Federation	

There is no requirement for legalisation of public documents originating from the following countries:

Aruba	France	Portugal
Austria	Germany	Slovenia
Belgium	Italy	Spain
Croatia	Luxembourg	Switzerland
Cyprus	Neth. Antilles	Yugoslavia (Serbia & Montenegro)

Triple legalisation is required for public documents from Ireland.

Sworn translation is required of public documents which are not made up in either Dutch, English, French, or German. In view of the above-mentioned it is recommended that legalised certificates are processed in good time. However, a delay of three months is granted in case of non-compliance with legalisation requirements.

(b) Housing

The property market is tight, especially in the Randstad area. In consequence, prices are relatively high, but mortgage rates have been declining steadily for several years now. The services of a licenced real estate agent of NVM (De Nederlandse Vereniging van Makelaars – The Netherlands Association of Real Estate Agents) are recommended or of Match Makelaars, a new competitive association. Licensed agents share a computerised information system covering the entire property market supply and demand. In real estate transactions two agents are involved (one for the seller and one for the buyer) who receive commission only from their client. Licenced agents are not permitted to take commissions from both parties. The same rule applies when representing lessors and lessees. The commission for agents of the buyer and seller is approximately

1.85% of the purchase price, plus 17.5% VAT for houses in a price range up to ƒ 250,000. For more expensive houses, rates are lower. The commission for agents of the lessor and lessee is 8% of the first year's lease, plus 17.5% VAT.

All legal transactions in connection with buying real estate property go through a public notary, who will also draw up the mortgage agreement. It should be noted, however, that verbal agreements are legally binding in the Netherlands. The sales transaction will cost the buyer an additional 10% of the purchase price: 6% real estate transfer tax and 4% commission and legal fees. Mortgage interest is income tax deductible. For those who have lived in the Netherlands for less than three years, it is probably economically wiser to rent, considering the income tax savings on mortgage interest. Rental contracts should include a "diplomatic clause" which enables the tenant, for example in case of a sudden transfer by his or her company, to terminate the contract within a couple of months in spite of a longer agreed term of tenancy. If a price quote is "inclusive" it means that the supply of energy (gas, water, electricity) is included, but never the telephone. On the basis of an estimate of annual consumption the energy supply is charged by the municipal power company every one or two months in advance. Meters are read each spring for annual settlement.

In many cases the rental of apartments and houses include service costs and/or the rent of furniture. Advance payments of the central heating bills may also be included. In a proper rental contract these items should be mentioned and specified separately.

(c) Importing household effects and motor cars

The rules and regulations governing imports differ between imports from an EC country and those from a non-EC country.

(i) Household effects

Tax exemptions are available for the import of household effects if the applicant will be domiciled in the Netherlands for at least 185 days per year.

Household effects from an EC country should have been used already as such and should not be intended for commercial purposes. Two lists of household items must be filled, signed and submitted at customs, together with a signed application form for tax exemption.

For household effects from a non-EC country a permit for tax-free import must be applied for in advance at the regional customs office where the person intends to take up residence. Household effects are declared on submitting the permit and a series of completed forms.

(ii) Motor cars

A car import procedure entails:

- applying for an exemption on BPM tax (see below) at the regional customs office;

- obtaining Dutch car registration documents and licence plates;
- paying motor vehicle tax;
- taking out insurance pursuant to the Statutory Liability for Motor Vehicles Act.

BPM is a tax on motor vehicles, both new and used, which are less than 8.3 years old. Payment falls on the person in whose name the vehicle is registered. This means that with a new car, or any car being registered in the Netherlands for the first time, the buyer pays the BPM to the dealer. The dealer hands over the payment to the importer who has the initial obligation to pay it to the tax office as the owner of the vehicle. Importers, manufacturers and dealers who request vehicle registration in the Netherlands are obliged to pay the tax at the point that the registration is issued on each individual vehicle. However, in the case of business people conducting ongoing transactions, it is possible to request a BPM number, which enables payments to be made on a monthly (or other time-frame) basis after statements have been submitted to the tax office.

Determination of BPM is made by the net (without VAT) Dutch catalogue price of the vehicle including any extra accessories, *i.e.* air-conditioning, electric windows, etc. A new passenger vehicle is taxed at 45.2% of the net catalogue price, reduced by a fixed amount of f 3,394. For diesel-burning vehicles the fixed reduction is f 1,278. For motorcycles with a net catalogue price of f 4,700 or less the BPM tax is 10.2%. For motorcycles over f 4,700 the BPM tax is 20.7%, reduced by a fixed amount of f 494. Calculations on used cars begin from the date the vehicle was first used. A 1% reduction is calculated for every month the car was used from the day of its manufacture. Example: a car is 15 months old and is being registered for the first time in the Netherlands. The catalogue price is f 30,000. The BPM tax is 45.2% = f 13,560 minus the fixed reduction of f 3,394, leaving the BPM at f 10,166. Devaluation stands at 15% because the car is 15 months old. The 15% is taken off the f 10,166 leaving a total BPM tax of f 8,641.

In order to be eligible for BPM tax exemption, a car must be at least six months old before it is brought to the Netherlands.

If car comes from a non-EC country the applicant must produce documented proof that he or she has lived outside the Netherlands for at least 12 months immediately prior to the application. The tax exemption is granted under the condition not to sell the car for one year after import. The exemption is granted to the car owner exclusively and is not transferable. As cars can only be exempted as part of the applicant's household effects, company cars – bought by and registered in the name of the company – cannot be exempted from BPM tax.

The car import procedure is comprised of a car check at a regional station of the Ministry of Transport (Rijksdienst voor het Wegverkeer) for car registration and submitting prescribed documents to the regional customs office for granting tax exemption.

(d) Driving licences

Those who have become Dutch residents by registration with the local immigration police and the population register must obtain a Dutch driving licence. Those with driving licences from an EC or EEA country, the Netherlands Antilles, Aruba or Japan can exchange their driving licence for a Dutch licence within the first year of registered stay. Applicants for exchange must prove to have been resident in the country of issue of the driving licence for at least 184 days immediately prior to that issue.

Those holding a driving licence from any other country will have to take the CBR (BNOR-Division) "special expedited" theory and driving test (duration 70 minutes) before they can apply for a Dutch driving licence. However, as of 1st January 1996 seconded employers and their family members who are entitled to benefit from the Dutch 35% tax ruling, are exempted from the exchange regulations. This means, that they can exchange their foreign driving licenses without any test whatsoever as soon as the 35% tax benefit has been granted.

(e) Schools

The Dutch education system is composed of:

- primary schools;
- special schools;
- secondary schools;
- institutes for higher education; and
- institutes for international education.

Full-time education is compulsory for children from five to 16 years of age. For children who leave school at the age of 16 additional schooling or training for one or two days per week is compulsory for another two years.

(i) Primary schools
Primary schools are for children aged from four to 12. Younger children attend playgroups or crèches. Schools are not locally "zoned"; parents are free to choose the type of schooling they wish for their children. The possibilities include Dalton, Steiner or Montessori education. In the final year of primary school education, all children take a State examination called "Cito-toets". This test is not for a school leaving certificate but is a method of establishing a child's level of knowledge in comparison with an average standard of knowledge throughout the Netherlands.

(ii) Secondary schools
There are three types of secondary schools:

- general secondary schools;
- pre-university schools; and
- vocational secondary schools.

Junior general secondary school education (MAVO) takes four years. It offers a basic level of higher education. Senior general secondary school education (HAVO) involves a five-year course.

Pre-university secondary schools (VWO) are called "gymnasium" and "atheneum". The six-year courses consist of classical languages and prepare children for higher vocational or university education.

Vocational secondary education is available at three levels: junior (LBO), senior (MBO) and higher (HBO). All courses are completed by written State examinations.

(iii) Higher education

Higher education involves higher vocational and university education. There are 14 universities in the Netherlands and seven theological colleges. As a constitutional right both private and State foundations are financed from government funds. Students with a VWO certificate can register at a university faculty depending on their qualifications. For faculties which are over-booked, a lottery system is used. As a rule, university courses last for four years. Students graduate as candidates for a doctor's degree, much like the Master of Arts qualification in the United States. At some faculties additional specialisation courses are available. A doctor's degree involves a period of individual studies and research during which a doctoral thesis is written.

(iv) International education

Although many benefits may be attached to sending children to Dutch schools, consideration must be given to the fact that unless parents have fully integrated themselves into the Dutch language, society and culture, they may be unable to assist their children's progress with regard to homework, Dutch literature and history.

Throughout the Netherlands, international schools follow the British, US, French, German, as well as international and European systems of education. There are a number of Dutch schools with special departments (e.g. "English streams"). These streams provide two possibilities: a gradual integration into the Dutch educational system or preparation for the International Baccalaureate.

Boarding schools, some of which are co-educational, offer not only International Baccalaureate, but also British and US qualifications. All international schools are specialised in accepting children in the middle of terms and are used to providing additional English language tuition, if necessary. Most schools teach Dutch as part of the curriculum. The European and "English stream" schools concentrate to a large extent on language skills. Entry to all schools is based on previous school records and/or entry examinations.

(f) Re-migration

When terminating residence in the Netherlands the local immigration police and the population register must be notified. Social security authorities must be notified by the employer.

It is advisable to file an income tax return with the tax authorities before departure. Income tax returns can only apply to the calendar year of departure. Pension rights under the General Retirement Pension Act are not payable until a person has reached the age of 65. Payment of a full pension is based on 50 years of residence in the Netherlands. Expatriates are entitled to a proportional share of the full pension based on the number of residential years in the Netherlands. It is not possible to receive payments as a lump sum.

Everaert Advokaten, Weteringschans 28, 1017 SG Amsterdam.
tel.: (31) 206271181. telefax: (31) 206273231

Contents of Chapter 14

PORTUGAL

Chapter 14

PORTUGAL

Joao Noronha Lopes

1. Country characteristics and general principles

The Republic of Portugal occupies an area of more than 92,100 square kilometres in the extreme south west of Europe. The territory of Portugal comprises mainland Portugal on the Iberian Peninsula, which it shares with Spain, and the Islands of Madeira and Azores in the Atlantic Ocean. The climate is mild, with average temperatures ranging from 11°C (52°F) in winter to 23°C (74°F) in summer. The population is approximately 10 million and the main cities are Lisbon (two million) and Oporto (one million).

The official language is Portuguese, which is also spoken in Brazil, Angola, Mozambique, S. Tomé e Principe, Cape Verde, Guinea Bissau, East Timor and Macau by more than 200 million people.

Portugal is a founder member of the OECD and NATO. In 1986 Portugal entered the European Community and has been so far an active member of the European Union. Membership of the European Union has had a major impact on the economy of Portugal, from easier access to European markets, the liberalisation of trade and investments, the availability of assistance through EU structural funds and the pressure on business to modernise in preparation for the Single European Market.

The Portuguese economy is based on the principles of free enterprise and private ownership. The State is about to conclude the re-privatisation of most of the companies which were nationalised in the aftermath of the 1974 revolution. The inflation rate was 5.4% in 1994 and the unemployment rate in the same period was 6.8%, one of the lowest in the European Union.

The main manufacturing activities are in automobile and auto parts, textiles, footwear and clothing, machinery, chemicals, wood, glassware and pottery. The main agricultural produce comprises cork, cereals, olives and fruit trees. The country is the world's seventh largest wine producer and is best known for its port and rosé wines. Forests cover 30% of the country and are a major source of export earning. Portugal is the world's largest exporter of cork and one of the larger cellulose producers in Europe.

Tourism is a major contributor to the Portuguese economy. An average 15 million tourists visit Portugal every year, and this activity is one of the largest foreign currency earners.

Portugal's main trading partners are Spain, Germany, France, Italy and the United Kingdom.

The system of government is a parliamentary democracy. The President of the Republic is the Head of State and represents the nation as a whole, but the day-to-day administration of the country rests with the Government, which is led by a Prime Minister.

The Constitution of 1976 enshrined the fundamental civil rights and public freedoms, and assigned legislative powers to Parliament and the Government, executive power to the Government and judicial power to the courts.

Portugal has traditionally been an emigrant country rather than a recipient of immigrants. Emigration to Northern Europe, the United States, Canada and Brazil reached a peak in the 1960s with more than two million Portuguese working and living abroad.

This tendency has however gradually decreased, and the country has witnessed, since the 1980s, the return of many emigrants and the influx of many foreigners attracted by the improved living conditions. These facts, combined with the process of unification of immigration laws in the European Union, have led to significant changes in the general principles of immigration law. The approach by Portuguese authorities to prospective immigrants draw gradually closer to procedures adopted by other EU countries, culminating in the signature and implementation of the Schengen Agreements.

2. Employment and inter-company transfers

Foreigners wishing to work in Portugal for a period not exceeding 90 days require a uniform visa in the Portuguese consulate of their country of residence.

Work for longer periods of time is subject, first, to the general conditions outlined for permanent residence (see **7** below). Besides those requirements, visa applicants are required to deliver to the Portuguese consulate of their country of residence a written advice by their future employer whereby it is clearly shown that they have been offered employment.

When considering a visa application, immigration authorities will consult with the Ministry of Labour, to ascertain the credibility of the employer, the compliance by the employer of its fiscal, social security and legal obligations, and the rate of unemployment in the field of activity to be undertaken by the foreign workers.

Resident companies employing more than five persons and whose staff is at least 90% Portuguese are qualified to employ foreign workers. In specific cases, such as activities requiring a high degree of technical knowledge, it is possible to obtain special authorisation to exceed the 10% limit on foreign employees.

Access to certain professions such as medicine, law, engineering and architecture require the approval of credentials by the competent Bar or Professional Association in Portugal.

3. Business

(a) General requirements

Foreigners wishing to take up residence and do business in Portugal for more than three months are required to apply for a residence visa.

Besides those requirements outlined for permanent residence (see **7** below) businessmen or women should produce to the Portuguese consulate of their place of residence, a "declaration of intent of investment" issued by ICEP (Portuguese Foreign Trade Institute) relevant to the enterprise they wish to establish/ purchase/join. Such declaration will give basic information on the features of the operation, and ICEP will not generally disallow investments provided they comply with certain minimum legal requirements.

In principle, there is no minimum amount to be invested in the business operation and the foreign investor may freely decide the allocation of funds for investment purposes. However, immigration authorities are more likely to grant a visa to foreigners whose projects feature, amongst others, the following characteristics: a considerable financial investment; the utilisation of the investor's own money; the management and direction of the business by that same investor; and the creation of employment for Portuguese citizens.

In any case foreigners will normally be required to produce documental proof showing that a bank account in Portuguese escudos has been opened in a Portuguese bank. The amount to be deposited may vary from case to case, and is defined by immigration authorities.

(b) Foreign investment

There are no general restrictions on foreign investment, although certain types of business such as water, gas and electricity require special authorisation from government.

Projects of investments are normally approved without major difficulties and authorisation is only denied in case of illegal or clearly unfeasible operations. Due to the implementation of EU programmes to develop Portuguese economy, there are many incentives to investments on industry, agriculture, tourism and infrastructures.

Fiscal incentives are also available for large investment projects, which are negotiable on a case-by-case basis with Portuguese authorities.

(c) Business entities

There are basically two ways of carrying on business in Portugal: through a branch office or by incorporating a new company.

(i) Corporation ("Sociedade Anónima" – SA)

This structure is more appropriate for larger and/or widely held enterprises. The minimum share capital required is five million escudos, and there must be at least five shareholders. Each shareholder's liability is limited to the amount of capital subscribed.

Shares are usually deposited with a bank and transfers are normally effected by the depository bank.

The management and control of a corporation normally consists of a board of directors which must contain an uneven number of members, and an audit board with at least three or five members, at least one of them being a statutory auditor. Resolutions by the general meeting may usually be passed by a simple majority, although qualified majority is needed for some specific matters.

Incorporation costs may be estimated to be equivalent to 1.5% of the company's share capital.

(ii) Quota company ("Sociedade por Quotas" – Lda)

This structure is more appropriate for small and medium-size enterprises and is the vehicle most commonly used by foreign investors.

The minimum share capital required by law is 400,000 escudos and only two quotaholders are necessary. These quotaholders are jointly liable for all financing stipulated in the articles of association.

These companies do not issue physical shares certificates but have interests (designated as "quotas") which are divided between the quotaholders. The transfer of quotas can only be made by means of a formal notarial deed and quotas and its holders are registered in the companies register.

Quota companies are run by directors and may or may not have an audit board. Only if certain turnover, staff and total asset value limits specified by law are exceeded during at least two years, will those companies be required to appoint a statutory auditor.

Resolutions by the general meeting are normally passed by simple majority, although a qualified majority is required for some matters, such as increase of capital and alterations to the articles of association.

Incorporation costs can be estimated to be 1.5% of the company's share capital.

(iii) Branch office

Branches conduct business in exactly the same way as companies but do not constitute a separate legal entity. Therefore, the foreign company is jointly liable for the debts of the branch.

In general, there are no minimum or maximum limits on the amount of capital needed for setting up branches. However, the Companies' Register is unlikely to authorise the setting up of a branch with no capital assigned, and in practice the branch must have the minimum 400,000 escudos as capital assigned. Setting up a branch involves less legal costs than incorporation of companies.

4. Persons of independent means/investors

The general conditions outlined for permanent residence (see **7** below) fully apply to these cases. Retired persons or investors wishing to stay in Portugal for more than three months are required to file their applications in the Portuguese consulate of their place of residence.

(a) Pensioners/retired persons

Pensioners or retired persons applying for residence in Portugal must produce in the consular office documental proof of their retirement indicating the amount that they receive and the availability of such amounts while living in Portugal. They may also be required to open a bank account in Portuguese escudos, the amount to be deposited varying in each case.

(b) Persons of independent means

Persons of independent means must provide some documental proof to the Portuguese consulate showing the nature and amount of their income and the availability of those funds while in Portugal. On the other hand, they may be asked to prove that a bank account in a Portuguese bank has been opened, issued by the bank concerned, the amounts of such account varying in each case.

(c) Property investors

Applying for residency by means of property investment has been considered the easiest way to obtain residence in Portugal. In spite of recent Directives aimed at controlling the overwhelming number of applications under this category, it still remains the most popular and simple form of applying for residence in this country.

Upon delivery of documents with the Portuguese consulate, foreign citizens are also required to produce a legalised copy of the property's promissory contract of purchase and sale. However, common experience shows that some consular offices ask the applicants to produce not only the document proving a promise to purchase, but the definite contract of purchase and sale (land title). Thus, those applicants must purchase the property prior to obtaining the visa for residence. In any case, the property has to be completely free of charges or encumbrances and cannot be allocated for rent. Property investors may, likewise, be compelled to show documental proof that a bank account in Portuguese escudos has been opened, issued by the bank concerned. The required amounts to be deposited may vary from case to case.

5. Spouses, children and relatives

One of the criteria for obtaining permanent residence (see **7** below) is family reunion. For this purpose, immigration authorities will facilitate the entrance and residence in Portugal of the spouse, children, adopted children and parents of the foreign resident or his or her spouse provided that they are shown to live as dependants of that same foreigner.

An applicant under these circumstances must produce documental proof that he or she is related to the foreign resident. Immigration authorities also demand official written proof of the relative's financial capability or a letter from the relative's employer confirming his or her appointment to be either on a temporary or permanent basis, detailing current salary. Finally, a residence permit of the relative established in Portugal is also needed for application purposes.

6. Temporary stays

(a) Visitors

Foreign citizens visiting Portugal for a temporary purpose (tourism, business, etc) may usually remain in Portugal for a period of three months without the necessity of a visa if they are nationals of most European, North American and some South Americans countries (the same applies to citizens from Australia, New Zealand, Japan, South Korea, Malawi and Swaziland). People coming from other parts of the world must produce to immigration officers a uniform visa which is normally applied for at the Portuguese consulate of their country of residence. This visa will enable the foreign visitor to stay in the country for a maximum period of three months per each semester, counted from the date of the first entry in Portugal.

(b) Students

Foreign nationals wishing to study in Portugal for more than three months must apply for a student visa with the Portuguese consulate abroad. When applying for such visa, they must produce a statement in which it is clearly shown that they are enrolled at a certain academic institution to attend a course. They will also be required to show some documental proof of the financial means they have secured for their maintenance in Portugal. On the other hand, in cases of scholarships or bursary holders, applicants must have a declaration from the establishment where they are going to further their studies, showing clearly the title of the body granting the scholarship or bursary and respective duration, this document being always endorsed by the competent department of the Portuguese Ministry of Foreign Affairs. The student visa is valid for two entries into Portugal and enables its holder to stay in the country for a maximum period of one year.

7. Permanent residence

"Permanent residence" is a stay in Portugal for a period exceeding 90 days.

Persons applying for residence under this category are normally required to submit their application for a residence visa with the Portuguese consulate of their place of residence. In some very limited cases foreigners may apply directly for a residence permit with the Foreigners Department ("Serviço de Estrangeiros") in Portugal, if they are able to prove that they do not have fixed residence in another country. However, in the latter case and in order to enter Portugal they should always previously obtain a short-term visa if they are not nationals of any of the countries referred to at **6(a)** above.

Immigration authorities will consider the following circumstances when considering the visa application:

- the purpose of the stay and its feasibility;
- financial capability (some consular offices may require copies of bank accounts, the opening of a bank account with a Portuguese bank or other evidence of the applicant's financial capability);
- housing conditions (some consulates may ask for a certificate obtained locally attesting the ownership or lease of a house);
- facilitation of family reunion;
- health and criminal records.

Children under 18 may be included in their parent's application.

After the residence visa is granted, the applicant enjoys a period of 120 days to travel to Portugal and apply for a residence permit with the Foreigners Department. The presence of the applicant in Portugal is not required and he or she may be represented before the Foreigners Department by a resident in Portugal duly empowered by a power of attorney given in accordance with the law.

Common experience shows that if a residence visa is granted, obtaining a residence permit is then a simple formality. In any case, the application for the residence permit must meet the following conditions:

- the existence of a residence visa duly granted;
- the existence of any new fact which, if known to the consular office, would have prevented the granting of a residence visa;

- the presence in Portuguese territory of either the applicant or his or her representative.

Residence permits are of three types:

(1) annual permit valid for one year and renewable for the same period of time;
(2) temporary permit valid for five years and renewable for identical periods, which may be issued in favour of foreigners who have legally resided in Portugal for more than five consecutive years;
(3) permanent permit valid for life, which may be issued in favour of foreigners who have legally resided in Portugal for more than 20 consecutive years.

The renewal of residence permits must be carried out at the latest 45 days before the term of their period of validity. When considering the renewal application, immigration authorities will take into account the following criteria.

- financial capability;
- housing conditions;
- compliance with Portuguese laws.

Foreign residents in Portugal are compelled to inform the Foreigners Department every time there is an alteration in their nationality, civil status, profession, residence, or in case they plan to be absent from the country for more than 90 days.

The residence permit may be withdrawn it:

- the foreign resident has stayed in Portugal less than six months in a period of one year;
- the foreign resident has failed to comply with his or her obligations as resident or has put in jeopardy public safety, national security or international relations with other EU Member States.

8. Nationality

(a) Birth

Children born of Portuguese parents (father and/or mother) in Portuguese territory, or abroad in case either of the parents is officially employed by the Portuguese State, are automatically considered as nationals of Portugal. Children born of Portuguese citizens while abroad and whose parents were not officially representing the Portuguese State, may, upon reaching full age, choose Portuguese citizenship.

Children born in Portugal of foreign parents who have been legally residing in Portugal for a minimum of six years (in cases of citizens from Portuguese-speaking countries) or 10 years (in cases of citizens from other countries), and who were not officially representing a foreign country, may also acquire Portuguese nationality provided that, upon reaching full age, they declare it to be their intention.

(b) Marriage

A foreigner married for more than three years to a Portuguese citizen may choose Portuguese nationality.

(c) Naturalisation

In order to apply for Portuguese citizenship under this category a certain number of conditions have to be fulfilled, such as:

- full age (18 years of age or more);
- legal residence in Portugal or Macau for at least six years (in cases of citizens from Portuguese-speaking countries) and 10 years (in cases of citizens from other countries);
- sufficient knowledge of the Portuguese language (the applicant in certain cases is required to take a test before a Portuguese official, or alternatively to produce a legalised diploma issued by a Portuguese school);
- existence of an effective connection with the Portuguese community;
- good character;
- financial capability (the applicant must prove that he or she is able to support his or her family and, in some circumstances, must produce documental evidence of his or her means of subsistence).

Applicants who have previously been Portuguese citizens, have Portuguese ancestors, are members of communities with Portuguese roots, or have rendered or are called to render relevant services to the Portuguese State, may be excused from complying both with the condition of the period of residence in Portugal and with the good character requirement.

The decision to grant citizenship is taken by the Ministry of Internal Affairs, which holds a considerable discretionary power in these matters. Naturalisation may be denied, among other reasons, if:

- there is no effective connection with the Portuguese community;
- the foreigner was previously convicted for a crime with a prison term that, in accordance with Portuguese law, is more than three years;
- the applicant was previously a public official of a foreign State or was voluntarily enlisted in its armed forces.

9. Refugees and political asylum

The right of asylum may be granted to:

- foreigners persecuted or seriously threatened with persecution as a result of activities in favour of democracy, freedom, peace or human rights;
- foreigners who have reason to fear that they will be persecuted on the grounds of race, religion, nationality, political opinions or integration in a certain social group, whether those activities were performed in the foreigners' country of birth or in their country of residence.

Persons who have been granted political asylum on these grounds are considered to have the status of refugees, within the meaning of the Refugee Convention of Geneva (1951) relating to the status of refugees.

Right of asylum will be denied to foreigners if:

- they have committed any acts against the fundamental interests and sovereignty of Portugal;
- they have committed war crimes, crimes against peace or crimes against mankind as defined in international Conventions;
- they have committed other serious crimes in accordance with Portuguese law;
- they have practised any acts against the principles of the United Nations;
- national or international security or the protection of the country's population so justifies.

The application for asylum must be filed with the Foreigners Department and may include the spouse and unmarried children under 18. If a foreigner has illegally entered Portugal for the purpose of obtaining political asylum he or she should file such request without further delay. Such request will suspend all proceedings eventually to be brought against the foreigner for illegal entry.

Foreigners enjoying refugee status are subject to the same duties applicable to other foreigners residing in Portugal, provided those duties are not opposed to the Convention of 1951 and the Protocol of 1967. They are therefore prevented from:

- interfering in Portuguese political life;
- developing activities which may jeopardise national or international security or the relations between Portugal and other countries;
- practising any acts against the general principles of the United Nations or which are contrary to international Conventions signed by Portugal.

Asylum seekers who can prove that they lack the minimum financial capability to support themselves and their family may benefit from social security assistance until a final decision on their request is reached.

In case asylum is denied, a foreigner has a maximum period of 30 days to seek asylum in another country. At the end of such period, the foreigner will be deported from Portugal.

10. Government discretion

In spite of the existence of specific laws regulating immigration to Portugal, a considerable degree of discretionary power is held by immigration authorities. In fact, provisions of law are purposely vague, most of the times generally referring to guidelines, leaving interpretation and application in the hands of government entities which decide on a case-by-case basis.

Therefore, even though from a "written law" point of view Portuguese legislation may appear more favourable to immigrants than other European jurisdictions, one must bear in mind that the wide discretionary powers held by immigration authorities tend to mitigate the benefits. On the other hand, Portuguese membership of the European Union has led to a process of unification of laws and procedures with the other Member States, leading to significant changes in the Portuguese legal system (*e.g.* the changes necessary to comply with the Schengen Agreement).

The Government has, however, continued to evidence a far more favourable approach to applications in cases of investment or establishing businesses in Portugal.

11. Sanctions

(a) Deportation

Foreigners are liable to deportation on the following grounds:

- illegal entry or stay in Portuguese territory;
- threat to national security or public order;
- threat to the interests of the Portuguese State or of Portuguese citizens;
- abusive interference in Portuguese politics;
- disrespect with regard to the laws relating to foreigners;
- practise of any acts which if previously known by the immigration authorities would have prevented entry into Portugal.

Deportation will also be imposed as an additional sanction in the following cases:

- on non-resident foreigners convicted of a crime with a prison term of more than six months;
- on foreigners residing in Portugal for less than five years where they are convicted of a crime with a prison term of more than one year;
- on foreigners residing in Portugal for more than five and less than 20

years, if they are convicted of a crime with a prison term of more than three years.

Deportation may be decided by judicial or administrative authority. Deportation by judicial authority will occur in the following cases:

- as an additional sanction;
- on foreigners who have legally entered and/or are legal residents in Portugal;
- on foreigners who have obtained refugee status.

Deportation by administrative authority (the Foreigners Department) will take place where foreigners have illegally entered or are illegally staying in Portugal.

Foreigners cannot be deported to a country where they may be persecuted for any of the reasons, in accordance with the Refugee Convention, which are grounds for obtaining refugee status. The burden of proof lies with the foreigner, who will need to convince immigration authorities that his or her fears are duly justified.

(b) Periodic presence at the Foreigners Department or police stations

Foreigners may be required to visit the Foreigners Department or police station in good time to show their identification.

(c) Detention

Until the enforcement of the decision to deport, foreigners may be detained in temporary installation centres if one of the following circumstances occur:

- they are subject to on the additional sanction of deportation;
- they have violated the duty of periodical presence at the Foreigners Department or police stations;
- they lack financial capability;
- where immigration authorities fear that foreigners are likely to disobey the deportation decision.

(d) Sanctions for third parties

Anyone encouraging or facilitating illegal entry of foreigners may be liable to a prison term of up to three years.

12. Tax and social security

(a) Tax

The complexity and breadth of fiscal mattes and their various implications justifies a detailed discussion on this subject. However, in view of the broader scope of this work, this discussion will focus only on the general features of Portuguese income tax. More information on local taxes can be found at **13** below.

The principal taxes in Portugal are levied by Central Government and include the following:

- corporation income tax (imposto sobre o rendimento colectivo (IRC));
- individual income tax (imposto sobre o rendimento singular (IRS));
- inheritance and gift tax (imposto sobre sucessões e doações);
- value added tax (imposto sobre valor acrescentado (IVA));
- real estate municipal tax (contribuição autárquica);
- real estate transfer tax (SISA);
- stamp tax (imposto de selo).

(i) Income tax

There is a single basis of assessment encompassing income from all sources to which different rates of tax are then applied, depending on the income source.

The classes of taxpayers are as follows:

- business entities with commercial, industrial or agricultural income (if non-resident, with a permanent establishment in Portugal);
- recognised professional resident freelancers, whether acting individually or in partnership;
- other individuals, whether or not resident.

Both corporations and individuals, depending on whether they are considered to be resident in Portugal, can be either unlimited or limited taxpayers. An unlimited taxpayer is one whose worldwide income is potentially subject to Portuguese tax, subject to exclusions under the relevant double tax Treaties. A limited taxpayer is subject only to tax on Portuguese-source income.

Corporations are regarded as unlimited taxpayers if their seats and/or places of management are in Portugal. Individuals are considered to be resident taxpayers as from the date of their arrival if they spend more than 183 days in any calendar year in Portugal; they are also deemed resident if they visit Portugal for a shorter period in any year and have residential accommodation available on 31 December of that year, showing their intention to keep and occupy it as permanent residence.

(ii) Corporations

The income tax system is unitary and aggregates worldwide income less allowable expenses. Double taxation relief may be available for foreign-source income under the tax Treaties concluded by Portugal.

Different withholding tax rates exist for residents and non-resident corporate entities in Portugal.

Taxable income is classified according to income source. Allowable deductions and tax credits are specific to each category of income. Corporations are at present taxed at the rate of 36%, increased in most cases to 39.6% by the addition of a 10% municipal surcharge (derrama).

(iii) Individuals

Resident individuals are taxed on worldwide income at progressive rates which have a maximum of 40% on the excess over 5,790 million escudos (1995).

Married couples are taxed on their combined income.

Double taxation relief for foreign-source income may also be available under the tax Treaties concluded by Portugal.

The following countries have signed tax Treaties with Portugal: Austria, Belgium, Brazil, Denmark, Finland, France, Germany, Italy, Norway, Spain, the United Kingdom and the United States.

(b) Social security

All workers and their families are covered regardless of nationality. Foreign workers can opt out of the system if they are temporarily employed in Portugal and can demonstrate that they are covered by a similar scheme in their country of origin.

Base remuneration for the purpose of calculating social security is widely defined and includes overtime, commissions, profit-sharing, and benefits-in-kind.

Contributions are deducted by the employer at source by withholding 24.5% from the payroll or by annual declaration and payment if the taxpayer is self-employed. In addition, employees will have to pay a contribution of 11% of gross pay.

A special regime is established for employees working in the capacity of general managers or directors. They may obtain an exemption from social security if (i) they are not remunerated or (ii) they are covered by an alternative social security system in Portugal or in the country of origin if they come from abroad.

Portugal has adopted the EU Directive concerning social security and has social security Treaties with EU Member States, with various other European countries, and with several non-European nations, including the United States. These Treaties generally allow exemption from social security contributions in the host country for up to a maximum of two years (with possibilities of extension) for employees who are working in Portugal on an assignment basis. These employees may remain insured under the social security system of their home country. The social security Treaties provide for inclusion of the insured periods in both countries, in the final retirement pension calculations and mutual recognition of health insurance for travellers requiring medical treatment.

13. Domestic considerations

(a) Civil registration

Non-resident foreign citizens entering Portugal through an uncontrolled terrestrial border are required to register with police authorities within three days after their arrival. Registration with their own country's consular office is also advisable.

(b) Housing

(i) Purchase
The formalities involved in buying property may seem complicated to foreigners, who should get local independent advice.

Searches should be conducted at the Land Registry Office and in the tax registration department to check whether the house is owned by the seller and whether there are any charges or encumbrances on the property.

A first promissory contract is normally signed between the parties. This binding agreement includes the terms of payment and usually involves a deposit, the balance normally to be paid on the completion date (notarial deed of purchase and sale to be signed before a notary public). After the notarial deed is signed between the parties, the transfer of ownership must be registered at the Land Registry Office.

Notarial and registration costs are payable by the buyer (approximately 1.5% of the purchase price). The sale of urban housing and land for development gives rise to real estate transfer tax (Sisa) at 10% on the higher of two values: the purchase price or the rateable official value of the property. The tax must be paid prior to the signing of the notarial deed.

(ii) Rental
Written rental agreements are not normally required, but are advisable. Special attention should be given to the choice of the type of contract and to its contents. The law provides for two types of rental agreements: limited or unlimited term agreements. Limited term agreements have a minimum term of five years and upon reaching their term the tenant is required to leave the property. Unlimited term agreements are contracts usually drawn up for less than a one-year period, but which, if the tenant so wishes, are renewed indefinitely provided the same tenant complies with the contractual obligations.

The execution of rental agreements is made by means of private document with no intervention of a notary public. No taxes, notarial or registration costs are payable.

(iii) Real estate municipal tax (Contribuição Autárquica)
This tax is assessed on the registered value of the land and ranges from 0.8% to 1.1%, and is paid on an annual basis.

(iv) Water, electricity, gas and telephone services

The supply of any of these services only requires the production either of the notarial deed of purchase or of the rental agreement.

(c) Employment

Labour relations in Portugal are normally founded on individual employment contracts which are signed by employer and employee. Terms and conditions of these agreements, which are voluntarily agreed between the parties, are specifically restricted by two principal statutes, the general employment law, which dates from 1969, and the provisions for collective employment agreements, which are usually applied on a sectoral basis in a particular industry or profession.

The law demands a written contract only where the employment is for a short term, involves casual labour, or there is a probationary period. In the absence of a written contract. an employee enjoys all the statutory rights of permanent employment from the start of his employment.

The working day/week period is: for industrial workers a maximum of eight hours per day; for office workers a maximum of seven hours per day and 42 hours per week. Most workers are able to enjoy two full rest days (Saturday and Sunday).

The Government establishes minimum wage levels for various sectors of economic activity, and these are reviewed periodically, usually on an annual basis. For 1995 the national minimum wage was 52,000 escudos per month, payable 14 times a year, to include a holiday bonus and a Christmas bonus. These bonuses are payable in addition to an employee's entitlement to a minimum of 22 and not more than 30 calendar days of holiday with full pay.

(d) Health

Portugal has a comprehensive free health service provided by the State and can be used by pensioners and workers covered by the social security system. Adequate insurance cover is also available.

(e) Schooling

Schooling is compulsory from the ages of six to 15. There is a State-run system of free education from grammar school up to university level. Private schools and universities are also available throughout the country.

(f) Motor cars

In the six months following their arrival, foreign residents who wish to drive in Portugal are required to obtain a driving licence from the Transportation

Department (Direcção-Geral de Viação), by producing a copy of their original licence and identification documents.

Automobile insurance against third parties is compulsory.

Jose Alves Pereira & Associados, Av. de Berna n°4 – 1°DTO, 1000 Lisboa. tel.: (351) 17938890/4. telefax: (351) 17938889

Contents of Chapter 15

SPAIN

Chapter 15

SPAIN

Jaime Valera y Martos

1. Country characteristics and general principles

Situated in the south west of Europe, Spain is the second largest country in the European Union, with a surface area of 504,750 square kilometres, and is the home of 39.5 million people approximately.

The greater part of Spain lies in the Iberian Peninsula, neighboured by Portugal in the west and France across the Pyrenees on the north east, which form a natural border. To the south lies the North African coast, only a few miles across from the Straits of Gibraltar. Spain also comprises the Balearic Islands on the Mediterranean Sea, the Canary Islands on the Atlantic Ocean and the towns of Ceuta and Melilla on the North African Coast. The largest cities are the capital city of Madrid, where most of Spain's financial and commercial activity takes place, and Barcelona, a major industrial and maritime centre. Other important cities are Bilbao, Valencia and Seville.

Immigration is not new to Spain. Due to its geographical situation, strategically enclaved between Europe and Africa, the Mediterranean and the Atlantic, throughout history Spain has been the crossroads of many different cultures and peoples: Phoenicians, Greeks, Carthaginians, Romans, Visigoths and Arabs all settled within, in more or less friendly terms with the original inhabitants.

As a result of its ancient history, Spain has a unique culture, both rich and diverse, the blend of the influences left by so many visitors. Spain is also the founder, together with Portugal, of one of the world's largest cultural communities, that of Latin America, with which it continues to have very strong ties.

The official language of Spain is Spanish or Castilian, although regional languages and dialects are also spoken in certain areas of Spain, particularly in Cataluña, Galicia and the Basque Provinces, where they are considered official alongside Castilian. Spanish is spoken worldwide by more than 350 million people.

A member of the European Community since 1986, of NATO since 1982 and the United Nations since 1955, Spain is an active role-player in the international scenario. Spain's economy, among the world's 15 largest, is gradually recovering from the worldwide recession of the early 1990s and has one of Europe's highest growth potentials. Its main industries are machinery, steel, textiles, automobiles and, of course, tourism. Spain is one of Europe's main tourist destinations and is visited by more than 50 million people every year.

Spain is a relatively young but stable democracy. At the head of the State is the King, and sovereign power is exercised by a bicameral Parliament before which the Government is responsible.

A political unity since the fifteenth century, presently Spain is divided internally into 17 autonomous communities (Comunidades Autónomas), all of which have their own parliament and government with varying degrees of autonomy.

Spain has recently become a target destination for economic immigration, particularly from Eastern Europe, North Africa and Latin America. The combination of strict legislation and permeable borders has resulted in large numbers of illegal immigrants.

While corporate immigration is welcomed and encouraged by flexible laws and the absence of foreign exchange controls, immigration laws are restrictive on the establishment of foreigners on Spanish soil. However, a large number of fundamental rights are guaranteed to foreigners who live in Spain by the 1978 Constitution. Due to its historic commitments, Spain is more lenient towards immigration from Latin America, the Philippine Islands and its old African territories, although having to adapt to common EU policy and legislation has considerably limited such an attitude. The Sephardic Jewish community, descending from the Jews who were expelled from Spain 500 years ago but who still preserve a strong hispanic identity, are also favoured by Spanish immigration laws.

2. Employment and inter-company transfers

Under this heading we refer to employment within a company, as opposed to self-employment, which is dealt with in **3** below.

(a) Work permits

(i) Different types of work permits
Foreigners who wish to work in Spain need to obtain an authorisation by way of a valid work permit.

The most important types of permits are known as b (initial), B (renewed), C, and permanent permits. These permits can only be obtained consecutively in that order, *i.e.* a worker can only initially opt for a b (initial) permit and upon expiry of the same may apply for a B (renewed) permit and so on until entitled to apply for a permanent permit (permanent permits are a novelty to Spanish law, only recently introduced by Royal Decree 155/1996 of 2 February 1996). We shall look at these permits more closely:

b (initial): expire after one year and entitle the holder to work in a particular activity and geographical zone and may be limited to a particular employer.

B (renewed): are available after expiry of an initial b permit and are issued for two years. These types of permits entitle the holder to engage in several activities during that time.

C: are issued for a three-year period and entitle the holder to work in any employed activity anywhere in Spain. They are only issued to foreigners who hold a renewed B permit after expiry of the same, and have, therefore, worked in Spain for three continuous years. This period is reduced to two years for certain categories of workers, among others, as follows: workers who are nationals of any Latin American country, the Philippine Islands, Equatorial Guinea, Andorra, or belong to the Sephardic Jewish community; foreigners who have resided in Spain during the previous five years; or the spouse or child of a C permit holder.

Permanent permits: entitle the holder to engage in any type of employed activity throughout Spain for an indefinite period. They can only be issued to C permit holders upon expiry of the same.

Apart from those already mentioned, other categories of permits exist such as collective permits (which may be granted to teams or groups of workers for a maximum duration of six months), A permits (which are adequate for seasonal jobs and are granted for a maximum nine months and cannot be extended or renewed) and extraordinary permits (which are available only to foreigners who have made an outstanding contribution to the economic or cultural progress of Spain and authorise the holder to exercise any type of employed activity for an indefinite period).

(ii) Obtaining a work permit

Initial permits (A or b initial)

The granting of an initial work permit to foreigners depends on the national employment situation generally, the absence of a skilled or qualified local workforce or the local rate of unemployment in relation to the particular activity and area for which a permit is sought. Only if the above circumstances are favourable will a permit be granted. The reciprocal provisions applied by foreign countries to Spanish nationals are also considered.

Certain applications for initial work permits are treated preferentially, with no regard paid to the national employment situation, either due to the nature of the post to be occupied or the applicant's personal circumstances. Thus:

- applications for workers involved in repairing or assembling imported equipment,
- applications for posts of special responsibility within a company (top executives), and

- applications when the prospective employee is the spouse or child of a holder of a renewed work permit or a permanent residence permit, or is an asylum seeker, a close relative of the prospective employer, has Spanish relatives under his or her charge, is the child or grandchild of a Spanish national, was originally Spanish and later lost Spanish nationality, or enjoyed the benefit of asylum, within one year of losing such status

are preferential and are considered regardless of the national employment situation.

Beneath the above categories, but also treated preferentially, are applications for work permits made by nationals of Latin American countries, the Philippines, Equatorial Guinea, Andorra and members of the Sephardic Jewish community, as well as applications by foreigners who have been legal residents for at least five years and applications by relatives of foreign workers.

The application is submitted by the prospective employer, who must prepare a dossier describing the nature of the post to be occupied and the reasons for which such a post should be occupied by a foreigner. An official offer of employment must also be presented reflecting the employment conditions which are offered to the foreign workers.

Applications for initial work permits will be denied when, due to the national employment situation, it is advisable to do so or when the conditions offered to the foreign worker are inferior to those established by law for the activity for which the permit is sought.

Non-resident foreigners who seek an initial work permit must also obtain a residence permit. The first step to be satisfied is the obtaining of a residence visa for employment purposes, which must be applied for at the Spanish consulate where the foreigner resides. The visa will only be granted after a work permit is issued by the competent authorities, the application for which will have to be made by the prospective employer. Among other documents which are common to applications for other types of residence visas (for which, see below), the applicant must submit a copy of the offer of employment presented by the prospective employer when applying for the work permit.

With respect to certain sectors of employment, which are not sufficiently provided for by the local workforce, yearly quotas are established by government to benefit non-EU nationals. These quotas are established on a country-by-country basis and the satisfaction of the same is canalised by the Spanish consular offices situated in those countries. To date, this system has applied to sectors such as agriculture, domestic service and construction.

Subsequent permits (B renewed, C, permanent)

The following circumstances are considered for the renewal of a work permit:

- whether the worker has held a regular and stable employment during the validity of the expired permit;
- whether the worker will continue in his or her present employment or will receive a new offer of employment;

- the reciprocal provisions applied to Spanish nationals in the foreigner worker's country of origin. Applications by nationals of countries where Spanish nationals are treated more disfavourably will be treated as applications for initial permits.

Permanent permits will be granted upon expiry of a C permit provided the worker continues to be active, whether as an employee or seeking new employment.

(b) Permit-free employment

Exceptionally, the following persons do not require a work permit:

- scientists who are invited or employed by the State;
- university professors who are invited or employed by a Spanish university;
- officers or professors of foreign cultural or educational institutions of well known prestige, recognised by Spain, to develop cultural or educational programs for their country;
- civil or military personnel of foreign States who come to Spain to act within an international cooperation scheme with the Spanish administration;
- correspondents of foreign media;
- members of international scientific missions which are authorised by the State;
- ministers, clergymen or representatives of religious groups which are registered in the Religious Entities Registry;
- artists who come to Spain for a particular performance.

3. Business

(a) Self-employment

(i) Work permits

Foreigners who wish to develop a business in Spain or live in a self-employed capacity (entrepreneurs) must obtain a work permit. These come in various forms and sizes.

- **d (initial)**: are limited to a single activity and are valid for one year. They may also be limited to a particular geographical zone.
- **D (renewed)**: upon expiry of a d permit, foreigners may apply for a D permit, which is valid for two years and is not limited to any particular activity. Exceptionally, these permits may be limited to a single activity and geographical zone.
- **E permits**: expire after three years but are otherwise unlimited. Application can be submitted after the expiry of a D permit. Exceptionally, the following

categories of foreigners may apply for an E permit one year in advance of the expiry of the D permit: nationals of any Latin American country, the Philippine Islands, Equatorial Guinea, Andorra; members of the Sephardic Jewish community; foreigners who have resided in Spain during the previous five years; the spouse or child of an E or permanent permit holder; and foreigners who have Spanish descendants or ancestors under their charge.

- **Permanent permits**: entitle the holder to engage in any type of activity throughout Spain for an indefinite period. They can only be issued to E permit holders upon expiry of the same.

- **Extraordinary permits**: are available to foreigners who have made an outstanding contribution to Spain's economic or cultural progress, and such permits are in all other ways similar to permanent permits.

(ii) Obtaining a work permit

Applications for initial permits (d (initial))

Work permits are valid only if held together with a residence permit. Thus, non-resident applicants must also obtain a residence permit. The first step towards obtaining a residence permit is to request a residence visa for self-employment purposes in the Spanish consulate where the foreigner resides. The residence visa for self-employment purposes is issued only after the labour authorities have granted the necessary "d"-type work permit.

When applying for an initial permit (or a residence visa for self-employment purposes) the applicant must forward, amongst other documents, a detailed report of the proposed business or activities to be carried out, with an analysis of the capital investment required and the activity's profitability and employment-creation potential, as well as evidence that any licences or authorisations which may be required in order to carry out the projected activity have been obtained or requested.

The creation of job opportunities, the importance of capital to be invested and the introduction of new technologies are all relevant factors for the granting of these permits. An application may be turned down if the proposed investment does not favour the creation of job opportunities or is otherwise considered as irrelevant to the economy.

Certain applications for initial work permits are treated preferentially, no regard being paid to the proposed activity's impact on the employment market. The following persons are entitled to this preferential treatment: the spouse or child of a holder of a renewed work permit; the holder of a permanent residence permit; a person who has requested the benefit of asylum; a person with Spanish relatives under his or her charge; the child or grandchild of a Spanish national; a person who was originally Spanish and later lost Spanish nationality; a person who enjoyed benefit of asylum, within one year of loosing such status.

Nationals of Latin American countries, the Philippines, Equatorial Guinea, Andorra and members of the Sephardic Jewish community, as well as foreigners who have been legal residents for at least five years, and more distant relatives of foreign workers than those mentioned above, enter a less-privileged category of persons, but are also treated preferentially with regard to the obtaining of these work permits.

Application for subsequent permits (D, E, permanent)
To obtain any subsequent permit the applicant must show that he or she is well established and has complied with all fiscal duties and social security regulations.

(b) Forms of business organisation

The more common corporate structures are the "Sociedad Anónima" (SA) and the "Sociedad Limitada" (SL). Both types of company limit their shareholders' liability to the capital invested.

The SA must have a minimum capital of 10 million pesetas, which is divided into registered or bearer shares with a par value. The SA is managed by one or more "administradores" or a board of directors, elected by the shareholders for a period of five years. The board of directors can, in turn, appoint executive officers who are responsible for the company's day-to-day management. The use of an SA is mandatory if its shares are publically quoted.

The SL provides a more appropriate structure for small and medium-sized companies and is becoming increasingly popular due to its greater flexibility. A new law governing the SL was enacted in 1995. Among the novelties introduced by the new law is the possibility for a single shareholder to incorporate an SL and no maximum limit to the number of shareholders. An SL must have a minimum capital of 500,000 pesetas.

4. Persons of independent means/investors

(a) Residence

We shall refer here to residence for non-working purposes, as the requirements to reside in Spain for employment or business purposes have been dealt with under other headings.

(i) Residence visas
A prior requirement for obtaining an initial residence permit is to obtain a residence visa. This is very important as foreigners who arrive in Spain in possession of a tourist visa will not normally be able to obtain a residence permit. Only very exceptionally can a residence permit be granted in the absence of a residence visa.

Application must be submitted in person to the Spanish consulate of the applicant's place of residence *before travelling to Spain*. Applications are then submitted by the Spanish consulate to the Ministry of Foreign affairs for its consideration.

To apply for a residence visa the applicant is required to provide, among other documents, a certificate of good conduct, a health certificate and, finally, proof of sufficient means or resources to provide for accommodation, maintenance and health costs for himself or herself and any supported relative.

In addition, the applicant may be required to attend a personal interview in order to verify his or her identity, personal and economic situation, and chances of adapting to Spanish society etc.

Obtaining a residence visa does not guarantee that a residence permit will follow.

(ii) Residence permits
There are three types of residence permit which vary in their duration:

- **initial permits**: which last for one year and may be renewed for a further two years;
- **ordinary permits**: which last for three years and may be extended for a further three years. They can be granted in favour of foreigners who have legally resided in Spain for at least three continuous years. The applicant must be in possession of an initial permit;
- **permanent permits**: may be obtained by foreigners who have legally resided in Spain for at least six continuous years. A permanent permit can also be issued in favour of foreigners who fall into one of the following categories:
  - foreigners who receive a retirement pension from Spanish social security or receive certain other pensions from Spanish social security;
  - foreigners who were born in Spain and upon reaching 18 can prove that they have legally resided in Spain for at least three years;
  - foreigners who were tutored by a Spanish public institution during the three years prior to their reaching 18;
  - foreigners who were Spanish by reason of birth and later lost Spanish nationality;
  - foreigners who have acquired refugee status;
  - foreigners who hold an extraordinary work permit (see above).

Children who are born in Spain will immediately acquire the same type of permit as that held by their parents.

(iii) Obtaining a residence permit
The application to obtain or renew a residence permit must be submitted to the local police station of the foreigner's intended place of residence.

Applicants are required to complete an official form and forward a series of documents similar to those which are required to obtain a residence visa (for which, see above).

In general, applicants must provide evidence that they possess sufficient means to support themselves during their intended residence period or that they will receive such means periodically and also that they have medical insurance. Where applicants have relatives under their charge they must also show that they will possess a home capable of accommodating the family.

Residence permits can be extended or renewed if the circumstances or reasons for which they were first granted still persist. If such circumstances have changed the application will be treated as if it were the first application. To renew a residence permit the applicant must prove that he or she has duly complied with all his or her fiscal obligations.

(b) Investors

Following EC Directive 88/361, "foreign" investments are those carried out by non-residents, regardless of their nationality.

Thus, investments by foreigners who legally reside in Spain are subject to the same conditions as those carried out by Spanish nationals.

Since 1992 most exchange controls and controls on investments were dismantled and substituted by reporting requirements. Exceptionally, the following "foreign" investments are subject to prior authorisation by the Council of Ministers:

- investments by residents in non-EU Member States in Spanish companies which are involved in any of the following activities: gambling, radio, television, air transportation, activities related to national defence;
- investments carried out by public entities of non-EU Member States;
- investments by non-EU residents, which could be harmful to national interests.

The invested capital and returns or profits obtained from an investment that was carried out in accordance with Spanish legislation may be freely transferred abroad.

5. Spouses and children

(a) Family reunion

The immediate relatives of foreigners who have legally resided in Spain for at least one year have a privileged access to residence in Spain.

Family reunion visas can be obtained for this purpose by spouses, children under 18, ascending relatives and children over 18 when legally or economically dependent, and disabled persons and minors under the care of a resident foreigner.

Application for a family reunion visa must be made by the above persons in the Spanish consulate of their place of residence, where they will have to forward documents to prove their kinship to or dependence on the relative in

Spain. The resident foreigner in turn must prove that he or she has sufficient economic means to support his or her relatives and can guarantee that their medical needs will be cared for.

Foreigners who enter Spain under a family reunion visa must subsequently request a family reunion residence permit. Spouses may obtain an individual residence permit provided they obtain a work permit or have lived in Spain with their spouse for two years, or their spouse died in Spain while a resident. Children obtain independent residence permits upon reaching 18.

(b) Dependants of EU nationals

EU nationals who have settled and are resident in Spain, have the right to be joined by their family members irrespective of their nationality.

Family members include the spouse, descendants of either of the spouses who are older than 21 years of age or dependent on them, or dependent relatives in the ascending line of either of the spouses.

Family members are entitled to obtain a residence permit of the same duration as that of their relative or person on whom they are dependent, and, except for the relatives in the ascending line, they are entitled to work in Spain as employees or in a self-employed capacity under the same conditions as Spanish nationals.

Family members who hold non-EU passports must apply for a residence visa before travelling to Spain. To obtain the residence visa they will have to prove their relationship with or dependence on the relative they wish to join.

6. Temporary stays

(a) Visitors

Visitors may remain in Spain for three months or, when a visa is required, for the time for which the visa is issued.

Visitors who are authorised to remain in Spain for a shorter period may request authorisation to extend their visit up to the three-month limit and, under exceptional circumstances, visitors who do not require a visa to enter Spain may obtain leave to remain in Spain for a period exceeding three months.

Visitors can be required, before entering the country, to prove that they have sufficient economic resources to pay for their stay and return journey home and to justify the reasons for visiting Spain. A medical examination may also be required unless appropriate health certificates are produced. A visa does not guarantee access into the country.

(b) Students

Foreign students who wish to take up long-term studies in Spain must obtain a student visa before travelling to Spain and, subsequently, a student card from the Ministry of Interior.

The visa and student card may be granted provided the applicant has been admitted as a pupil, student or researcher in an authorised centre for a period of at least three months, and is able to show sufficient means to pay for his or her studies, stay and eventual return journey home.

7. Permanent residence and nationality

(a) Permanent residence

Traditionally "permanent residence" was not available to foreigners, the maximum authorised period of residence being 10 years.

Recently enacted legislation (February 1996), introduced the concept of permanent residence to Spanish immigration law. The requirements to obtain a permanent residence permit are dealt with under **4** above.

(b) Nationality

There are several different ways of acquiring Spanish citizenship although the more natural way is by being born the child of a Spanish father or mother (*iure sanguinis*). Being born in Spain will only exceptionally lead to the acquisition of Spanish citizenship when the child's parents are unknown, or do not have a nationality of their own, or one of them was, in turn, born in Spain (*iure solis*).

In all other cases, being born on Spanish soil will only lead to a privileged access to citizenship through naturalisation. Below we shall refer only to naturalisation through residence.

Spanish citizenship can be obtained through a period of residence in Spain. Foreigners are ordinarily entitled to apply for Spanish nationality after residing in Spain for 10 years. This period is reduced to five years for those who enjoy the benefit of asylum and to two years for Latin Americans, Portuguese, Filipinos, Equatorial Guineans, citizens of Andorra and Sephardic Jews.

Only one year of residence is needed to apply for citizenship for those who were born in Spain or who have been married to Spanish nationals for at least one year provided the spouses are not legally or *de facto* separated, or who are widowed from a Spanish national provided they were not separated at the time of their spouse's death. One year is also sufficient for those who were under the legal care of a Spanish citizen or institution for two consecutive years and for children born abroad when one of their parents was originally Spanish.

In all the above cases the necessary period of residence must be legal and continued and take place immediately before the petition is filed. The prescribed period of residence entitles the foreigner to apply for nationality. The applicant will also have to prove good conduct and that he or she is sufficiently adapted to Spanish society (a good knowledge of Spanish is a must in this respect).

Applications for Spanish nationality can be refused for reasons of national interest or public policy or if the applicant fails to prove a sufficient degree of adaptation to Spanish society. Reasons for the refusal must be justified. The applicant is entitled to appeal against the refusal in court.

8. Refugees and political asylum

The benefit of asylum is the protection granted by Spanish law to persons who are considered as refugees in accordance with the 1951 Geneva Convention. This protection is also extended to the refugee's spouse and direct descendants, and persons under their charge.

The refugee under asylum is entitled to:

- reside in Spain;
- receive appropriate documents for identification and travelling purposes;
- obtain a work permit.

The application for asylum can be made within Spain, at the Spanish border posts or before a Spanish consulate. The applicant will be provided with a form explaining his or her rights and an application form.

Applications are considered in a two-phase procedure. The first phase has been designed to examine within a short time-limit whether there is any basis to the application and will either go through to the second phase, or will be refused. The applicant is entitled to request a reconsideration of the petition and is also entitled to be assisted by an interpreter and a lawyer when in Spanish territory.

If the applicant is refused after the first stage, the applicant will be rejected at the frontier or expelled from Spanish territory, or asked to leave upon expiry of his or her legal stay in Spain. Exceptionally, an authorisation either to enter or remain in Spain can be granted for humanitarian reasons.

During the second phase the application will be thoroughly examined. The applicant will be provided with provisional documents and entitled to certain social and sanitary services, and even a temporary work permit. The outcome of this examination will be either recognition of refugee status and the benefit of asylum, or the denial of refugee status, and, consequently, the eventual expulsion from Spanish territory.

9. Government discretion

Ministerial discretion can be widely exercised in relation to individual cases or to the general application of immigration rules according to national interest, but such discretion must not be confused with the possibility to act arbitrarily.

Acts or decisions which affect immigrants or foreigners in Spain are subject to the provisions of general administrative law and must therefore be subject to as many appeals as provided by the law, and the affected party is entitled to be heard before the decision or act is taken.

10. Sanctions

(a) Deportation

A foreigner is liable to deportation by administrative authority (State Security Director) on the following grounds:

(1) remaining in Spain after the expiry of his or her legal stay or residence permit;
(2) working without a work permit;
(3) being involved in or carrying out illegal activities or activities which are contrary to public order, national interest, internal or external national security or which can damage Spain's relations with other countries;
(4) having been sentenced in Spain or abroad to an imprisonment term of more than one year for the commission of a criminal offence, unless his or her criminal record has been cancelled;
(5) not informing the authorities of his or her personal situation in the way prescribed by the law;
(6) lacking legal means of support or begging to earn a living.

If the circumstances listed in (1), (3) or (6) occur, while the deportation decision is pending the foreigner can be detained and held in a special detention centre for a maximum period of 40 days.

The deportation of a foreigner must be decided by judicial authority when the foreigner is being prosecuted for a minor offence (sanctioned with an imprisonment term of six years or less). A judge can also decide that a foreigner be deported instead of serving an imprisonment term if he or she is found guilty of such an offence.

11. Tax

(i) Corporate tax

Companies and other legal entities which are resident in Spain are subject to corporate tax at a rate of 35%

Corporate tax is levied on the company's worldwide income from all sources, including gross income and capital gains, less deductable expenses and capital losses.

(ii) Personal income tax

Residents of Spain

Spanish tax legislation considers an individual to be resident in Spain when he or she spends more than 183 days during the year in Spain or when the greater part of the individual's professional or entrepreneurial activities or economical interests are based in Spain.

Residents in Spain are taxed globally for the income they obtain worldwide with no regard to the place where it is obtained. They are entitled to a deduction on account of double taxation when these incomes have already been taxed elsewhere.

This is a progressive tax in which the highest rate (in 1995) was 56%, applicable to the income obtained in excess of 9,500,000 pesetas.

Non-residents

Non-residents are taxed only for the returns and capital gains which are produced in Spain. These include profits or returns obtained from work or entrepreneurial or artistic activities carried out in Spain and capital gains or returns obtained from real estate property situated in Spain. Certain exceptions aside, capital gains which arise from movables are exempt.

Non-residents are taxed at a general rate of 25% for returns or profits and at 35% for capital gains.

Spain has entered double taxation Treaties with most Western European countries. The provisions contained in these Treaties prevail over the general rules set out above.

(iii) Wealth tax

Residents in Spain are taxed yearly on the net value of the properties, assets and rights which they own regardless of their location. They are exempt from this tax when the said net value does not exceed 17 million pesetas (1996).

Non-residents are taxed only on the properties and rights which are located or are to be exercised in Spain. They do not enjoy the same exemption as residents.

12. Domestic considerations

(a) Civil registration

A Central Foreigner's Registry is kept in Madrid in which the granting of residence permits, work permits and extended stay permits is registered together with any relevant information regarding the beneficiaries of such permits.

Foreigners who enjoy a residence permit of any kind are obliged to inform the local police station of any changes in their nationality, working situation or address within 15 days. They must also provide other information regarding their personal situation when required to do so by the competent authorities, within the same time-limit.

Failure or delay in providing the authorities with the prescribed information or providing false information can result in the foreigner's deportation.

When granting a residence or extended stay permit the authorities will provide the foreigner with a personal identification number.

(b) Employment

Employment is strictly regulated in Spain and labour laws are, in general terms, generous to the employee. Workers are guaranteed a number of statutory rights such as the right to join trade unions of their choice, the right to collective bargaining, the right to strike, protection against discrimination on basis of sex, race, age, religion etc.

The standard working week is 40 hours and the retirement age is 65 for men and women. Workers are entitled to social security, and high rates of social insurance is paid by the employer.

Rules regarding the duration of employment contracts and dismissal and redundancy are very strict. Standard employment contracts are unlimited in their duration, although an increasing number of temporary contracts can now be entered into depending on the employee's age, qualifications or the nature of the post, or the employer's situation. Verbal contracts are presumed to be unlimited unless proved otherwise.

Employment contracts can be terminated for a number of statutory reasons. Termination by the employer can take place for disciplinary reasons due to grave misconduct or fault on the part of the employee and also for reasons of an economical, technical or organisational nature, in which case the employee is entitled to an indemnity.

The dismissal of an employee for reasons other than those accepted by law or carried out without complying with the formalities prescribed by law entitles the employee to an indemnity or readmission, at the employer's election. Readmission is mandatory if the dismissal was for reasons of illegitimate discrimination or was in breach of the employee's constitutional rights.

(c) Housing

A recent survey revealed that 70% of Madrid's families own the houses in which they live. This proportion is similar and even higher throughout Spain. Owning a house is regarded by Spanish families as a safe investment and as a guarantee of stability. However, the purchase of a house is by no means inexpensive. While prices collapsed during the recession in the early 1990s, they are steadily rising again, which has been seen as an indicator of economic recovery.

Normally, the transfer of real estate property is carried out by means of a public deed signed before a notary public and later registered in the Land

Registry. The signing of a public deed before a Spanish notary or Spanish consul is mandatory if the purchaser is a non-resident. Professional legal advice should always be sought when purchasing real estate property.

Fernando Scornik Gerstein, Abogado, Alberto Alcocer 7, 3° Izda 28036 Madrid. tel.: (34) 9 13507262. telefax: (34) 9 13507306

Contents of Chapter 16

SWEDEN

Chapter 16

SWEDEN

1. Country characteristics and general principles

Sweden, Finland and Austria became full members of the European Union on 1 January 1995. Norway gave a no-vote in November 1994 resulting in a new EU-frontier between Sweden and Norway.

The Schengen Agreement came into force on 26 March 1995. The Swedish Government wants Sweden to become part of the agreement if full guarantees can be obtained to maintain the Nordic Passport Union between Sweden, Norway and Finland. Sweden and Finland do not yet benefit from the Schengen Agreement, which now means free movement between the EU Member States. Nordic cooperation will continue and Sweden will strengthen Nordic cooperation by means of the European Union.

In Sweden's view, the European Union must be an open union that does not raise walls between other countries. There is no contradiction between Sweden's commitment to Europe and its long-standing involvement in global development work and the United Nations.

In September 1995 the Swedish people elected the 22 members who will represent their country in the European Parliament.

The discussion below concerns primarily the possibilities and problems with which third-country nationals (from outside the European Union) may be faced.

Sweden has a total area of 459,000 square kilometres (similar to Spain and California and twice as big as the United Kingdom) and a population in 1994 of 8,800,000, of which some one million are of foreign origin. The number of inhabitants per square kilometre in Sweden is only 19, compared with the Netherlands (362), in Germany (249) and France (102).

The warm Gulf Stream in the Atlantic gives Sweden a milder climate than other areas equally as far north. Sweden and Alaska are on the same latitude.

Nearly 100,000 lakes dot Sweden's surface, of which 50% is covered with forest and 10% farmland. Around 90% of the population belong to the Church of Sweden, which is Lutheran. Swedish is Germanic language. The average life-expectancy is 76 for men and 81 for women.

Sweden has rich natural supplies of forest, water power, iron ore, uranium and other minerals, but lacks significant oil and coal deposits. The vast forests of spruce, pine and other softwoods supply a highly developed sawmill, pulp, paper and finished wood-product industry, of which 60% is exported. Sweden is among the world's biggest spenders in industrial research and development and industrial groups such as Volvo, Saab, Ericsson, Astra, ABB, SKF, Atlas Copco etc are well known all over the world.

Sweden's main trading partners are Germany, the United Kingdom, the United States and the Nordic countries, making up 14%, 10%, 9% and 22% respectively of total exports. The average hourly wage earnings of adult earners in 1994 was SEK 82 (Swedish Crowns = "kronor") for men and SEK 72 for woman.

Due to the recession in the 1990s the jobless rate has risen considerably and amounted to 13% in 1995. Employment in the service sector between 1960 and 1995 rose from about 1,700,000 to 2,800,000, while manufacturing employment fell from around one million to less than 800,000.

Since the 1940s, immigration has accounted for over 40% of the population growth. Thus, there has been a certain amount of immigration to Sweden during many different periods of history. Sweden today is a country of greater ethnic diversity than ever before, with nearly 10% of the population being immigrants or those who have immigrant parents.

Swedish policy on immigrants and ethnic minorities is based on three objectives:

(1) equality between immigrants and Swedes;
(2) freedom of cultural choice for immigrants; and
(3) cooperation and solidarity between the native majority and various ethnic minorities.

The general election on 15 September 1991 put the Social Democrats in opposition after almost 50 years (except for a short period) of socialism in Sweden. After the 1994 elections the Social Democrats were returned to power and formed a Minority Government, with 162 of the 349 seats in Parliament.

2. Employment and inter-company transfers

(a) Employment

For some years Sweden has held a very restrictive policy with regards to the immigration of labour. In 1994, only 400 citizens from other countries were granted a permanent residence permit for labour market reasons. Many more were granted residence and work permits for a limited period in order to carry out special assignments.

Sweden has no "guest-workers" policy but does not withdraw work permits already issued during periods of economic stagnation.

Specially skilled workers and specialists of foreign origin will encounter no problems in obtaining a work permit (Arbetstillstånd (AT)) when a Swedish company or scientific institution requires them for work or research in Sweden.

A work permit is not required for an alien who has;

- a permanent residence permit (usually given after one year);
- married a Swedish citizen;
- not reached the age of 16 if the custodian has a residence permit.

(i) Exceptions on grounds of Swedish ancestry

There are no exceptions on grounds of Swedish ancestry.

(ii) Permit-free employment

Foreigners working on Swedish ships on Swedish territory or abroad do not need work permits, provided the shipping company has been given a permit to employ the alien in question.

(iii) Trainees

Trainees who wish to enter the country as temporary immigrants, who intend to work for a Swedish or foreign company and who can prove that the offer of training is satisfactory, should have no problems obtaining a short permit.

It is presumed that the company can prove that the trainee has sufficient means of support and intends to return abroad after the completion of the training. No ordinary employment is permitted after the training period.

(iv) Sole representatives of overseas firms

The Swedish Aliens Act does not yet recognise the concept of "person of independent means" or "sole representative". However, article 1, chapter 4 of the Swedish Aliens Ordinance (SFS 1989:547) states that a foreigner who, due to employment in Sweden, works in Sweden as the sole representative for a foreign company, can be exempted from a work permit if staying for less than three months.

However, it is possible for a foreign company to rent an office in Sweden for a sole representative and request a residence permit for a period exceeding three months – which will be granted on request to the Immigration Board.

(v) Doctors and dentists, overseas journalists and broadcasters

Specially skilled workers and specialists of foreign origin will have no problem acquiring a permit when a Swedish company or scientific institutions requires them for work or research in Sweden.

There is no formal hindrance to an entrepreneur or self-employed person to apply for a residence permit if he or she can show an extremely well-documented business plan.

(b) Inter-company transfers

A company which wishes to introduce staff members to work in its subsidiary in Sweden can present the offer of work directly to the Swedish embassy in its own country.

Swedish embassies have been given the right to grant residence and work permits for up to two years if the applicant is going to work as:

- an assistant manager;
- a controller (head of economy department);
- a marketing manager;
- a sales manager; or
- a departmental manager.

If the applicant does not belong to one of these groups, a special licence must be obtained from the Labour Market Board before the decision of the Immigration board. A Swedish embassy will forward the application to the Swedish Immigration Board for its statement or decision. The permit will be restricted to a specific employer and workplace. These permits are given for six months and for up to a maximum of four years. The permit holder will not qualify for a residence permit. The spouse of the permit holder will automatically be given a work permit.

Since the Swedish Immigration Board is under reconstruction and lacks staff familiar with the new policies and legislation, it is advisable that the applicant is represented by an advocate (member of the Swedish Bar Association) specialising in this field of law.

3. Business

(a) Businessmen and women

People of the business community will usually have no problems acquiring "business" visas to Sweden. The Swedish Immigration board will issue a questionnaire to the Swedish company involved and will, after receipt of an answer, grant a visa for one to three months, which can be prolonged.

A bilateral agreement between Sweden and the United States of 13 February 1992 introduced reciprocity between the two countries for the purpose of the issue of non-immigrant investors and traders visas.

An entrepreneur's application to a Swedish embassy or consulate should contain detailed accounts of the business plans. Full particulars of anything which may be considered of importance must be included, such as the names of any reference persons, bankers, business experience, prospects of success etc.

The embassy/consulate will then forward the application to the Swedish Immigration Board, which will make a decision. Notice of the Board's decision will then be sent to the embassy/consulate at which the application was submitted. It may take up to three month before a reply to the application is received. Representation by a Swedish advocate specialising in this field of law is strongly recommended.

(b) Foreign investment regulations

Sweden has an open attitude towards foreign investment from any country of the world.

Following the September 1991 election a coalition of four non-socialist parties took power in Sweden. This meant a new orientation in Swedish economic policy. Many of the restrictions on foreign companies wishing to establish operations in Sweden were abolished. Members of the Business Community of the World for the first time in 45 years of socialism now have no difficulties investing and working in Sweden. The return of the Social Democratic Party after the 1994 election made no major changes to this policy.

Foreign investment in Sweden has increased rapidly, and more wealthy foreigners than ever now live in Sweden.

The four freedoms in the EU Treaty can no longer be disregarded now that Sweden is a member of the European Union.

The principle of non-discrimination lies at the very heart of the Treaty of Rome. The principle is explicitly stated in Part 1, Article 7 of the Treaty and its special provisions regarding the free movement of goods, people, services and capital.

The same conditions for foreigners buying shares in Swedish companies have been introduced as those applied to Swedish companies and individuals acquiring foreign property.

The Control of Foreign Investment in Swedish Companies Act 1982 was annulled in 1992 and the Permission for Foreigners to Acquire Real Estate Act 1916 was amended so that there is now no licencing requirement on commercial real estate, industrial or office buildings or office space, when investing in Sweden.

An alien's ownership prohibition clause in corporate by-laws meant that a foreign subject was only entitled to acquire shares up to 40% of the capital stock or 20% of the number of votes in a company. The permit for acquisition of shares was previously set at 10%, 20%, 40% or 50% of the capital stock or number of votes. This is no longer applicable to takeovers. Even if that discrimination is now removed, it is important to remember that no permits have ever been needed for a foreign company to form a Swedish subsidiary company.

Only Swedish citizens domiciled in Sweden (or Swedish legal persons) may establish a new corporation unless the Government or other appropriate authority waives this restriction. In practice, this means that a foreigner must first arrange to have the corporation set up by Swedes, and then buy it from them.

As part of the current process of adapting Swedish laws to EU requirements, and to encourage foreign investments in the Swedish business sector, during 1991 Parliament voted to repeal the Foreign Acquisition of Swedish Companies Act. Since 1 January 1992 foreign legal entities have thus been entitled to acquire shares in Swedish companies without the permission of any Swedish public agency. In addition, the Ministry of Justice presented a proposal to repeal the Foreign Acquisition of Swedish Real Property Act from 1 July 1992. The interest to buy business opportunities in Sweden rocketed after 1992, and Sweden has been named a "tax heaven" in a report published in August 1994 by the OECD.

A corporate tax rate of 28% should be compared to 55% in Germany and 52% in Italy! Sweden is considered a good country to invest in, and a number of steps are being taken to update Swedish business law to the standards of EU legislation.

The corporation (Aktiebolag (AB)) is the dominant form of business in Sweden and is usually the most suitable for a foreign enterprise wishing to establish operations here. All shares in a corporation must be of equal par value and must amount to at least SEK50,000. A corporation's articles of association may specify that certain shares will receive preference with regard to dividends, participation in new issues of shares, or other transactions. Certain categories of shares may also be accorded voting rights up to 10 times as much as those of other categories of shares.

The rules on restricted shares was repealed on 1 January 1993, and all existing restricted share clauses in corporate by-laws ceased to be valid at the same time. From 1 January 1993 it is not possible to bring legal action to invalidate any previous acquisitions which violated an alien ownership restriction clause. A distinction between private and public limited liability companies and also a number of changes to the Act took effect on 1 January 1995 (*e.g.* to private and public companies, minimum share capital, increase of share capital, reduction of share capital, acquisition of a company's own shares, validity of a company's obligations, and mergers and disclosure).

The right to invest in Sweden will also give the investor a right to live here in order to control the investment. Swedish legislation will no longer be in conflict with EU legislation.

4. Persons of independent means/investors

(a) Persons of independent means

Non-active persons, *e.g.* persons of independent means, cannot expect a residence permit in Sweden. Probably due to 50 years of former socialism, Sweden does not yet acknowledge the right of an alien to "buy" a place in Swedish society.

Citizens of a EU Member State can retire in Sweden without restrictions. As stated above, the Swedish Aliens Act does not yet recognise the concept of a "person of independent means" for a non-EU citizen.

(b) Investors

Sweden does not formally acknowledge the right of an alien to "buy" a place in Swedish society through investment. There are no legal rules on the subject, as there are, for example, in Canada, where an alien who can make an irrevocable investment of a certain amount for at least three years which will contribute to the creation and continuation of employment opportunities for Canadian citizens, or, for example, in the United Kingdom, where an individual can bring a certain amount of money with him for possible investment, and will almost automatically be given a permanent residence permit. There is no "point system" for wanted immigrants in Sweden.

Following a bilateral Treaty between Sweden and the United States, Swedish firms and nationals are now eligible to apply for Treaty trader/investor non-immigrant visas (E-1 and E2) and the same restriction has been removed for citizens of the United States (March 1992).

5. Spouses and children

(a) Marriage

Family or relatives of an immigrant who has become an Swedish citizen or who lives in Sweden with a residence permit (PUT) can expect to reunite with relatives in Sweden in the following circumstances.

On an application from abroad, a husband or wife or minor of a Swedish citizen or a foreign citizen legally settled in Sweden cannot be refused. The relation should be well-established. The Immigration Board often demands two years' cohabitation abroad or that the spouses have a child together. Cohabitations without marriage are treated in the same way, and, in practice, children under 20 years of age are accepted if not married.

If the cohabitation has lasted less than two years, a residence permit can be granted for six-month periods, with a police investigation after each period.

Marriages where one of the spouses is under the age of 18, and polygamous marriages are discriminated against and never lead to approval of the application.

(b) Children

A foreign unmarried child under 16 years of age does not need a residence permit if the parent in custody is a citizen of Sweden, Denmark, Finland, Iceland, Norway or is settled in Sweden with a valid residence permit. Children between 16 and 20 can be denied a permit where they have not been living together with the Swedish parent from an early age.

A parent of an immigrant who has become a widow or widower and who has a minor (under 16) is normally given a residence permit if a majority of the adult children lives in Sweden.

A single parent is normally given a permit to settle with his or her children domiciled in Sweden. Any children in the home country or the number of children in Sweden is of no importance. The parent in question must be at least 60 years old. If it is obvious that the intention is to live on maintenance from the Swedish social welfare this could be a reason to refuse the application.

Reunion with both parents is permitted if all the children are domiciled in Sweden and if the parents are at least 60 years old or there are strong humanitarian grounds.

The remaining member of a nuclear family can be given a residence permit.

6. Temporary stays

(a) Visitors

Aliens furnished with a passport and visa can enter Sweden and stay for three months without a special permit. Usually no questions are asked at the border control, and no forms need to be filled in. A foreigner without the means to live or for the return ticket home runs the risk of being refused entry. Citizens of some countries must have a visa before entering Sweden, which must be applied for at the Swedish consulate or embassy in those countries. A visa will not be issued at the Swedish border.

If furnished with a valid passport, entry clearance gives the right to stay in Sweden as a tourist for three months provided sufficient means of maintenance are shown at entry.

Sweden does not have, as in United States, different types of business or other visas, but does have different types of residence permits.

(b) Business visitors

People of the business community will usually have no problems acquiring a (business) visa if they come from a country which is on the visa list. The Swedish Immigration Board will normally issue a questionnaire to the Swedish company involved and will, after receipt of the answer, grant a visa for one to three months to allow visitors to attend meetings and briefings which can be prolonged for the purpose of transacting business (*e.g.* fact-finding, negotiations, making contracts to buy or sell goods and services).

(c) Medical visitors

Medical visitors must apply for visa if they intend to stay for medical treatment for longer than three months. Visitors from some countries must apply for a visa at the Swedish embassy or consulate in their country before entry.

(d) Students and prospective students

Guest students must have reached the age of 18 and must have had at least 11 years' education previously. A student must have been admitted to the university before making an application for a visa at the Swedish consulate or embassy in the country concerned.

At the interview the applicant must show means for living expenses for the full intended time of studies. The amount varies and the study-plan must be fixed and realistic. Sufficient proof of competence from the domestic school is also required. The applicant is asked to sign a declaration to return to his or her home country after finishing the studies.

(e) Spouses and children of students

Spouses and children of students are entitled to the same permit as the student if it can be shown beyond reasonable doubt that they can be maintained and accommodated without recourse to public funds.

(f) Au pairs

Swedish authorities do not allow unmarried persons between 18 and 25 without dependants to work in Sweden, even for a short time.

(g) Working holiday-makers

Swedish authorities do not allow the entry of working holiday-makers.

7. Permanent residence and nationality

(a) Permanent residence

A permanent residence permit (Permanent Uppehållstillstånd (PUT)) gives, in practice, permission to stay in the country without limitation of time and can be applied for by an alien who has had:

- a work permit for more than one year;
- a residence permit for more than one year and who is married to a Swedish citizen, or who has an alien's passport (Främlingspass) and who does not require a work permit;
- a residence permit for more than one year and who, after application, would be granted a work permit if applied for, for example a person who is married to a holder of a residence and work permit.

Accepted refugees are given a permanent residence permit automatically.

The concept of temporary residence permits for refugees was introduced in 1995.

(b) Nationality

Some 550,000 aliens were naturalised in Sweden between 1948 and 1995. The application for naturalisation varies depending on the immigrant's country of origin and the way in which he or she came to Sweden.

Changing citizenship does not mean as much to a Nordic or EU citizen, who can move freely across Nordic boundaries, as it does to a refugee from, *e.g.* Somalia or Peru. A refugee, on the other hand, may hope to return home once the political situation in his or her own country has changed, so may not wish to change his or her nationality.

The basic principle in Swedish nationality law is in line with the European Conventions on limitations of plural citizenship. The basic principle in Swedish nationality law, based on the nationality principle, is that dual citizenship should be avoided.

After an application for citizenship is made at the local police board, the applicant will have to wait about 18 months for the final decision. The Immigration Board usually needs at least eight months to process the case. This has been strongly criticised by Parliament since it obstructs Parliament's decision to shorten the qualification time for Swedish citizenship. Certain parts of the investigation may need to be made twice, if the original information given is out of date.

Naturalisation
The Swedish Immigration Board decides on 20,000 citizenship applications a year, including some 500 from the Nordic countries. An application boom is expected due to recent immigration waves.

About 85% of the applications are sanctioned and about 3,000 are refused because of insufficient periods of residence, or misconduct. Approximately 30% of these are appealed to the Aliens Appeal Board.

The present processing time is 14–18 months from the date on which an application is given to the local police board.

The basic rules for naturalisation of non-Nordic citizens are that:

- the applicant must have attained the age of 18;
- the applicant must have been domiciled with a valid permit in Sweden for the past five years;
- the applicant must be of good character.

A citizen of a Nordic country must have been in Sweden for two years.

A non-Nordic national must have lived in Sweden for five years with a valid permit. A non-Nordic national married to a Swedish citizen must have been in Sweden for three years and married for two years.

Persons who are stateless or classified by the Immigration Board as refugees can usually obtain citizenship after four years' residence.

Domicile is defined as "permanent living with the intention to stay". Intention to stay is stated in the application for residence permit, and time runs from then.

If an illegal entry results in a residence permit, the starting time is from the day of the decision. An interruption in the domicile time under 30 days or for military service, for example, is not deducted. The determining factor here is the intention of emigration.

A crime leading to expulsion will break the domicile, but if this is impossible to execute, domicile counts for the first day of the residence permit.

A legally binding deportation order which is impossible to carry out means that domicile counts from the day of annulment of the deportation order.

An investigation of good conduct is carried out by the local police board.

Criminality, or owing money to the State for alimony or taxes, can disqualify the applicant. Physical impossibility is disregarded, but lack of willingness to fulfil natural obligations will be taken into consideration.

The following is a list of the periods of delay which will result as a consequence of sanctions imposed for crimes committed.

Crime Sanction	Delay
Fines (determined on the basis of the defendant's income – higher number indicates a more severe crime – number is then multiplied by 1/1000 of defendant's annual income):	
30–60	1 year after committing the crime
60–100	2 years after committing the crime
100–	3 years after committing the crime
Imprisonment:	
1 month	4 years after committing the crime
4–8 months	5 years after committing the crime
8 months–1 year	6 years after committing the crime
1–2 years	7 years after committing the crime
2–4 years	8 years after sentence carried out
4–6 years	9 years after sentence carried out
6 years–	10 years after sentence carried out
Suspended sentence	3 years after sentence
Probation	4 years after sentence

Repeated criminality means a much longer waiting period, and any foreign criminal sentence will also be taken into account.

The applicant for citizenship must prove loss of previous citizenship within the last two years. Exceptions are political refugees and persons who are denied release from their first nationality. This is also the case where an application for release is not answered within a reasonable time. In these cases Sweden must accept dual citizenship.

The certificate of citizenship costs SEK 500. It is not necessary for the applicant to have any knowledge of the Swedish language. The applicant does not have to pass any examination whatsoever.

(c) Immigration categories leading to permanent residence

These categories are dealt with above.

8. Refugees and political asylum

On 15 June 1990 a meeting of EU Ministers in Dublin adopted a new Convention on asylum legislation. This established which European country should be responsible for the investigation of an asylum case. Refugees will not be allowed to travel from one European country to another to apply for asylum and will only be given one chance within the European Community. In the case of a negative decision no other nation within the Community will have any obligation to deal with the case again.

On 19 June 1990, five EC countries signed the Schengen Agreement, which came into force on 26 March 1995, enabling refugees fleeing from torture, war and bad conditions to apply at the EU closed border when seeking asylum in Europe. The concept of the European Fortress was founded.

Sweden, however, had already adopted the established rule of "first country of asylum", which entitles the police and the Immigration Board to return an asylum applicant to the country where he or she may have stopped on the way to Sweden if that country is a signatory of the Geneva Convention and does not intend to repatriate the refugee. A normal transfer through a country is usually not considered to be a "stop", but the Schengen Agreement interprets the concept negatively for the refugee.

"Persecution" is defined as persecution of a severe nature directed against the life or liberty of an alien or otherwise (political persecution). Asylum in Sweden is also available to conscientious objectors and can be granted on humanitarian grounds.

A refugee can also be an alien who "although not a refugee, was unwilling to return to his home country on account of the political situation there, and is able to plead very strong grounds in support of his reluctance".

The criteria for determining refugee status under the 1951 Refugee Convention of Geneva and the 1967 Geneva Protocol relating to the status of refugees has been severely violated in Sweden over the last three years. The Government has claimed that the criteria do not adapt to the reality of today, and the political parties are in favour of harmonisation of all legislation on refugees within the European Union. The Alien's Appeal Board turn down some 95% of all appeals. The "European Fortress" is under construction, although some 90,000 refugees from war-torn former Yugoslavia have found new homes in Sweden.

Amnesties allowing refugees permanent residence permits without investigation have been passed on 31 May 1989, 1 October 1989 and 14 April 1994, giving long-term asylum seekers and families with children new homes in Sweden. A Bill presented in Parliament on 26 September 1996 could result in substantial changes to the Aliens Act from 1 January 1997. A more strict interpretation of the Geneva Convention in line with EU harmonisation is suggested.

9. Government discretion

The exercise of ministerial discretion outside the immigration rules is unknown in Sweden and directly forbidden in the Swedish Constitution. The Minister of Immigration cannot intervene in an individual case. On rare occasions the Immigration Board or Alien's Appeal Board can send a "pilot" case to the Government to set out future practice.

10. Sanctions

(a) Deportation, illegal entry and detention

A foreigner who resides in Sweden without a residence permit or who takes up employment or works in some capacity without a work permit is subject to a fine. A Swedish citizen or holder of a permanent residence permit employing an alien who is illegally living in Sweden runs the risk of imprisonment for up to one year.

An alien or refugee giving false information to the Immigration Board can be imprisoned for up to six months. This is also the case for a person helping a foreigner to enter Sweden illegally.

A person trying to hide a foreigner who is then deported from Sweden can be sentenced to imprisonment for up to one year.

Organised smuggling of aliens who do not hold residence permits can be punishable by imprisonment for up to two years.

Government funds to deport rejected asylum seekers were granted in August 1993 when the Government allocated SEK 100 million to the police to seek and deport some 5,000 "disappeared" refugees – cleared for deportation.

11. Tax and social security

(a) Tax

A foreigner who plans to work in Sweden for several years or for an indefinite period is normally considered as resident for tax purposes. Sweden has entered into bilateral agreements to avoid double taxation with most countries.

Foreign employees do not have to report formally to the tax authorities unless they intend to stay in Sweden more than one year, in which case they must register within two weeks of arrival. However, because a personal registration number is essential in Sweden a visit to the tax authorities to obtain a personal registration number is recommended.

Foreigners working in Sweden do not receive special tax treatment.

The level of income tax until the Swedish tax reform of 1991 was the highest in the world. Employment income and business income (earned income derived by an individual) is taxed progressively. From 1995 the following approximate tax rates apply. Where the taxable income (assessed income reduced by a standard deduction) does not exceed SEK198,700, the individual is liable only to municipal income tax at an average rate of approximately 31% (which varies according to the municipality). In 1991 about 83% of taxpayers having earned income were liable only to municipal tax on such income. For a taxable income exceeding SEK198,700, there is an additional State tax of 20% which gives an overall marginal tax rate of approximately 51%.

The new system for taxation of capital income represents one of the major novelties in tax reform. For different reasons, the taxation of such income has been separated from the taxation of other income. Nominal capital income is taxed at a flat rate of 30%.

One of the most significant changes in the capital income taxation is that the tax rate of 30% is applied on essentially all nominal capital gains.

The corporation income tax rate is lowered to 30% and the tax base is broadened through the abolition of most reserve options. In addition, the tax base is also broadened through a fully nominal taxation of capital gains on shares and real estate.

Corporation income has always been taxed twice until recently (at corporate level through the corporation tax and at shareholder level through the tax on dividends). This double taxation effect was abolished in 1992 and a lowering of corporation income tax to 25% has been discussed in Parliament. A deduction corresponding to the value of new issued shares is also permitted following the tax reform. This deduction is limited to dividends distributed on new issued shares, at a maximum of 10% per year of the value of the new shares, for a maximum period of 20 years. In principle, only dividends distributed to shareholders liable to tax in Sweden are deductible, *e.g.* shareholders resident in Sweden and non-residents and corporations liable to withholding tax.

The new tax rate of 30% applies to all legal entities and corporations, as well as co-operative associations, unit trusts, foundations and non-profit associations.

The corporation income tax rate coincides with the tax rate on capital income earned by individuals and – approximately – with social security contributions on payroll paid by corporations (28%). Thus, uniformity is improved between direct and indirect household savings and between taxes on capital and employment income in the corporate sector.

(b) Social security

Both comparative statistical and qualitative studies of welfare states consistently show Sweden as the leader among advanced industrial countries in the strength and reach of the social safety net and its redistributive impact.

The growth of the National Debt shows that the Swedish welfare state stands at a crossroads.

All residents in Sweden are covered by national health insurance. If a person is ill or must stay home to take care of sick children, he or she receives a taxable daily allowance, of 65–90% of lost income, depending on the length of absence.

County councils, together with the heath insurance system, pay most hospitalisation costs and laboratory fees. Above a ceiling of SEK 1,600 per year, treatment/drugs are free of charge.

When a child is born the parents are legally entitled to a total of 12 months' paid leave from work, which can be shared between them and used at any time before the child's eighth birthday.

A national occupational injury insurance system pays all health care costs for work-related accidents.

A basic old age pension financed by both employees and employers is payable to everyone from the age of 65. The State also pays an income-related supplementary pension financed from employers' payroll fees.

12. Domestic considerations

(a) Introduction

Sweden is a homogeneous, well-ordered society where a business meeting starts on time and gets right down to business.

Social attitudes emphasise the importance of the group rather than the individual. Leadership style is consultative. Bosses consult with their employees. Labour legislation restricts overtime work to 200 hours a year and grants everyone five weeks' vacation.

Equality is an important factor in Swedish society. Half of all students are women and both men and women in the labour force work outside the home and share chores at home. Children are treated well and their views are respected.

Swedes enjoy meeting and working with people from other countries. They are delighted if given the opportunity to practise their foreign language abilities, which are often considerable.

(b) Housing

Good quality housing is available in Sweden. The number of square metres of housing per capita is the highest in the world. Most people in major towns live in flats, although many live in single-family dwellings usually in the suburbs. Expatriates usually rent a flat or a house during their stay in Sweden; agencies can provide assistance in finding accommodation.

A foreign citizen must apply for special permission to buy real estate in Sweden. The nationality of the applicant is not decisive.

Exceptions are made for persons domiciled in Sweden or who have been domiciled in Sweden previously for more than five years. The procedure is very liberal when the intention is to provide a permanent residence for the buyer and his or her family.

Acquiring a summer house may be more restricted.

No permission is required for a foreigner to buy shares in a housing corporation or a housing cooperative whereby the shareholder/member obtains an apartment in the corporation's/cooperative's property.

There are no restrictions whatsoever on EU nationals.

(c) Health care

Good health and equal access to health services for everyone are the goals of the Swedish health care system.

A fundamental principle of the health care system is that it is a public sector, with responsibility to provide and finance health and medical services for the entire population. The social insurance system today includes the following main categories of insurance, as well as a number of miscellaneous allowances: health and parental insurance, pension insurance, work injury insurance and unemployment insurance (see **11(b)** above).

(d) Schooling

The Government operates most of the educational system. Children normally start school at six or seven and receive free education in public schools for nine years, with free instruction, books and lunches. Many people continue their studies at universities or technical colleges and generally receive subsidies. Private schools are also available.

Private, government-subsidised adult education associations arrange study circles for 2.5 million course participants a year.

INDEX